KAREN CURRY PARKER

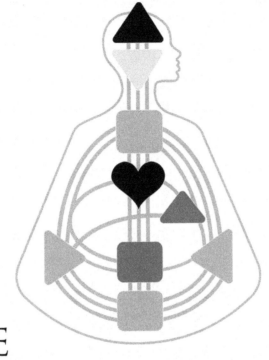

THE
ENCYCLOPEDIA
—— OF ——
QUANTUM
HUMAN DESIGN™

Edited by Debby Levering
Cover Design by Jessica Murrell

An Imprint for GracePoint Publishing (www.GracePointPublishing.com)

GracePoint Matrix, LLC
624 S. Cascade Ave, Suite 201
Colorado Springs, CO 80903
www.GracePointMatrix.com
Email: Admin@GracePointMatrix.com

SAN # 991-6032

A Library of Congress Control Number has been requested and is pending.

ISBN (Paperback) 978-1-951694-92-0
ISBN (Hardback) 978-1-951694-96-8
eISBN: 978-1-951694-94-4

Books may be purchased for educational, business, or sales promotional use.
For bulk order requests and price schedule contact:
Orders@GracePointPublishing.com

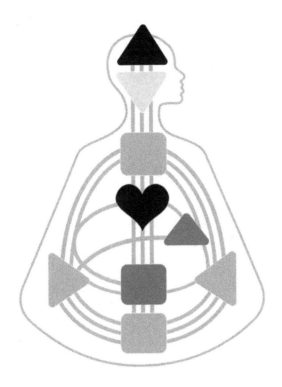

To learn more about Quantum Human Design,
enroll in our Free Course: Quantum Human Design Basics.
QuantumAlignmentSystem.com/QHDBasics

Other Books and Resources by Karen Curry Parker

Abundance by Design

Human Design Workbook

Inside the Body of God

Introduction to Quantum Human Design™ 2nd Edition

Quantum Human Design™ Activation Cards

*Quantum Human Design™ Activation Cards
Companion Book*

QHD Quantum Activation Card Deck (iPhone App)

Human Design and the Coronavirus

*The Quantum Human: The Evolution of Consciousness and the Solar Plexus
Mutation in Human Design*

Understanding Human Design

Quantum Human Design™ Evolution Guide 2022

Follow Karen and Quantum Human Design on social media
@KarenCurryParker

To the Generals in the Army of Love, Kristin, Betsy and Jamila. I am grateful to you and to whatever quantum field of information unified us and brought us together on this mission. Without you, none of this would be possible.

Table of Contents

Introduction

We are standing at the cusp of a creative revolution that will be as transformational and world-changing as the scientific revolution.

The scientific revolution was rooted in a desire to interpret the material world. By understanding how the world worked and measuring and finding patterns that created reasonable truths about the nature of material reality, scientists worked hard to banish fear with data and take control over superstitious practices and dangerous beliefs.

This creative revolution promises to bring us a new way of understanding our world. With the emergence of quantum physics in the early 1900s, we learned that the appearance of an ordered and relatively finite reality is actually, at a quantum level, quite malleable, imperceptibly interconnected, and mind-blowingly infinite. Vibrational frequencies align with fields of information that cause our material reality to "manifest."

As the famous inventor Nikola Tesla said, "If you want to find the secrets of the universe, think in terms of energy, frequency, and vibration."

We are conquering a new way of creating. Quantum physics liberated us from the idea that using sheer will and force is the path through which we build our world. We are learning that serendipity and synchronicity are artifacts of this "new" quantum creativity. We are learning that we can consciously draw into our experience solutions to the challenges of our life without having to spend our energy and our time "figuring" things out with our minds.

We are learning that our thoughts DO create our experience of reality. We are being schooled in understanding our innate creative power. As we become more and more skillful at consciously harnessing frequencies of energy, we grow in our ability to find elegant solutions to the challenges facing humanity today.

All of this requires that we completely transform our conditioned way of creating. We have to start by letting go of ideas that cause us to measure and strive for a definition of value rooted in the scientific revolution's old metrics. The numbers that once defined our value—the amount of money you have, how much stuff you own, the number of years of education you have, the numbers on the scale, or the size of your pants no longer measure the value of who you are.

This process of harnessing our innate creative power requires us to redefine who we are. We are no longer simply a product of our upbringing or our genetics. Through the process of deconditioning our identity, we are learning that we are who we think we are, that our thoughts can literally change our lives and even regulate our DNA. By taking control of our identity, we increase our power to influence our experience of the world.

The words "I am" have been known by mystics for thousands of years to be the most powerful and creative words we can speak. The Aramaic phrase, "Abracadabra," used by stage magicians, when translated, means, "I am that I speak." In the Old Testament, when God first appears to Moses as a burning bush, Moses hears a voice that he attributes to the Divine. When Moses asks the voice to identify itself, the Divine proclaims, "I am that I am."

Who we proclaim ourselves to be and consequently aspire to become evokes our essential divinity. It is part of our soul curriculum and human experience to consciously define and explore who we are in this lifetime.

Learning to redefine the pain of the past and unwind ourselves from old patterns and conditioning that keep us disconnected from the truth of who we are is a natural part of this process of proclaiming and reclaiming who we truly are. It's also an essential part of the work we do on an individual level that helps heal the planet and to initiate a wave of creative activations all around the globe.

When we live aligned with our true self and proclaim an identity worthy of who we are, we elevate our vibrational frequency and live in a state of coherence. This state of coherence gives us a better capacity to self-regulate and enhances our state of emotional, mental, and physical wellbeing. It also makes us more receptive to Life's Intelligence flowing through us, supporting us in walking a deliberate and guided evolutionary path.

This high vibrational frequency and state of coherence are also contagious. Vibrational states entrain each other. Higher frequencies of energy entrain lower frequencies of energy, lifting them up. This vibrational elevation creates greater energetic openings for others to elevate their vibrational alignment.

In other words, the more we do the work of clearing our past conditioning and limiting patterns, the easier we make it for others to do the same. Our personal, microcosmic transformation and activation become a part of creating a collective, macrocosmic transformation and activation.

This process sounds like a complex and challenging task, but your natural story-telling ability is the answer to changing the world.

You were born a storyteller.

You learned about life, the values of your family, and who you are from the stories you were told as a child. As you grew, you began to tell your own story about who you are, what you're here to do, and what you're capable of. The narratives you crafted from your conditioning—your life experiences—set the tone and the direction for your life.

Words create. They endure. They allow for Unity. They transmit. They are the interface between the Divine and the Human. Words are Power. They translate the infinite to the finite. Together words together create a code for a story. Words carry frequencies of energy, and our DNA responds to that language.

We have the power to use words, language consciously, and, ultimately, stories to create a template for our dreams and the expansion of our potential. We tap into resilience and courage when we consciously craft stories that are powerful enough to call us forward and inspire us. The power of these stories can help us maintain momentum, even when we are struggling with the day-to-day challenges of our own personal growth and evolution.

When Ra, the founder of Human Design, first shared his transmission of the system, he did so in a way that penetrated and shocked people into waking up. He used language that had the power to speak into the 'Not-Self' to get people's attention quickly, and it worked.

Having personally known and worked with Ra and, after over two decades of teaching Human Design, I have been Divinely inspired and guided to do what Ra wasn't given the time to do before he suddenly passed away from a heart attack in 2011. I intend to share this knowledge respectfully, an "awakened" Human Design I Ching, with an empowering, higher vibrational frequency language that I call Quantum Human Design.

As a nurse and a life coach since the 1990s, I have seen first-hand the power of language to heal people. My purpose for this new language is to give you a more aligned way to tell the story of who you are, find healing in these words, and find the language that helps your soul feel truly "seen." I have deliberately engineered the Human Design vocabulary to a powerful, positive, higher vibrational frequency of energy to help you fully activate your potential.

Since 1999 I've been teaching, writing, and sharing Human Design as a tool in my coaching and healing practice. I've spent a lot of time in readings rewording the information on the chart to make it more inspiring and uplifting. The Encyclopedia of Quantum Human Design is an index of language you can use to craft a personal narrative that is strong enough to inspire you and call you forward, even when the going gets tough. My intention for this codex is to give you a tool that, through the language of ancient and modern archetypes, gives you the power to craft a personal narrative that tells the TRUE story of who you really are.

The evolution of the BodyGraph, both with the split from seven to nine Energy Centers in 1781 and the emerging Solar Plexus Mutation in 2027, enhances our ability to influence our life path consciously. Language and the meaning we give it trigger photon storms in the brain. These photon storms cause the brain to produce neurotransmitters, which cause the body to experience an emotional response. This emotional response calibrates the heart creating a state of coherence, sometimes called "The Zone." When we are in "The Zone," we feel connected to our deepest selves, to others, and to life itself. Heart coherence occurs when our mind and body are entrained and operate at the same frequency.

Not only do we create flow and the experience of being in The Zone, but heart coherence also influences what we attract into our lives. From Human Design, we know that a magnetic resonance field is generated in the G-Center, the Magnetic Monopole. The Magnetic Monopole attracts opportunities and sets the tone and direction for our lives depending on the quality of emotional energy we generate.

In addition, the words we use program our brains to "see" what we expect. The brain can process as much as 400 billion bits of information a second, but we are aware of only about 2,000 bits a second. Regarding visual processing, the brain can effectively process only about 1 percent of the information it takes in. This is because specific neurons, called the Reticular Activating System (RAS), selectively filter out unimportant visual information. The language we use programs the RAS to "see" things in our outer reality that match what we've programmed our minds to pay attention to. Your perception of reality is influenced mainly by your language and the stories you tell.

Human Design shows us the energetic pathway that programs the Magnetic Monopole and creates a state of heart coherence.

The power of thinking and imagining influences the emotional wave. The emotional wave flows through the Will Center to the Identity Center calibrating the Monopole.

The wave influences the quality of your self-worth and your sense of lovability. The Gates of the Will Center and the Identity Center contain a code that helps you calibrate your Magnetic Monopole to its highest potential.

Human Design shows us that our sense of self-worth is rooted in integrity. There are five kinds of integrity in the Human Design chart. If we question our value, we may also experience a breach in any of these five areas of integrity.

The five kinds of integrity are:

1. Physical Integrity is experienced when our bodies are healthy and vital.

2. Resource Integrity is when we sustainably use our material resources.

3. Identity Integrity is experienced when we feel that we can fully manifest the value of our authentic identity and we don't compromise who we are for the sake of money.

4. Moral Integrity is the courage to do the right thing and ensure that your actions are honest and aligned with high principles and values.

5. Energetic Integrity is experienced when we consistently and deliberately rest and take care of ourselves so that we have the energy to engage with life sustainably.

The Identity Center, the seat of the Magnetic Monopole, shows us that the quality of Love we have for ourselves and each other also influences what we attract. The Gates of the Identity Center give us a code that helps guide us in creating deep alignment with our original intention for our life. Our higher purpose is encoded into the Identity Center, and the Gates of the Identity Center help us unlock the energies necessary for us to fulfill the full potential of our life and soul purpose.

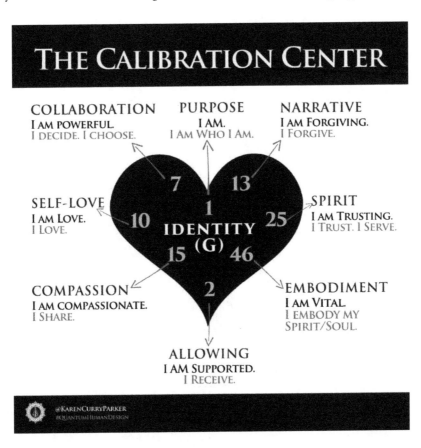

When we love ourselves, feel empowered, express ourselves authentically, release the past, and consciously choose our own personal narrative, when we feel connected to Source and the more profound meaning and purpose of our lives, when we fully embody the amazing body we are given, when we trust in our support enough to expect to receive what we need to fulfill our life path and purpose and when we freely share who we are and what we have in the world, we are not only living out the highest expression of being human, we calibrate our Monopole to keep attracting experiences that match these themes.

Finding the language that speaks into these themes in a way that helps you anchor your intention to live aligned with this potential is the purpose of Quantum Human Design.

I hope Quantum Human Design will provide you with a new way to see your Human Design chart and tell a bigger and better story about what's possible for You!

From my Heart to Yours,

Karen

How to Use This Book

This book is a reference guide for those who already have a basic knowledge of Human Design. Each section of the book will refer to the traditional Human Design names for the parts of the system and then give information and insights about reframing and renaming the traditional definitions into Quantum Human language. This difference in renaming is represented throughout the book like this:

Traditional Human Design | Quantum Human Design

I recommend you start by gaining a traditional understanding of your Human Design chart. Traditional Human Design is a powerful tool to help you understand what you are "not" and how you may have been conditioned to make choices in your life that have not felt aligned or correct for you, even though they may have been "reasonable" and traditional choices.

If you are brand new to Human Design, start first with my book, *Human Design Workbook*. This book offers a straightforward, basic introduction to your Human Design chart. If you're ready for more depth and more insights into Centers, Profiles, Circuitry, and Gates, my book *Understanding Human Design The New Science of Astrology: Discover Who You Really Are* will give you a good, solid understanding of the basics of the traditional Human Design system.

Your understanding of your chart gives you a personal narrative about who you are, how you operate, and what you can give to the world. To craft a story that is truly worthy of who you really are, you need a language that has the power to build a story big enough to inspire you and call you forward. I have created a template you can use as a writing prompt for creating the story of your chart. You can download a fillable and printable version of the Quantum Life Purpose template under the student resources section of my free Your Quantum Life Purpose course, found here:

karencurryparker.teachable.com/p/your-quantum-life-purpose

Scanning the QR code will take you directly to the course.

Use the template there and the new language to write a new story that is truly worthy of the once-in-a-lifetime-cosmic-event that you are.

The Types

Manifestor | Initiator

Spiritual Purpose: Translate Divine Inspiration into action.

Quantum Purpose: To initiate people into the frequency of transformation and creativity through direct access to the Quantum Pulse.

Emotional Theme: Anger.

The Initiator has a direct, non-verbal connection to Divine Inspiration. When an Initiator feels the internal alignment and a sense of right timing for action, the role of the Initiator is to follow through on the inspiration with the matching action.

If an Initiator cannot follow through with the matching action or if they are interrupted in their creative flow and forced to stop their creative follow-through or explain, with words, what they're doing, the Initiator can experience the emotional theme of anger.

Anger signals that the Initiator's creative flow has been interrupted. The anger is the force of their creative energy that has nowhere else to go because it is no longer being channeled into action.

Optimal Expression:

An awakened Initiator is deeply connected to Divine Inspiration and the flow of Spirit as the result of a deep connection to the value of the unique role that only the Initiator can play. A skilled Initiator is aware of their power, informs those who their actions will impact, and moves forward when the timing is right. They own their power, never allow the judgment of others to impede their creative flow and are honoring and aware of the initiating force they bring to the world. They serve the creative muse and are transformational agents of change.

Unbalanced Expression:

The unbalanced Initiator either hides their power and fails to initiate or feels the need to overcompensate for their internal feelings of powerlessness by power struggling. The unbalanced Initiator fails to inform out of fear of being stopped, controlled, or having their power questioned. The failure to inform creates the energy of anger and resentment in their relationships, further creating the possibility of power struggles or shutting down of their personal power. Misusing power can result in burnout, depletion, and a deep sense of feeling misunderstood and alone.

Lesson/Challenge:

The challenge of the Initiator is to learn to use their creative essence sustainably. To be sustainable and to truly serve their purpose of initiating others, the Initiator must heal their relationship with their personal power, reclaim their power, cultivate an internal alignment with their own truth and their own creative flow and learn to be at peace with the idea that they are uniquely connected to a creative force in a way that not many others share. Once an Initiator can integrate the value of their power and their role in the world, they can also heal their feelings of being alone and embrace their unique role in waking the world.

Contemplations:

- How do you feel about being powerful?
- Were you allowed to "follow your own flow" as a child?
- Was your power acknowledged and supported by those around you?
- Do you feel comfortable being powerful?
- Is anger a theme in your life?
- Does your fear of anger or your suppression of anger stop you from doing what you want in life?
- What needs to be healed, released, aligned, and brought to your awareness for you to fully embrace the value of your unique initiating role in the world?
- Are you out of physical, resource, identity, moral, or energetic integrity?
- What do you need to do to be in integrity with yourself, your energy, or others?
- What needs to be healed, released, aligned, and brought to your awareness for you to trust your own powerful connection to your own right timing?

Affirmation:

I am a powerful creative force. I trust my inner sense of timing to act on my creative intentions. I follow my creative flow and inform those who may be impacted by my actions so that they can support me and clear the path for me to do what I need to do. I recognize my value and know that when I follow my creative flow, I am not only bringing something new into the world, I am initiating others into new possibilities. I value the unique role only I can play. I honor my power and commit to nurturing my energy, so I can act with great power when the timing is correct. I am a transformational force, and my actions change the world.

Generator | Alchemist

Spiritual Purpose: Turn inspiration into form.
Quantum Purpose: To physically manifest creativity and express through devotion.
Emotional Theme: Frustration.

The Alchemist has the role of turning inspiration into form. The Alchemist is here to become the expert of self-fulfillment. The process of turning inspiration to form is not about ruling over a particular skill or job but knowing how to navigate life itself with skilled confidence—knowing how to know and knowing how to learn and then following through until one becomes accomplished.

The Alchemist has the role in the world to do the work to build the world. It is vital for the Alchemist to have work that feels fulfilling or fulfills a purpose that supports a more significant purpose beyond a job.

The Alchemist is designed for dancing responsively with life. It is not the job of the Alchemist to figure things out but to engineer a course through life by allowing opportunities and experiences to show up and to follow the ones that feel good and correct. The Alchemist must train themselves to tune into their own inner gut-level feeling of what feels right and follow it, even if it defies the plans they made in their mind.

To become especially skilled, an Alchemist must do things repeatedly, to work towards perfection. The Alchemist has a stair-step learning curve. Once an Alchemist responds to an opportunity, they usually experience an immediate growth cycle and surge in skillful accomplishment. It is expected for the Alchemist to feel stuck and frustrated once an Alchemist has learned all they can from a particular experience or cycle.

This part of the learning cycle is essential to the Alchemist process. This plateau is a cycle of building momentum, and the energy of frustration that builds up during this part of the learning process is necessary for the next surge in learning.

The challenge for the Alchemist is not to quit because of the frustration. When the Alchemist hits the plateau in the learning process, it is essential to do nothing except realign and explore potentials, envision what's next, and wait for clues and signs about what to do next. Sometimes a plateau indicates it's time to quit, but Alchemists must respond to an opportunity to quit—not simply get frustrated and throw in the towel. When the time is right, the next step in the process will reveal itself, and the Alchemy process begins again.

Frustration indicates that the energy for the next opportunity or the next growth cycle is building. It's a signal to Alchemists to recalibrate, set clear intentions, and then nurture their energy while they wait for the next step in their genius to appear.

Optimal Expression:

The skillful Alchemist understands that their life is an arena within which they explore their elevated education. Through responding, enduring, sustaining, practice, repetition, and correction, the Alchemist learns who they are and how they best respond to life and uses their life to fully embody the story of who they are.

The Alchemist understands that there is no "figuring out" their next right step. They cultivate a deep and aligned relationship with their purpose and path and trust that the next level of skilled accomplishment will be revealed to them when they are ready.

It is through allowing and responding that the Alchemist learns to fulfill their life's purpose. Their deep connection to their Sacral will enable them to either stay with an experience and continue to grow or to accept that they have gleaned the necessary lessons and wait for the next opportunity for growth.

Unbalanced Expression:

The unbalanced Alchemist has a pattern of quitting before reaching genius level. Frustration leads to quitting, which leads to greater frustration. The pain of the unbalanced Alchemist is the struggle to find the right path for total self-control.

The unbalanced Alchemist will often respond to frustration with quitting, refuses to wait for the next opportunity, and can waste enormous amounts of time and energy trying to figure out what to do next. This leads to depletion and a cycle of joy-less living that can cause the Alchemist to shut down their access to their own life force energy—their Sacral Center.

Lesson/Challenge:

To learn to wait for the next right step. To conquer the ability to sit with and be with their frustration, recognizing that frustration signals that momentum for change is growing. To learn to trust their inner Sacral response and let the trajectory of their skilled accomplishing to unfold with ease and grace.

Contemplations:

- How do you experience frustration?
- Where do you feel it in your body?
- What is your habit when you feel frustrated?
- Are you frustrated about your life right now?
- What is your response to your current frustration?
- Do you trust your Sacral?
- Do you trust that your next right step will show up for you?
- How do you feel about waiting?
- What can you do to cultivate more patience and alignment?

Affirmation:

My life gives me an arena within which to explore myself and who I am. I let my inner alignment with my truth and what feels good and right to guide me and reveal to me the next right step. I strengthen my self-trust and courage so that I can confidently follow my path. I use the power of my mind to inspire me and allow for the gentle unfolding of my life path. I trust in the cycles of growth in my life, knowing that my destiny is to be the fulfillment of who I am. I listen to the signal that frustration gives me, knowing that my frustration informs me that change is coming.

Manifesting Generator | Time Bender

Spiritual Purpose: Turn inspiration into form.

Quantum Purpose: To physically manifest creativity and speed up the quantum process and linear time.

Emotional Theme: Frustration and Anger.

The Time Bender is a hybrid of sorts, a blend of the manifesting energy similar to that of the Initiator and the proficiency of the Alchemist.

Like the Initiator, the Time Bender has an internal non-verbal creative flow. But, unlike the Initiator, the Time Bender cannot initiate but must wait for the inner signal, the Sacral response, making them, first and foremost, a Generator Type.

Once the Time Bender has something to respond to, they can spring into action with the same speed and inner alignment as their Initiator cousin. The speed of the Time Bender gives them the role of finding the fastest, easiest way to complete tasks and to experience self-proficiency. It is the role of the Time Bender to speed up the experience of time by finding the fastest route and the quickest path.

Like the Alchemist, the Time Bender experiences the cycles of frustration that indicate change is on the horizon. Like the Initiator, the Time Bender also experiences the anger that comes from a disruption in the internal, non-verbal creative flow. Frustration and anger for the Time Bender signal that change is coming and that they need to improve their advanced skill over their creative flow by informing those impacted by their actions.

When Time Benders align with their inner signal of timing and their creative flow, they are powerful forces who promise to bring to the world an expedited way to create something new.

Multitasking is essential to most Time Benders, not because they can create multiple things simultaneously (they can!), but because they need to be busy to expend their excess energy. Not everything that the Time Bender starts will be completed, which others can often judge as sloppy. The expectation that they should finish everything they start can lead to the experience of frustration and anger in the Time Bender if they fail to realize that some creative projects simply serve the function of burning off extra energy.

Optimal Expression:

The proficient Time Bender is aware of their power and speed. They are deeply conscious of those around them who will be impacted by their fast response to life. They are tuned into the inner signal of their Sacral Center and wait for something to respond to before they leap into action.

The Time Bender's capacity to "do" changes the story of what can be done in time and on time. The inner alignment of the Time Bender binds them to a creative flow that brings change, transformation, and creativity to the world in new ways. The wisdom of the Time Bender is that, through their own experience, they are wise about which steps are necessary to create in a skillful way and which steps can be skipped.

When responding, the awakened Time Bender has the capacity to bring creative projects to fulfillment and become more skillful over how to work directly with their creative flow and experience of time. Their ability to "do" transforms people's perceptions of what's possible.

Unbalanced Expression:

The unbalanced Time Bender struggles with the same theme of quitting before reaching genius as the Alchemist. The frustration of the Time Bender is more intense and edgier, mixed with the anger of creative disruption. This is a symptom of the quality and quantity of energy the Time Bender naturally carries within their energy field.

The unbalanced Time Bender can build up intense amounts of energy in their bodies that they sometimes have to work hard to shut down, disconnecting them from their inner creative flow and natural power.

Time Benders who are disconnected from the response mechanism of their Sacral wisdom can often create from the ideas in their minds, causing them to expend massive amounts of energy with little return, triggering frustration and anger.

Time Benders who force themselves to only focus on creating in a limited way, who believe that they are scattered and unfocused if they multitask, will also build up energy in their bodies that can cause them to experience deep frustration and anger.

Lesson/Challenge:

To learn to wait for the next right step and to inform before acting, and to accept that not all actions will result in the success they envision. To recognize that the role of the Time Bender is to find the most efficient way to create. To embrace the inner sense of timing married with action unique to the energy of the Time Bender and to follow at their own correct speed without self-judgment.

Contemplations:

- How do you manage your energy?
- Are you getting enough physical activity?
- What does your body feel like if you don't move enough?
- What role does frustration play in your life?
- What frustrates you?
- How do you manage your frustration?
- What role does anger play in your life?
- What makes you angry?
- How do you manage your anger?
- How do you feel about yourself if you work on something that doesn't work out the way you hoped?

- What can you do to be more gentle and self-accepting?

Affirmation:

I move faster than most people. My speed and ability to create many things simultaneously give me a unique perspective on getting things done on the planet. Because I have a lot of energy, I need a lot of movement to stay healthy and strong. It's healthy for me to multitask; I need to do more than one thing at a time to move my energy. Not everything that I do will create the result that I'm envisioning. The purpose of multitasking is to burn off my extra energy. The things that are mine to complete and bring to the world will align with my inner sense of timing married with action. I am careful to let the people around me know what I'm doing so that they can stand back and let me create at my own speed.

Projector | Orchestrator

Spiritual Purpose: Here to anchor the energetic template of what we are here to create, to align the energy of the world and heal the planet's energy.

Quantum Purpose: To hold the energy template of what's to come and clear the vibration of the collective consciousness.

Emotional Theme: Bitterness.

The Orchestrator plays a very special role in the world. They carry knowledge, insights, and wisdom that have the potential to transform and improve the way we build the world. They process and work with energy and, as such, intuitively understand how energy works and energy flows. This awareness gives them insights into how to translate the world's energy into form.

The Orchestrator's internal energy and wisdom are activated through recognition and invitation. They need to be seen and valued to be heard and to be able to transmit their wisdom effectively.

Energy is of a premium for the Orchestrator. Because they rely on the trajectory of the creative process of others to best serve the world, if the Orchestrator is not engaging in the correct alignment with the creative process, they run the risk of using their own energy to try to force a project into form. Consequently, they can burn themselves out pushing for recognition, doing all the work instead of allowing others to do the building, and offering up their wisdom with people who don't cherish the value of what the Orchestrator is offering.

An exhausted Orchestrator can be bitter. Bitterness signals two vital things in the Orchestrator experience. When an Orchestrator is bitter, it means that they are not valuing themselves enough to wait for the people who genuinely cherish their insights and wisdom to activate their energy, or it can mean that the Orchestrator requires rest.

When an Orchestrator is not valuing their own wisdom, they can be so thirsty for an opportunity that they drink from every cup handed to them. Drinking from the wrong cup can be poisonous to the energy of the Orchestrator and can leave them feeling exhausted and bitter.

When an Orchestrator waits for the right opportunity and recognition, their energy is unlocked and amplified, and their ability to lead and guide is purposeful and valuable.

Optimal Expression:

The awakened Orchestrator nurtures and cares for their mind, body, and spirit with great deliberation. They understand that timing and waiting work in their favor, and they use the time between activations to rest and restore their energy.

An awakened Orchestrator knows their value, and they stand in their value with the awareness that what they have to give will only serve its purpose if they share it with the right people at the right time. They recognize that timing is not about their personal value but about the readiness and timing of the opportunity. They trust in right timing and understand that when the timing is right, and the value is correctly placed, the right opportunity will reveal itself.

The Orchestrator that values themselves and properly harnesses their energy is aware that they are most impactful when they share their knowledge and wisdom and do not necessarily have to do the physical work of bringing a creation into form. They allow others to do the work and they manage, guide, and delegate accordingly to conserve and use their energy effectively.

Unbalanced Expression:

The unbalanced Orchestrator desperately seeks recognition and attention to try to manipulate and facilitate an invitation or an opportunity. This effort to be seen, heard, and invited can cause the Orchestrator to burn themselves out.

The unbalanced Orchestrator, in their excitement and eagerness to see the end results of their creation, can sometimes end up doing all the work if they forget the true nature of their unique role in the world.

Lesson/Challenge:

The lesson of the Orchestrator is to learn to value themselves and their wisdom enough to wait for the right opportunity to share their knowledge and insights. To facilitate the correct experiences that reflect their value, the Orchestrator needs to maintain a high sense of self-worth and cultivate their energy by resting and replenishing themselves to be sustainable.

Contemplations:

- Are you bitter? What do you feel resentful about?
- What message do you think your bitterness is giving you?
- Do you value yourself?
- What do you need to heal and release to increase your sense of value and self-worth?
- What is the quality of your spiritual, mental, emotional, and physical energy?
- Do you think you have the energy available for the opportunities you seek?
- What do you need to do to cultivate your energy?
- Do you need to rest?
- Think about some of the greatest invitations you've received in your life.
- How did it feel to be invited or recognized correctly?

Affirmation:

I am a powerful resource for the world. My intuition, insights, awareness, and knowledge help manage and guide the energy of the world and the next phase of growth and evolution on the planet. What I have to offer the world is so powerful, necessary, and valuable that I recognize I am carrying the seeds of evolution within my being. I wait for the right opportunities that reflect the value of what I carry and bring into the world. When the opportunity is correct and I am valued, I share my knowledge and wisdom and facilitate the work necessary to build the next phase of the human story. In between opportunities, I rest and replenish my energy, so I'm ready to serve when I am called again.

Reflector | Calibrator

Spiritual Purpose: To be the barometer of the alignment of humanity with Heart.

Quantum Purpose: To mirror to others the Human condition and Human potential.

Emotional Theme: Disappointment.

The Calibrator has the role of experiencing, in an amplified way through their completely open centers, the potential of what's possible for humanity to be creating and fulfilling. Through their experience of the current level of fulfillment of the potential of humanity, they then reflect it back to the world.

The theme of disappointment for the Calibrator has two important sources. The first source is disappointment in the world around them. Through their nine open centers, the Calibrator has a deep, visceral knowledge of what is possible for all of humanity. They can sense and feel deeply the potential that lives within all of us. When Calibrators look at the world and perceive the gap between our potential and what we are actually creating, they experience disappointment.

This disappointment is genuine not only on a collective level but also on a personal level. This can often lead to the Calibrator falling in love with a person's potential and being disappointed that their loved ones don't fulfill the potential that the Calibrator sees in them.

Without a clear understanding of how their energy works, the Calibrator can often merge with others and struggle to fulfill their own potential. They can sense that they need and want something different. Still, their experience of the energies of others can cause the Calibrator to lose connection with their own energy, direction, and identity. Often the Calibrator experiences this as a disappointment in themselves.

Disappointment signals the Calibrator that they may not be in the right place with the right people and may need to change their community to reflect a different potential for fulfillment.

The second source of disappointment for the Calibrator involves the need for time. The Calibrator's decision-making process involves taking enough time to clarify what they need and want in the context of all the energy from the world outside of themselves that they are amplifying at any given time. Time, usually at least one entire lunar cycle (and sometimes more than one!), provides the Calibrator with a chance to connect with their own needs and wants versus the amplification of their experience of the needs and wants of others.

Calibrators also need time to talk through their decisions and choices with others while they wait for clarity. They need to see their decisions reflected in their dialogues with others to get more clarity about what to do.

If Calibrators don't give themselves the gift of time—a difficult thing to do in our fast-paced world—they can often jump the gun and feel compelled to make a speedy choice that eventually turns out to be unfulfilling.

Optimal Expression:

The awakened Calibrator is aware of their surroundings and the experience of the energy of their surroundings within them. They feel in alignment with their community. They experience the people they surround themselves with and the environment they place themselves in as "home." The awakened Calibrator knows the impact of the energy of others and values themself enough to take the time to find the alignment with what is right for themselves in the midst of the experience of the energies of so many other people. They are aware of the reflection and can simply "be" with the reflection. They are witnesses, and the power of what they see and reflect is the purpose of their lives. They know that, even though they can see the potential, it's not their work to fix it, just to simply reflect it back.

Unbalanced Expression:

The unbalanced Calibrator feels ALL of the world and takes on the task of fixing the world as a whole. Without awareness of the reflection, the Calibrator uses the full force of their powerful energy to try to heal the experience of the pain of others. With their deep awareness of other people's energy and potential, they put all of their power into inspiring, coaching, serving, and nurturing others into healing and fulfilling their potential, even when others aren't willing to see the potential and do the work to change. This massive effort on the part of the Calibrator is exhausting and disappointing.

Lesson/Challenge:

The lesson of the Calibrator is to learn to let go of the need to fix what isn't working, to share and experience what they see and feel, and to trust that the Universal flow of right timing will support the world in doing the transformation necessary to create alignment and peace. Calibrators have the job of embodying what they feel and sense and use their lives as a mirror of awakening for others, but to remember that it is not the job of the Calibrator to do the work of fixing others.

Contemplations:

- Are you disappointed?
- What/who are you disappointed in?
- What needs to be healed, released, aligned, and brought to your awareness for you to recover from disappointment?
- Do you feel responsible for fixing and healing the pain of others?
- Do you need to release yourself from this responsibility?
- Do you feel responsible for helping others meet their potential?
- Do you need to release yourself from this responsibility?
- Are you in the right place? With the right people?

- Do you need to change your environment?
- Are you giving yourself the time you need to make good choices?
- Do you have people in your life who can serve as your sounding board as you talk through your decisions in life?

Affirmation:

I am a karmic mirror. Through my experience and expression of the energy around me, I reflect back to others their potential and their misalignment. Through my reflection, others can see what they need to bring back into alignment to fulfill their path. I understand the depth of the potential of possibility for humanity. I know it is not my job to fix the world but to simply mirror the current energies. I trust in Divine Timing, and I know that with time the potential of the world will be fulfilled. I am patient and honor myself. I give myself the time I need to make right choices and to place myself in the right location with the right people. I trust my inner sense of feeling at home where I belong and stay aligned with where I feel most at home.

Authority

Authority influences what you need and, sometimes, the timing to use your Strategy effectively to help you make decisions. Depending on which software you use to generate your Human Design chart, there are many different ways to talk about Authority.

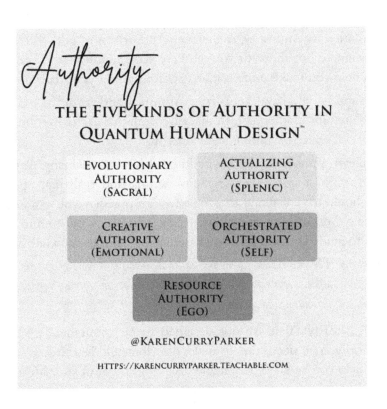

All Generator Types have Sacral Authority, called Evolutionary Authority in Quantum Human Design. When you have Sacral Authority, it means that your in-the-moment gut response is letting you know whether something is right for you or not. The biggest challenge with Evolutionary Authority is learning to trust your instinctual response. Please read the Alchemist and Time Bender Sections to learn more about Evolutionary Authority.

Quantum Definition: The gut-level pulse of Evolutionary Authority informs the Alchemists and the Time Benders about what needs to be done to further the Divine Imperative and the evolution of the world.

In the name of keeping it simple, there are four other basic kinds of Authority:

1. Actualizing Authority (Splenic Authority)

2. Creative Authority (Emotional Authority)

3. Orchestrated Authority (Self-Authority)

4. Resource Authority (Ego Authority)

Different Human Design software programs list other kinds of Authority, but these variations are simply sub-categories of the three basic types of Authority.

1. Actualizing Authority: Actualizing Authority means you are designed to know, in the moment, what feels right to you (or not). Having Actualizing Authority means that you can be spontaneous with your decisions. You don't need time to contemplate or sit with decisions. You will know what is true for you immediately.

Much like Evolutionary Authority, Actualizing Authority is a "gut" level sense of what feels right or aligned. For those of you who are not Evolutionary Types, Actualizing Authority can help you make more minor decisions about your daily life choices.

For example, suppose you have Actualizing Authority and are at the health food store searching for a vitamin supplement. In that case, your Self-Actualization Center might give you a sense of which vitamin is right for you.

Often, we achieve Actualizing Authority in hindsight. Actualizing Authority is that feeling of "knowing" something is right or wrong and realizing, upon reflection, realizing you should have listened to yourself. With practice, you can begin to notice your Actualizing Authority in the moment, allowing the wisdom and awareness of your intuition to guide you and give you essential insights about what you need.

Quantum Definition: The instinctual awareness to know when it is time to expand resources, align with greater integrity, take actions to sustain or increase value or your own value, and fully self-actualize your gifts, experiences, and talents.

2. Creative Authority: You are not designed to be spontaneous when you have Creative Authority. You need time to make decisions and learning to wait for clarity is essential to help you avoid experiencing disappointment in your life's choices.

Creative Authority can influence the way the Strategy for your Type works. The Strategy for your Type is still essential, but if you have Creative Authority, you have to check in with your Strategy and sense how you feel over time.

You tend to have a lot of emotional energy when you have Creative Authority. You are passionate and experience big feelings to various degrees depending on other aspects of your chart. (For more insights, read the section on the Creativity Center). This internal emotional energy makes it essential to take your time to make decisions. It's easy to leap into things in the moment when they feel good, only to wake up the next day doubting whether you made the right choice. Waiting for clarity helps avoid some of the regrets you may have experienced in your life.

With Creative Authority, your decision has to stay consistent over time. If you are all over the place with how you feel about your choice while waiting for clarity, it's probably not the right decision to make.

Here's how this might look. Let's say you get invited to speak at an event sponsored by a group that you like but are not crazy about being around. You love speaking, but you don't necessarily enjoy this particular group. When you get the invitation, you're so excited to land a speaking gig that you immediately accept the invitation. The following day when you wake up, you question your decision, and you have a slight anxiety stomachache from worrying about whether you did the right thing.

Over the next couple of days, you try to convince yourself that it was the right choice. You manage to stir up enthusiasm along the way, but you can't quite get your energy aligned with the opportunity. When you finally give the talk, several group members want to hire you, but they end up being clients you don't really enjoy, and you're left continuing to feel obligated to do business in a way that doesn't feel good to you.

If you had followed your Creative Authority when you got invited to speak, you might have answered, "Thank you. This sounds like a lovely invitation. I need to check my calendar and get back to you. When do you need to know my response?" Your answer would have bought you time to check in with your feelings to see if this was the right choice for you, and you would have been aligned with whatever felt correct.

The most important thing to remember with Creative Authority is that your decision has to stay consistent over time. Suppose you feel a "yes" in response to an opportunity; that "yes" has to stay true over the course of a couple of days. If you're all over the place with your feelings, it's not the right decision for you.

Quantum Definition: The ability to consciously cultivate a baseline emotional frequency that allows you to sense through feeling the right timing and alignment for decisions and actions.

3. Orchestrated Authority: Orchestrated Authority is a catch-all phrase for a few different, less common Authorities. When you have a chart that says Self-Projected Authority, No Authority, No Inner Authority, or Mental-Projected Authority, it means you need to talk through your choices to get clarity.

You don't need advice. You simply need a sounding board, a good friend, or someone you trust to listen while you talk through your options. Having this kind of Authority means that you are gifted at seeking the potential of all possibilities. Talking through the potentials helps you gauge where the energy flows, the conditioning field, and your own alignment with what needs to happen to fulfill the potential in your own life.

Orchestrated Authority is common for Orchestrator Types and is true for all Calibrators.

Quantum Definition: The ability to see the potential in all choices, which requires externalization by talking it through to determine which potential is correct and aligned with action.

4. Resource Authority: Resource Authority means you have a defined Resource Center, and you don't have Creative Authority.

Because the Resource Center is about having sustainable energy and resources (or not!), if you have Resource Authority, you won't decide to do something unless you have the energy or the resources. It also can signal whether a choice is aligned with integrity or not.

This can present challenges because it means you have to have healthy self-worth in order to be comfortable saying "no" to something if you don't have the energy or the resources for it or if something about the decisions feels out of integrity. If you're in a pattern of trying to prove your worth by pleasing others, you may find that you have to strengthen your sense of value before you can truly follow the Authority of your Resource Center.

Quantum Definition: The ability to know when a choice is in alignment with available resources, sustainability, and integrity.

The Profiles

The Lines of the Profiles

When you look at the numbers (Gates) next to each planet symbol on your chart, you will see that each Gate number has a smaller number next to it. For each Gate there are six different lines, each line being a further expression of your uniqueness. The lines of the Gates do not show up on the BodyGraph itself and their meaning can be revealed to you during a Human Design Reading.

Each line has a specific expression or personality. The position of your Gates is expressed also in lines, giving you even more insight into how that Gate will be expressed in your life. Each line has a specific energy that will influence how the Gate is expressed.

TRANSPERSONAL LINES ARE ENERGIES
THAT ARE ALL ABOUT EXPERIENCES IN
RELATIONSHIPS WITH OTHERS.

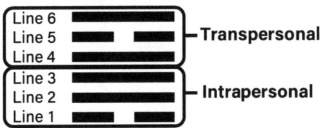

INTRAPERSONAL LINES ARE ENERGIES
THAT ARE SELF-FOCUSED AND ALL ABOUT
PERSONAL EXPERIENCE AND
UNDERSTANDING.

@KarenCurryParker

Lines 1 through 3 in the profiles are intrapersonal lines and are energies that are self-focused and all about personal experience and understanding. Lines 4 through 6 in the profiles are about transpersonal energy and all about experiences in relationships with others. Some people, by design, are focused more on their own life process, and others are more oriented towards relationships.

Line 1: Investigator | Resource

Purpose: To lay the information foundation for the security and safety of all of us.

Needs: To build a foundation of information to feel prepared.

Drive: Curiosity.

Fear: Not knowing enough or fear of the unknown.

Optimal Expression: To learn to value and trust your curiosity. Knowing that when you feel curious and inspired to learn about something, it signals that the information you gather will ultimately serve a need. To know there is a Cosmic Intelligence that points you in the right direction to gather the information that is yours to share with others and to know that you will know what you need to know when you need to know it. To learn to celebrate and value the depth of your knowledge.

Unbalanced Expression: To let the fear of the unknown or your fear of not knowing cause you to be frenetic in your gathering of data. To not trust in the Divine unfolding of the next right step and to overcompensate for your fear by over-preparing or getting lost in the data.

Lesson/Challenge: To learn to trust that when the time is right, the right information will appear. The challenge of the First Line is to embrace your role as a resource for others and to discover where to learn and how to gather information so that the unknown simply becomes a new opportunity to learn something new.

Contemplations:

- Do you trust that you'll know what you need to know when you need to know it? Why or why not?
- What is needed to deepen your trust in the flow of information and your ability to know how to know?
- List some ways that you have served as a resource for others. Do you value what you know?

Affirmation:

I am a wealth of information for the world. My natural curiosity inspires me to explore information to build a strong foundation of understanding about how the world works and what is necessary to ensure wellbeing, abundance, and the fulfillment of potential. I know how to access information, and this knowledge allows me to surrender to the deep knowing that I'll know what I need to know when I need to know it.

Line 2: Hermit | Responder

Purpose: To integrate knowledge, energy, and wisdom and wait for the readiness of others to call you out to share your wisdom.

Needs: Alone time to rest, integrate and regenerate so that you're ready when it's time to share what you know.

Drive: To become skilled at the balance between alone time and being out in the world.

Fear: Disappearing and being isolated.

Optimal Expression: Cultivating a mature understanding of the need for alone time as a way to integrate wisdom, knowledge, and experience. To know that alone time is essential for you to build your understanding and maintain your energy so that when others call you out to share what you know, you'll be prepared with the right information, and you will have cultivated the right amount of energy with which to deliver it—the introverted extrovert.

Unbalanced Expression: To fail to balance self-expression with self-renewal, and burnout creates a deep need to hide as the pathway to healing.

Lesson/Challenge: To find the balance between self-renewal and self-expression. To not let the desire to be alone keep you from building connections. To not be over-committed and fail to retreat for the sake of integration and regeneration.

Contemplations:

- Do you know the internal signals that let you know when you need alone time for renewal?
- Do you follow those signals?
- What can you do to cultivate your alone time better?
- Are you burned out?
- What do you need to do to heal your burnout?

Affirmation:

I am here to respond to the needs of others. My energy field signals the world when I am ready to share what I know and my understanding of my experiences. To serve at my highest level, I honor my need for alone time. My requirement for self-renewal and integration allows me to serve others better. I am skilled at finding the balance between alone time and honoring the timing of the call to respond to the needs of others. I trust my connection to my energy, and I sustain myself first to serve others better. When I nourish my own energy, I can give and share more.

Purpose: To explore and experience possibilities and share your experience with others to protect and serve them.

Needs: To experiment and try things.

Drive: To try things to see what works and what doesn't and to discover how to make things better based on experience.

Fear: Failure.

Optimal Expression: To follow the flow of curiosity and exploration. To embrace the exploratory journey as a challenge and expect to have to adjust and respond to the results until you arrive at the solution that is the most elegant and effective. To share those insights with others so they don't have to go through the same "trial and error" experience.

Unbalanced Expression: To stop exploring because you're too afraid of making mistakes. To judge yourself as a failure because you let the exploration process define your success rather than allowing yourself to keep working until you find the solution. Explore without doing the work to bring things to completion, leaving a trail of chaos behind you.

Lesson/Challenge: Learn to embrace the experimentation process with the full awareness that it will involve exploring what works and what doesn't. Learn that part of the experimentation process is about experientially discovering what doesn't work. Learn to trust the learning process and not judge the outcome until you've had enough time to work out all the details.

Contemplations:

- What am I good at?
- How did I become good at the skills that I have?
- Do I judge my explorations and experiments?
- Am I holding myself back because I'm afraid of failing?
- What needs to be healed, released, aligned, and brought to my awareness for me to embrace my curious nature and my exploratory wisdom?

Affirmation:

I am an explorer on the leading edge of consciousness. My curiosity compels me to try things out. The wisdom of my experience allows me to lead and guide others. I help them navigate the unknown and new experiences with the knowledge I've learned from my path. I have never made a mistake in my life. My explorations have led me to the right place at the right time to better lead and serve others. I need time to find the most elegant path through life challenges, and I'm gentle with myself as I work out the most effective and efficient ways to create in the world.

Line 4: Opportunist | Stabilizer

Purpose: To build and be a part of a community and to prepare the way for sharing and spreading ideas.

Needs: Stability and consistency.

Drive: To build the support and opportunities necessary to be prepared for any situation. Always have a backup plan ready, just in case.

Fear: The fear of loss and limbo.

Optimal Expression: The ability to skillfully accomplish the cadence and rhythm of change. To learn what must be done to facilitate change and to be in the flow of change. To use this knowledge to help guide others in creating easy and graceful change. To bring stability to the community with your wisdom. To know how to access contingency plans and implement them to maintain stability, even when the circumstances are dramatically different.

Unbalanced Expression: To be terrified of change. To be over-prepared for every potential. To be so afraid of change that you spend your energy calculating all the worst-case scenarios so that you're prepared for disaster. To fail to make change because the fear of change is overwhelming.

Lesson/Challenge: To discover what is trustworthy. To learn how to navigate change with grace and ease. To learn to trust that, with experience, you will discern with skill how to make change in a way that gives you confidence and grace when faced with the unknown or sudden shifts in the landscape. To learn how to build a new foundation confidently.

Contemplations:

- How do you feel about making change?
- What strategies have you cultivated to help you navigate change?
- What are your non-negotiable when creating a stable foundation during a disruptive cycle?
- Do you fear change?
- Do you trust that you'll know what you need to know when you need to know it?

Affirmation:

I cultivate an inner foundation of trust and connection to Source, allowing me to navigate transformation and change gracefully. I am fully present to all that life brings me, and I live in the moment, knowing that I'll know what I need to know when I need to know it. The stability that I AM co-regulates the people around me and brings calm and resilience to my community of loved ones.

Purpose: To serve as a karmic mirror for others and to support the healing process through the reflection by teaching and sharing the highest potential of humanity. To teach, lead and inspire.

Needs: To be seen and heard for who you are by people who respect your leadership and wisdom.

Drive: To experience and learn from life and to take those experiences and share what you know with others.

Fear: Not being or feeling truly seen or heard. Being subject to the false expectations of others.

Optimal Expression: To lead others to the fulfillment of personal and collective expectations sustainably and healthily. To see what's possible, to gauge where people are and what they need to be led towards, and to do so in a way that is inspiring and uplifting. To teach, lead and inspire those who are ready and to be able to gauge who you are here to lead.

Unbalanced Expression: To be so afraid of the expectations and projections of others that you hide out. To fail to lead. To take the unhealthy expectations and projections of others and internalize them.

Lesson/Challenge: To not let the expectations or the projections of others cause you to hide out to the degree that you can't be "found." To learn to watch and reflect and not to take the perspectives of others personally. To see the potential of others but not fall in love with it or to coach and coax it into fulfillment at a cost to yourself. To cultivate a high enough sense of self-worth and value that the unhealthy opinions and expectations of others don't hurt you.

Contemplations:

- How healthy is my self-worth?
- Do I have trauma to my sense of personal value that needs resolution?
- How do I handle the projections of others?
- Am I hiding out?

Affirmation:

People see in me what they need to heal in themselves. I hold their reflection with love, and I do not take it personally. My gift is my ability to see people's potential and to treat them accordingly. I stand firm in my value and my ability to lead others. I nurture myself and fulfill my potential with the knowing that the more I embrace my value, the more value I have to give to others.

Line 6: Role Model | Adept

Purpose: To experience, integrate and demonstrate the highest potential of consciousness on the planet and to quietly show us how to live it.

Needs: To be living in alignment with your life purpose.

Drive: To make the world a better place.

Fear: The fear of failing your life purpose.

The Line 6 Profile has three distinct life phases based on age and planetary cycles. Phase One is from birth to the first Saturn return at approximately 28.5 years of age. Phase Two, called "being on the roof" is from the first Saturn return until the Chiron return at approximately 50 years of age. Phase Three starts following the Chiron return.

Optimal Expression:

Phase One: To fearlessly experiment and explore to discover what works best. To realize that your "mistakes" are simply part of your experiential learning process and that your role is to find perfection through experimentation.

Phase Two: To allow yourself to integrate all that you have learned. To realize that this cycle is essential for your wellbeing and to be self-generous and allow for rest, healing, learning, and exploring your own internal creative plane. To vanquish being at peace with trusting the unfolding of your life and your life plan and to surrender to the unfolding.

Phase Three: To live as a ruler of aligned and authentic living. To trust that you are having a profound impact on others when you model for them what it looks like to live in alignment and be relentlessly authentic. To show the world how to live by walking your talk and trusting that you are fulfilling your mission when you are aligned.

Unbalanced Expression:

Phase One: Failing to try something new out of fear of failure and judging yourself for making too many mistakes.

Phase Two: Failing to rest, heal or integrate because you let the pressure of needing to "do" dictate what's next in your life. Pushing too hard, hustling too much, and, ultimately, burning yourself out by not waiting for the right timing to fulfill your purpose.

Phase Three: Using will, force, and mental machinations to try to force yourself into a leadership position. Believing that the ends justify the means, pushing yourself out into the world and failing to live with integrity, or giving up and letting the fear of failure overwhelm you. Failing to fulfill yourself as a role model.

Lesson/Challenge:

Phase One: To learn to allow yourself to experiment and explore for the sake of discovering what works (and what doesn't). To not let your fear of failing stop you from exploring.

Phase Two: To let yourself rest, heal, learn, contemplate and integrate all of your life experiences without letting the pressure of feeling like there is something you need to be doing cause you to burn yourself out.

Phase Three: To let the intelligence of Life reveal to you the right next step for you to take to fulfill your life purpose. To stop letting the pressure of feeling like you're failing cause you to forget that your alignment with your Authentic Self is essential to your purpose. To remember that HOW you live is more important than WHAT you do.

Contemplations:

- How do you feel about experimenting and "getting it wrong"?
- How do you feel about resting? Do you trust in Divine Timing?
- What does integrity mean to you?
- What does "walking your talk" mean to you?
- Are you living authentically?
- What needs to change to bring your life into alignment?
- What phase of your Sixth line life are you in?
- Are you in alignment with your current phase?
- Are you resisting?
- What needs to change?
- How do you manage your fear of failing at your life's mission?
- Do you see evidence of where you are getting it right?

Affirmation:

I am a role model of conscious living. Me—being the full, unlimited expression of who I am—is my life purpose. Others look to me to see what authentic living and integrity look like. My life has given me experience and wisdom to show others how to live in alignment with right timing, authentic self-expression, honesty, self-generosity, and be of service to the world. There is nothing that I have to do unless I am called to do something. It is simply in me being myself that I show the world how to live.

The Centers

The Mechanics of Creating (Excerpt from *The Quantum Human*)

Each new generation is the culmination of the whole of evolution. We are born on the leading edge of consciousness. You are here at this vital time because you are a part of the shift that is happening on the planet right now. The work you do on your personal growth and expansion is essential to the evolution of the world.

How we create and the drivers for what we create on the planet are changing. Most of us learned that to create success in the world, we had to work hard. We measured success with numbers. Our personal value has been measured by how much material value we have earned. We learned that if you want more, you have to work harder.

There were formulas for success. You set goals. You work hard. You fight for your share.

In the last 30 years, we began to play with the idea that there was more to creating than sheer will and effort. The idea that your thoughts create your reality began to take hold and gain traction in the mainstream. In 2006, the movie The Secret was released, and the verb "manifest" became part of our cultural conversation. Vision boards, positive thinking, and affirmations were incorporated as part of goal-setting strategies for creating. (You could even buy The Secret's companion book at Walmart!)

The story of Human Design tells us that our energy field and how we interact with the material world are about to undergo a significant upgrade. We are on the edge of a creative revolution. Our bodies and DNA are evolving to hold higher frequencies of energy that support a shift in our ability to create.

We are learning to consciously harness energy frequencies and manifest in the world in alignment with the frequencies we hold. We are breaking free from material consciousness rooted in binary thinking and finite resources that must be gathered through hard labor. We are learning to create with the power of our minds, hearts, and consciousness in a new way that will help us find the solutions to humanity's challenges.

Quality of life, not numbers, will measure success in this new world. Your success will be measured in how much wellbeing you cultivate for yourself and how much wellbeing you add to the world.

You are an essential part of this story. Your own shift in consciousness and the work you do to heal the karma of your sense of value initiates a code of energy that has the power to lift others. The energy frequency you carry as you heal yourself reverberates in your community and impacts those you love and anyone you connect with. Your personal evolution changes the world around you.

As more and more people have access to higher frequencies of energy, the more this evolutionary shift is transmitted. This is the key to unlocking our evolutionary code of ascension and healing the pain of a planet trapped in chronic trauma cycles.

These cycles have resulted in people forgetting their unique, vital, and irreplaceable role in the world and their true creative potential.

We are not victims of our reality, living our lives without choice or influence over what happens. We are rather co-creators, translating Divine Inspiration into action and third-dimensional form. Our thoughts, conditioning, and lives are giant feedback loops for the expansion of consciousness in manifested form.

If we are going to change the nature of reality on this planet and create a world of equitable, sustainable peace, then we have to heal ourselves first. Each and every one of us carries the seed for the potential of this shift. The more we elevate our own frequency of energy as a result of our healing, the more we can seed the energy of integrity and alignment into the world.

The more we decondition ourselves from the stories we've been telling that limit who we are and our creative potential, the more we choose how we will experience the shift on the planet. The work you do creates choice, not only for yourself but also for the world.

We are standing on the brink of a decisive choice point on the planet. The evolution we face is inevitable, but we have to choose how we will evolve. We have the potential to claw, fight and scramble our way to our evolution, or we can heal, align, and peacefully shift the world, one conscious thought and action at a time.

To understand what's going on in this shift we're experiencing; we must start with some basic assumptions about how we create and experience the material world. We're going to start by looking at the essential parts of the creative equation and the mechanics of how we manifest the experience of the lives we're living.

Quantum Physics

In the early 1900s, a powerful new field of science, quantum physics, was recognized as an official branch of physics. Quantum Physicists study the building blocks of matter—atoms and the smaller particles that make up the elements of the material world.

Quantum Physicists realized early on that the building blocks of matter don't act in the same way we know matter to behave. Specifically, they began to discover that the act of observing quantum particles actually affects how the quantum particles behave. Expectation influences the experience of reality.

In a study reported in the February 26, 1998, issue of *Nature*, researchers at the Weizmann Institute of Science conducted a highly controlled experiment demonstrating how a beam of electrons is affected by the act of being observed. The experiment revealed that the greater the amount of watching, the greater the observer's influence on what actually takes place.

Quantum Physicists also noted that they could either measure the movement of a quantum particle wave (a potential) or they could measure the location of a quantum particle but never both at the same time.

Potentials are not made manifest until we observe them. The location or "manifestation" of a quantum particle, turning potential into matter, is influenced by our observation and our expectation of its behavior. When we observe a potential wave of quantum particles, they transform from a state of potential to a state of material manifestation.

Let's translate that into practical understanding. Your life is filled with potential. The story of who you are is a collection of innumerable potentials, most of which you won't manifest into reality simply because life is too short for you to fulfill all the options available! Your current reality is a collection of the potentials that you have made manifest. The meanings we hold about the elements of our life influence which moving waves of potential we materialize into our physical reality.

Imagine for a moment that you are swimming in a sea of potential. A potential is essentially a neutral concept—an archetype—one that has the possibility to be fulfilled in many different ways. Your perception and the meanings you have about a potential determine how you experience that potential in your life.

Let's look at a specific example. Close your eyes for a moment and think of the word *creativity*.

Creativity, in this sea of potentials you are swimming in, is a neutral concept. Creativity is simply the ability to create something.

How you perceive the idea of creativity, your experiences of being creative in your life, and the beliefs you are conditioned by influence how you manifest the potential of creativity in your life.

Let's say you, like all children, were born with a deep connection to your natural creative ability. You spent your free time daydreaming and thinking about all the things you'd love to do with your life. One day, while you were in school, you were looking out the window and dreaming about what it would be like to ride a horse when the teacher came by, took her ruler, and banged it loudly on your desk, startling you out of your creative daydream.

This experience left you so startled that you made a conscious choice not to dream in school again, shutting down a core element of your creative power. (You also never gave yourself permission to ride a horse in your life…).

In your family of origin, you grew up with parents who were practical, who believed that all dreams were born of hard work and that if you wanted to do fun, creative things with your life, you had to earn them after you got your work done first. Creativity was a luxury, and in your family, it was a luxury you couldn't afford. Your family's work ethic entrained you to put your dreams on the back burner, hoping that someday you'd earn the right to manifest them into reality.

At sixteen years of age, you fell in love with literature. You'd always been a voracious reader, but as you matured and you began to really understand the elegance and power of the written word, you decided that you'd like to become a professional writer.

When you shared your dream with your father, he scolded you for being impractical, informed you if you majored in literature in college, he wouldn't pay your tuition, and you'd better pick a more profitable and practical career path if you wanted to get anywhere in your life.

You compromised, majored in education, and got a job teaching school. Now, as an adult, anytime you think about pursuing your passion, creating what you really want in your life, and the prospect of fulfilling your creative urges, you push those desires down. Sometimes you think about writing when you retire. In your daily life, you never give yourself the gift of fulfilling the full expression of your creativity.

All of these experiences, coupled with the collective consciousness around the idea of creativity that you grew up with, are carried in your mental and emotional body—where you hold the memories that make up the narrative you are telling yourself about your creativity and your creative power.

This is the filter through which you observe and perceive the potential of creativity in the Quantum Field. Your filter influences how you manifest creativity in your life.

Instead of telling yourself a story about your innate creative ability, when you allow yourself to dream about your dream of being a writer, you shut down your connection to your dream because your filter won't let you even entertain it as a possibility. Consequently, you never manifest the possibility of fulfilling that dream in your reality.

The New Thought Movement, which started in the early 19th century around the same time quantum physics gained recognition as an official branch of physics, seeded the collective consciousness with the idea that your thoughts create your reality.

Our deeper understanding of genetics, neurobiology, and peak potential activation has demonstrated that there is more to creating your reality than your thoughts. At its core, the idea that YOU create your reality is true.

To gain influence over your experience of reality, you have to know how your mental and emotional body filter is conditioned. Who is the you who is creating your reality, and what parts of you might you need to realign to create the reality you want?

Human Design refers to the idea that we are all conditioned to be who we think we are. In this next section, I want to explore the concept of conditioning and many of the factors that go into forming your current personal narrative—the narrative that is influencing what you choose to create out of the Quantum Field.

Five Key Areas of Conditioning

1. Openness in the Human Design Chart

Traditional Human Design teaches that the centers you have open (white) on your chart receive and amplify energy and information from the world around you. The energy you are receiving is amplified and experienced intensely. When you are in a consistent energy field, such as in your family of origin, where you experienced the same energy for your entire childhood, it's easy to confuse the energy of others as your own.

This confusion causes us to engage in predictable behavioral patterns that become coping mechanisms for managing the intensity of the energy that we experience in our openness. The intensity of the energy causes us to identify with it, and we form an identity around our openness. We think we have energy that does not belong to us.

Let's say, for example, that you have an open Emotional Solar Plexus. That means that you take in other people's emotional energy, and you amplify it. If you grew up in a family with an aura of a defined Emotional Solar Plexus, you grew up in an energy field that always held emotional energy. As a person with an open Emotional Solar Plexus, you amplified that emotional energy, and because you experienced this intense energy configuration over the span of your childhood, you may have grown up thinking you are a dramatic and emotional person when, according to your Human Design configuration, you are not.

2. Imprinting

Your Human Design chart represents the mechanics of how you interface with the world, but your life experience informs you as to how you utilize these mechanics.

Our neurobiology plays a vital role in the formation of who we are. We are not only imprinted by the energy field in which we grew up; we are imprinted by our parents' behaviors, their belief systems, and our family culture. A big part of your identity is based on what you learned from watching and being imprinted by your family.

This imprinting influences how you respond to stress, what you eat, what you believe, your level of physical fitness, your self-talk, your resilience, and more. We cannot escape the need to explore our family of origin and how they influenced our life choices if we are going to decondition ourselves.

3. Intergenerational Family Dynamics

Human Design shows us that we inherit our unique energy configuration from our grandparents. This sets us up for the potential of long-term intergenerational dynamics that cause us to live out different sides of the same family interaction over and over again, both as parents and as children.

If we are energetically similar to our grandparents, that means that our parents had to confront similar energy themes that they experienced from their own parents through us as their children. We, in turn, have to deal with the same "replay" of energy themes through our own journey as parents and so on and so on…

Let's say, for example, your family had a dynamic that included the Gate 21, the Gate of Self-Regulation. The Gate 21 often has a relationship dynamic that involves controlling or feeling controlled.

If your grandparents carried this theme in their chart, your mother may have struggled with feeling controlled by her parents. In response, your mother may have adopted a very permissive parenting style. If you carry the Gate 21 in your own chart, you may have experienced this energy as a deep need for structure, consistency, and rules to feel safe and valued.

If your mother's permissive parenting style left you with too much freedom and a need for better boundaries and structure, you might go on to be too controlling or rigid with your children, setting your family up to repeat the intergenerational theme of control.

When we heal the more painful aspect of these intergenerational family dynamics and learn to live out the higher potential of the interaction between the configurations in our family energy constellation, we have the potential to not only heal our own wounds but to shift the dynamic in our families for generations to come.

4. Genetics

Your DNA, the gene code carried inside your cells, influences many aspects of who you are and who you think you are. Certain aspects of your personality are part of your genetic structure.

Your DNA is much more malleable than you probably were taught in school. Protein coats on our DNA called epigenes control the expression and regulation of our genes. Epigenes contain information about our environment. They also can hold information about the environment and experiences of our ancestors. Your ancestral memories' are stored on an epigenetic level and can influence how some of your gene code is activated or deactivated.

For example, in 2015, Dr. Rachel Yehuda, director of the traumatic stress studies at the Mount Sinai School of Medicine, found that the children of the survivors of the Holocaust had epigenetic changes to a gene that was linked to their levels of cortisol, a hormone involved in the stress response. This epigenetic change made these people more vulnerable to anxiety disorders and generalized stress response to life.

Even your epigenetic profile is malleable. Simple lifestyle changes, diet, exercise, and even consciously changing the thoughts you have can shift your genetic programming and, again, change the nature of what you pass down to generations to come.

5. The Personality Crystal, the Design Crystal, and the Magnetic Monopole

Human Design adds a few other components to the creative equation that help us deepen our understanding of how we create and the story of who we think we are.

In order to understand these key players in the creative equation, we have to go back to the moment of conception.

Your life and soul purpose are encoded in two crystalline bodies of energy called the Design Crystal and the Personality Crystal. These aren't actual physical crystals but codes of information that help define who you are in this lifetime.

At the moment of your conception, your father's energy calls forth a crystalline code of energy that resides in the earth. This crystalline code of energy, called the Design Crystal, contains the code for your human life story and purpose. It initiates and manages the process of the development of your body as you grow from undifferentiated cells into a baby. The Design Crystal carries your gene codes, your epigenetic programming, your ancestral memories, and all the things that make your unique human story.

The Design Crystal is bundled with a special magnet called the Magnetic Monopole. The Magnetic Monopole is a magnetic force that only attracts. Your Magnetic Monopole is encoded with the information that will attract into your life all the experiences you are destined to have that are essential to your life story. The Magnetic Monopole is also the source of the Law of Attraction.

The events in your life that have seemed fated or part of an unavoidable destiny are encoded in your Magnetic Monopole. As we evolve, our ability to consciously program our Monopole is growing, and we are gaining more control over what we attract into our lives.

The third component, the Personality Crystal, contains the code for your soul purpose. It enters the body at the moment of your birth.

At birth, the Design Crystal takes up residence in the Ajna Center. The Magnetic Monopole resides in the Identity Center, and the Personality Crystal is located in the Head Center.

The combination of the Design Crystal, the Personality Crystal, and the Magnetic Monopole help define the field of choices you are choosing from over the course of your life. The full range of potentials you can choose for your life is extensive, and you certainly won't run out of options in what you create in your reality! This limitation of possibilities is significant because it helps define who you perceive yourself to be in your current incarnation.

This combination of codes also makes you a unique once-in-a-lifetime Cosmic Event!

Most of what you think about who you are is based on your conditioning and what you carry in your mental and emotional body. The meanings you hold about ideas and potentials influence how they manifest in your physical reality.

The most important thing you can do right now to support the creation of an equitable, sustainable, and peaceful world is to begin a systematic exploration of the meanings you hold about who you are, why you're here, and what you're capable of. The most significant part of our work at this time, as volunteers here to birth this new world, is to untangle humanity from old collective and personal beliefs about lack and limitation.

Our Human Design shows us that the highest potential expression of humanity is rooted in Love. We are designed to love ourselves, love each other, and create from a deep connection to a loving spiritual Source. This is true for all of us, personally and collectively.

But we can't bring this ideal into form if our perception of who we are, our filter, doesn't support this as a possibility that we choose within the Quantum Field. If we don't hold a narrative that creates an infinitely loving identity, that believes in the possibility of an equitable, sustainable, and just peace, we can't manifest love on the planet.

The most important thing we can each do right now to midwife the birth of a new world is to align our personal identity with the true story of who we really are. We must consciously and deliberately inventory our identity, heal past traumas that keep us stuck in stories and meanings that are less than who we can be, and reclaim our personal value.

Your personal deconditioning journey is the key to unlocking the evolution of consciousness on the planet. As you heal and align yourself, you transmit a frequency of energy that unlocks the hearts of others. Higher frequencies of energy modulate lower frequencies and lift them up, opening doorways for new potentials to manifest in the world.

The evolution of the world is inevitable. The code for the transformation of humanity is already complete. The challenge we are facing now is determining how we will translate that code into action.

With old collective beliefs rooted in lack, "not-enough-ness," and fear, the meanings we hold have the potential to craft an evolutionary journey that is rooted in war, poverty, hoarding, and more, making the road to our evolution rocky and frightening.

If we shift these old meanings and beliefs, starting first with ourselves, we have the power to change the quality of the journey we are on. We can accelerate and amplify the potential for a gentle shift in the story of humanity, creating an easy transition to sufficiency and support for every sentient being on the planet in the fastest, most enduring way possible.

We will evolve. That part is inevitable.

The question is, how are we going to get to where we're going? When enough of us generate meanings and beliefs that support the idea—the dream—of a sustainable, equitable, and peaceful world, we change the filter through which we choose potentials, and we begin the process of manifesting the new world in a gentle and easy way.

The work you do on a personal level, the act of rewriting the personal narrative you tell about who you are, might not seem revolutionary. Still, it is the most vital work we must do on the planet at this time to build a critical mass of high-frequency energy that will usher in the transformation and shifts we need to activate to create a peaceful transition to a new world of peace.

Contemplations:

Take some time to contemplate or journal about the following questions. Your answers are simply giving you insights into what meanings you may be holding right now. Notice your responses with loving curiosity and without judgment. This is merely a series of questions designed to give you awareness. Awareness is the first step to transformation.

- What meanings do you hold about peace on the planet?
- Do you believe that peace is possible?
- How are you creating peace in your personal life?
- Are you peaceful?
- What old beliefs do you have about fighting, getting your share, and setting boundaries?
- How do these beliefs manifest in your life?
- What meanings do you have about sharing?
- Do you think there are enough resources to share in the world?
- Do you experience fear about giving too much?
- Do you share freely?
- Do you hoard?
- Do you trust Source?
- Do you believe you are enough?
- Do you believe that you are supported?
- Do you think you can always be supported?

The Energy Centers

The Centers in Human Design correlate to the Hindu Chakras. Each Center represents archetypal characteristics that set up the dynamics for the Soul Curriculum of the chart. The configuration of the centers in the chart tells you about how your energy works in the world, what you're here to learn from others, and what you're here to give to the world.

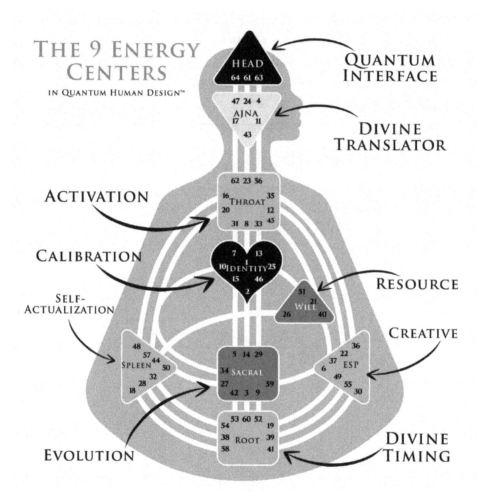

The energy flow between centers, both interpersonal and transpersonal, reveals an enormous amount of information about how a person is conditioned. Understanding the conditioning themes of both the open centers and defined centers in your chart and how they play out in relationships gives you critical insights into where you may have cultivated patterns and habits that hold you back from fulfilling your true potential.

The flow of energy between the centers also outlines the creative process, the way in which we harness the infinite potentials of the Quantum Field and experience them in our third-dimensional reality. To understand this creative process, we have to reframe much of the understanding that we have about the centers and also about the random nature of our creative drive.

There is an implicit bias in the Cosmos. The nature of life is to create a state of coherence, unity, and higher states of complex organization (evolution). When we de-condition and live according to our design, we express this implicit bias, allowing the whisperings of Life's Intelligence to work with us to create the next phase of our growth and expansion.

The concept of "thoughts" creating "reality" is outlined in the interplay between the centers. The list below is a summary of how the creative process flows through the centers in the chart.

1. Inspirations are experienced in the Head Center and processed through the Ajna. These inspirations are designed to trigger dreaming, imagination, and possibility thinking. They do not always provide answers or instructions. The more you de-condition the mind, the more you can discern the differences between thinking, which is the result of conditioning, and that which is pure inspiration.

2. The dreams, imaginings, and thoughts generated by the mind trigger a photon storm in the brain, causing the body to produce neurotransmitters which, in turn, stimulate a specific emotional response in relation to the thoughts.

Suppose you are having good thoughts that feel exciting. In that case, you will trigger positive emotions and generate either a "high" or "low" energy frequency in the Emotional Solar Plexus, depending on the quality of the emotions generated. The opposite is also true.

3. This emotional frequency calibrates the heart—comprising the Will Center and the G-Center—which then programs the Magnetic Monopole to attract in to your life experiences and opportunities that align with the emotional frequency of energy you generated in response to your thought.

The Will Center will process the frequency of emotional energy you generate and filter it through your sense of self-worth. If you are deeply connected to your value and

THE
MECHANICS
OF HEART
RESONANCE

are living in integrity with your self-worth, you'll allow yourself to receive and create in alignment with that value.

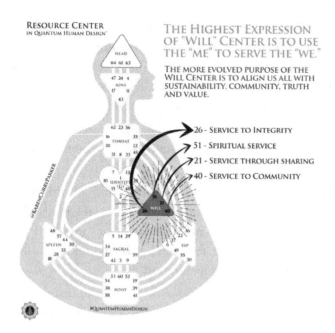

THE HIGHEST EXPRESSION OF "WILL" CENTER IS TO USE THE "ME" TO SERVE THE "WE."

THE MORE EVOLVED PURPOSE OF THE WILL CENTER IS TO ALIGN US ALL WITH SUSTAINABILITY, COMMUNITY, TRUTH AND VALUE.

26 - SERVICE TO INTEGRITY
51 - SPIRITUAL SERVICE
21 - SERVICE THROUGH SHARING
40 - SERVICE TO COMMUNITY

If you're struggling with your self-worth, your Will Center will modulate your emotional frequency and calibrate the Monopole to attract experiences into your life that will be a reflection of the current status of your self-worth, not to punish you, but to help you see what needs to be healed, released, aligned and brought to your aware-ness for you to align with a higher state of integrity and a more profound sense of your own value.

The G-Center, the seat of the Magnetic Monopole, holds the energy of Love. Much like the Will Center and your sense of self-worth, the G-Center holds the energy for the quality of love you generate in your life.

The Gates of the G-Center show us our direction in life. The experiences we attract are influenced by: the quality of love we have for ourselves; our sense of empowerment; the willingness we have to be relentlessly authentic; our trust in Source; the narratives we tell about who we are and what we deserve; the love we hold for our bodies and how well we take care of them; our willingness to allow ourselves to receive all the good that we deserve; and how much compassion we have to share and give to the world.

THE CALIBRATION CENTER

COLLABORATION
I AM POWERFUL.
I DECIDE. I CHOOSE.

PURPOSE
I AM.
I AM WHO I AM.

NARRATIVE
I AM FORGIVING.
I FORGIVE.

SELF-LOVE
I AM LOVE.
I LOVE.

SPIRIT
I AM TRUSTING.
I TRUST. I SERVE.

7   13
10 1 25
IDENTITY
15 (G) 46
2

COMPASSION
I AM COMPASSIONATE.
I SHARE.

EMBODIMENT
I AM VITAL.
I EMBODY MY SPIRIT/SOUL.

ALLOWING
I AM SUPPORTED.
I RECEIVE.

Your self-worth and lovability will calibrate your emotional energy accordingly to program the Magnetic Monopole to attract experiences and opportunities that reflect how you feel about yourself.

4. The Root Center, the Center that regulates the time and timing of right action, will give you a signal when the time is right to take the actions to create what you're intending.

5. The Sacral energy will sustain any work that needs to be done. Your Quantum Human Design Type will influence the kind of work you'll be called to do.

6. The Spleen Center will let you know if there is anything you need to do to keep yourself fulfilled and safe.

7. The entire process is then expressed through the Throat Center and, again, will be heavily influenced by QHD Type.

Resiliency Keys

The Human Design chart shows us that resiliency, the end goal of deconditioning, consists of nine key traits. These key traits give you a way to assess your level of conditioning and deconditioning.

Self-Trust: The degree to which you trust your inner wisdom and trust in your own abilities.

Empowerment: How much control and power you feel like you have in creating your life.

Lovability: How much love you believe you can receive, experience, and give.

Courage: How well you can navigate through fear without letting it paralyze you.

Authenticity: How free you feel to fully express your Authentic Self.

Decisiveness: Your ability to know how to make good and right decisions for you.

Emotional Wisdom: Your ability to use emotional energy as a creative source of power and to be deliberate, not reactive.

Self-Worth: Your self-esteem and sense of your own value.

Vitality: How much energy you have to do the things you want and need to do in your life.

The more we work on living the high expression of these energies, the more control and choice we have over how we work with the changes at hand. Awakened, resilient people always have choices. People living out the script of their conditioning have no choice but to react with old patterns and relive the same story repeatedly.

Each of the centers is associated with specific Resiliency Keys. The more we decondition the centers, the more resiliency and choice we cultivate.

Head | Quantum Interface

Biology: Pineal Gland, Eyes

Chakra: Crown

Resiliency Keys: Decisiveness, Self-Trust

Quantum Purpose: To use inspiration and possibility thinking to trigger imagination and the frequency of creative energy.

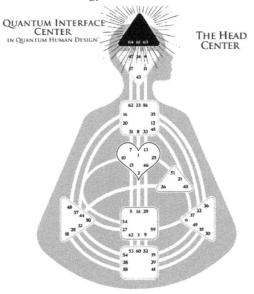

Defined: A conduit for inspiration.

Optimal Expression: To use inspiration with great deliberation and awareness of the possibility of what you inspire others to do.

Unbalanced Expression: To be uninspired.

Lesson/Challenge: To learn to use inspiration with responsibility and awareness. To recognize your role as an inspirational force in the world.

Contemplation:

- What do I want to inspire in others?

Affirmation: I am a conduit for inspiration in the world. My presence, words, and thoughts inspire others. I use inspiration with great deliberation and intention. I am inspiring.

Open: A vessel for inspiration.

Optimal Expression: To be an observer of inspiration. To learn to trust that the inspirations that are yours to follow will reveal themselves on the material plane.

Unbalanced Expression: Confusion, feeling lost, mental pressure, self-doubt, the pressure to figure things out.

Lesson/Challenge: To use ideas to inspire aligned thoughts and imaginations.

Contemplations:

- Am I afraid of the unknown?
- Do I trust the Universe to reveal the next right step?
- Am I under pressure to figure things out?

Affirmation: I amplify inspiration and use it to stimulate my imagination. I use inspiration as an energy that I cultivate. I trust and wait that when the timing is right, the inspirations that are mine to follow will reveal themselves to me.

Ajna | Divine Translator

Biology: Sinus, Mouth, Teeth, Face, Pituitary Gland

Chakra: Ajna

Resiliency Keys: Decisiveness, Self-Trust

Quantum Purpose: To translate inspiration into potential third-dimensional applications and to imagine possibilities to stimulate a creative (emotional) energy frequency.

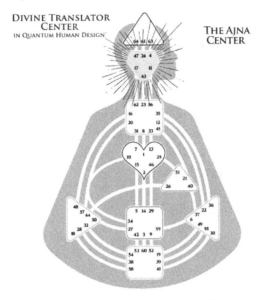

Defined: The ability to conceptualize and hold onto fixed visions.

Optimal Expression: To generate expansive ideas and concepts and envision them until the details of how to materialize these ideas reveal themselves.

Unbalanced Expression: To be locked in negative thought patterns that are fixed and minimizing. Closed-minded.

Lesson/Challenge: To learn to use the power of the mind to expand on possibilities and potentials. To hold a vision that is creative and expansive.

Contemplation:

- Are your beliefs serving your highest good?

Affirmation: I use my thinking as a spark that ignites possibility. I repeat and focus on the ideas and thoughts that create expansion and increase potential in my life. My mindset is open. My beliefs support my growth and reflect the value of who I am and what I'm capable of.

Open: The ability to see all potentials and possibilities from multiple perspectives. Open-minded.

Optimal Expression: To see ideas from many different perspectives and be open-minded in how you envision and imagine. To embrace unlimited possibilities and to make peace with the unknown.

Unbalanced Expression: To feel under pressure to figure things out. To exert effort to try to hold onto a fixed vision. To experience fear of the unknown.

Lesson/Challenge: To learn to be at peace with different visions and possibilities. To embrace the value of seeing perspectives from multiple angles. To learn to be comfortable with the unknown.

Contemplations:

- Are you afraid of the unknown?
- Are you struggling to be certain about fixed ideas and beliefs?

Affirmation: I embrace my innate ability to see ideas and beliefs from many different angles. This open-minded perspective is part of my creative power and helps me see opportunities and potentials that others can't see. I enjoy the open flow of my mind. I trust that when I don't know an answer that the next right step will be revealed to me, and I am at peace with the unknown.

Throat | Activation

Biology: Throat, Neck, Cervical Vertebrae, Thyroid, Parathyroid

Chakra: Throat

Resiliency Keys: Authenticity, Vitality

Quantum Purpose: To use language in empowering, loving, creative ways to stimulate and initiate sustainable, abundant possibilities.

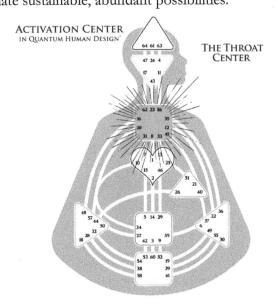

Defined: The ability to speak and share a specific message regulated by whichever Center the Throat is connected to. If motorized, you can initiate a conversation.

Optimal Expression: To wait for the right cues and clues to know when to share information or words that elevate and increase potential.

Unbalanced Expression: To speak without waiting for the right timing. To not mediate or regulate what information is shared. To use words irresponsibly.

Lesson/Challenge: To learn to transmit messages that elevate, transmit, and expand on possibilities when the timing and the circumstances are aligned.

Contemplations:

- Do I choose my words carefully?
- How can I better use my words to build more love, coherence, unity, and expansion in the world?

Affirmation: I use the power of my words to stimulate and elevate the energy around me. I use my words to build a template of possibility and judiciously choose them so that they reflect the potential of growth, unity, and coherence.

Open: To learn to experience the communication needs of the environment and to modulate your words to best meet the needs of others when the timing is right.

Optimal Expression: To learn to trust in the Divine flow of information. To trust that when the timing and the environment are correct, you'll be able to share what you know with words that best meet the needs of others.

Unbalanced Expression: To feel the pressure to speak and share as a strategy for gaining access to energy and to prove your value and your lovability. To not wait for right timing and to leak communication energy with the wrong people at the wrong time. Burnout.

Lesson/Challenge: To not push or force your communication or action if the timing isn't correct. To learn to allow your communication and action to be activated through recognition and attention. Wait for the recognition and attention that best reflects your value and values. Stop tying your self-worth or your lovability to the receptivity of others.

Contemplations:

- Do you feel invisible?
- Do you speak your truth?
- Do you value yourself and your words?

Affirmation: I am a conduit for information and language that initiates sustainable and abundant possibilities. The words I speak, the information I carry, and the inspiration I'm here to share are all dependent on timing and the readiness of others to hear them. I honor my own energy and my wisdom enough to only share what I know when the timing is right and with the right people who are ready for the information that I bring.

G | Calibration

Biology: Blood, Liver

Chakra: Heart

Resiliency Keys: Lovability, Decisiveness, Courage, Authenticity

Quantum Purpose: To give direction to love, sustainability, leadership, release, empowerment, Spirit, embodiment, natural order, compassion, and peace. Holds the magnetic resonance field of the Magnetic Monopole.

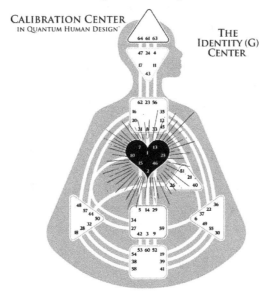

Defined: To have a fixed path for the fulfillment of your purpose. To have a consistent sense of self that can be an immutable beacon that gives direction to others.

Optimal Expression: To recognize that you are designed to love, to be empowered, to self-express, to control your own personal narrative, to use your life in service to your Higher Self, to stay vital, to explore how much goodness you're willing to allow and to share compassionately with the world. To trust that when you express your Authentic Self, you are moving in a direction that supports your sustainability and abundance and energetically shows the way to others.

Unbalanced Expression: To be afraid you won't be loved for expressing your Authentic Self.

Lesson/Challenge: To stay connected to your Authentic Self.

Contemplations:

- Do you feel accepted for who you are?
- Do you compromise who you are to please others?
- Do you feel safe to be yourself fully?

Affirmation: I was born with a powerful direction for my life. While my life path may take me many places, each of my life experiences is being integrated as part of my powerful personal narrative. I consciously and deliberately craft a personal narrative that fully tells the true story of who I am. I use my story and relentlessly authentic self-expression to give direction to my life and show others how to fully express their true Selves.

Open: To experience a variety of personal narratives as a way of gauging and learning about authentic self-expression. To deeply feel the stories of others. From your experience of the stories of others, consciously choose your own life path.

Optimal Expression: To be deeply wise about the potential of the story of humanity. To choose which elements of the human condition and narrative you want to integrate as part of yourself. To know who you are is evolving and expanding. To use other people's narratives to consciously calibrate your own direction.

Unbalanced Expression: To question your lovability. To struggle with direction. To allow your direction and the calibration of your Magnetic Resonance Field to be conditioned by others. To struggle to feel at home in the world.

Lesson/Challenge: To not experience the narrative of another as your own. To learn to sample people's stories and expressions and gauge which ones feel aligned with your value and values. To integrate elements of these stories into your understanding of your unique life path. To learn to place yourself in the right location and be embedded in the stories that reflect your lovability and authentic self-expression.

Contemplations:

- Do you feel lovable?
- Do you feel lost?
- Do you know the difference between your narrative and the narrative of others?
- Do you over-identify with others?
- Do you know how to feel someone else's story and not become it?

Affirmation: I experience myself as fluid and dynamic. I enjoy and savor the stories and experiences of others as a witness, never allowing myself to get lost in someone else's story. I choose the elements of the story of humanity that reflect my own value and values. I allow myself to let my personal narrative evolve with experience and embrace all the many delicious directions my life takes me. I allow myself to settle where I feel most at home, knowing that this may change as I gather the pieces of my narrative that I need to gather to continue my journey of growth and evolution.

Will | Resource

Biology: Cardiovascular System, Stomach, Thymus, Gallbladder, Heart

Chakra: Heart

Resiliency Keys: Self-Worth, Vitality, Empowerment

Quantum Purpose: To create sustainability, community, alignment with Truth, and value.

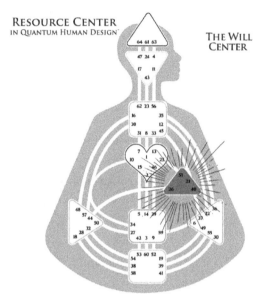

RESOURCE CENTER
IN QUANTUM HUMAN DESIGN™

THE WILL
CENTER

Defined: The ability to create enduring and sustainable value. To use the power of your Will to increase the value-base and resources of others. To become fully resourced in order to help others have access to more resources. To use your energy to heal and help others align with more aligned states of integrity.

Optimal Expression: To give from abundant resources and stay consistently resourced to avoid cycles of depletion and exhaustion. To live and create from a place of knowing your value and taking the right actions to take up your right place and right space. To live and create in physical, resource, identity, moral, and energetic integrity. To use conscious rest and re-Sourcing yourself as a way of sustaining integrity. Knowing who you are serves a unique and vital role in serving others.

Unbalanced Expression: To push and use the force of Will as a way of overcompensating for low self-worth. To give without replenishing and to deplete and exhaust your reserves. To misuse and overcompensate with actions or material goods. To measure value only on the material plane and fail to create from a place of alignment with sustainable wellbeing. Burnout. Egotistical.

Lesson/Challenge: To learn to sustain the power of your Will. To create sustainably and cultivate right value and values that keep you creating with integrity. To find the balance between rest, repose, and action.

Contemplations:

- Do you value yourself?
- Do you trust Source?
- Do you push with your power instead of waiting for right alignment?
- How do you measure your value?

Affirmation: I am an influential force that has the power and ability to transform the global metric of value. By fully embodying my own value and taking appropriate actions to regenerate and resource myself in an enduring and sustainable way, I create a force field of integrity that lifts others up to live in alignment with their own unique and vital role in the world. I use my resources to increase the resources of others.

Open: To learn to define value on your own terms. To learn to create in flow, not through willing your way through.

Optimal Expression: To evaluate the integrity and alignment with value in others. To gauge your level of investment in circumstances that do not match your own value and values. To have the freedom to consciously choose what you consider to be valuable and to build your life around it. To live from an internal sense of your own value. To learn to trust in sufficiency. To fully embody "enoughness" (I AM enough…)

Unbalanced Expression: To engage in actions and choices to prove your value to others.

Lesson/Challenge: To stop defining your value by the expectations and formulas of others. To experience a variety of different values and consciously choose your own values. To define success on your own terms.

Contemplations:

- Do you know your value?
- Do you trust Source?
- Do you live your life in alignment with your values?

Affirmation: I define value and what is truly valuable on my terms. I decide for myself what is valuable and construct a life that reflects my values. I trust in Source and the flow of sufficiency in my life. I know I have a unique, vital, and irreplaceable role in the Divine Plan. I follow my right path in the fulfillment of this right place, and I trust I'll have all I need when I need it.

Emotional Solar Plexus | Creative

Biology: Adrenals, Kidney, The Vagus Nerve, Solar Plexus Neuron Network, Pancreas

Chakra: Solar Plexus

Resiliency Keys: Courage, Emotional Wisdom, Empowerment, Decisiveness

Quantum Purpose: To hold the frequency of energy for abundance and faith.

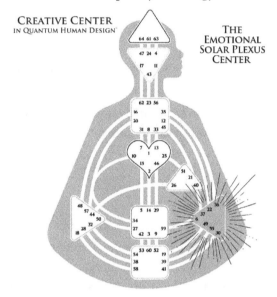

Defined: The ability to feel your way into alignment with a potential or possibility. To consciously cultivate a baseline frequency of abundance and to use that frequency to inspire abundance and faith in others.

Optimal Expression: To know how to envision a deliberate outcome and to wait to ensure the desire for the outcome stays consistent no matter how your mood may fluctuate.

Unbalanced Expression: To make emotional decisions in the moment that create disappointment, anger, frustration, or bitterness in yourself or others.

Lesson/Challenge: To learn to evaluate your creative desires and mood and know when the timing is right (or not) for the right aligned action.

Contemplations:

- Do you trust in right timing?
- Do you trust in the abundance of the Universe?
- Do you understand your emotions?

Affirmation: I carefully attend to my emotional baseline frequency. I nurture myself. I hold an abundant mindset that supports me, trusting deeply in Divine and right timing and the infinite supply of the Universe. I know that when I consciously calibrate this frequency of energy over time, even if it shifts on a daily basis, I am an emotional regulator whose emotional frequency has the capacity to lift others up.

Open: The ability to hold your own emotional frequency no matter what others may be experiencing. The ability to be calm in the midst of an emotional storm. To be emotionally empathic.

Optimal Expression: To hold your emotional frequency even when others struggle to sustain theirs.

Unbalanced Expression: To allow your emotional wellbeing and baseline frequency to be influenced by others. To give up what you want and need to keep others happy. To compromise on your values, value, and dreams for others because you can't hold your own baseline frequency.

Lesson/Challenge: To not let the emotional energy of others hijack your emotional energy. To use your emotional awareness to cultivate empathy and compassion.

Contemplations:

- Is your baseline frequency abundant?
- Is it okay for you to speak your truth?
- Can you disconnect from other people's emotions?

Affirmation: I am an empath. One of my greatest strengths is my ability to read the emotional energy and alignment of others. I observe emotional energy and only allow myself to accept emotional frequencies of my choice that are closely aligned with my own. I speak my truth and ask for what I want without worrying about the impact of other people's feelings on my own needs and desires. I am compassionate and empathetic. My emotional clarity and detachment are my gift to others.

Sacral | Evolution

Biology: Ovaries, Testes, and all reproductive organs

Chakra: Sacral

Resiliency Keys: Decisiveness, Courage, Vitality, Empowerment

Quantum Purpose: To respond with action to the needs of others to support the evolution of community and the expression of abundance and compassion.

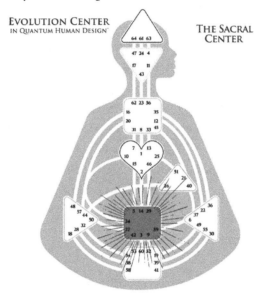

EVOLUTION CENTER
IN QUANTUM HUMAN DESIGN

THE SACRAL
CENTER

Defined: The ability, through responding, to have access to the sustainable energy necessary to build abundance and wellbeing. The ability to sustainably nurture and care for others.

Optimal Expression: To trust your inner alignment and innate responding nature to allow the unfolding of Life's Intelligent plan of action through you.

Unbalanced Expression: Pushing too hard, too fast in pursuing ideas that are not in response to what shows up, compromising on your inner wisdom because you allow your mind to dictate the plan of action, and perpetually quitting before you self-actualize.

Lesson/Challenge: To learn to respond as a critical way of navigating all life's possibilities. To learn to sustain your actions even when frustrated.

Contemplations:

- Do you trust in the unfolding of the Divine Plan?
- Do you trust you'll know what to do when it's time to do it?
- Do you know how to interpret frustration?
- Has quitting kept you from doing what you came here to do?

Affirmation: I am a sustainable force of action. When the timing is right, Life's Intelligence brings me the right clues, cues, and signs that let me know when and what

I need to do. By responding, I take the actions that allow me to fulfill the evolution of the world. I have a quality of energy that can sustain me and drive me. I am vibrant and vital when following my inner guidance, and I'm letting the signals of the Universe guide me. I relax and trust that I'm in the flow of doing what needs to be done to evolve the world, and I have the energy to sustain my actions.

Open: To use your sensual experience of workforce and lifeforce energies to know what needs to be done and to guide others to do it.

Optimal Expression: To experience life force energy and vitality and to use it to guide and direct others to do the work. To know what needs to be done and how to tap into the resources to facilitate getting it done without actually having to do it yourself.

Unbalanced Expression: To take in vitality and life force and use it as if it's your own. To not know when enough is enough and burn out by overdoing.

Lesson/Challenge: To learn to allow others to do the building while you do the guiding. To learn to know when enough is enough when it comes to hustling and work. To work with your energy ebbs and flows without burning out.

Contemplations:

- Do you know when enough is enough?
- Are you burned out?
- What strategies do you have to rest and renew your energy so that you don't burn out?
- Do you trust that you'll be supported?
- Do you value rest?
- Do you judge yourself for resting?
- Do you allow the judgments of others to keep you from the vital rest you need?

Affirmation: I am wise about how to use workforce and lifeforce energy. I see the potential of the work that needs to be done, and I delegate and manage others doing the work. I recognize when enough is enough, and I nurture, renew and regenerate my energy as needed in order to stay sustainable. I am a vital and wise resource to others, and I work with those who see my gifts, strengths, and values. My ability to see the potential of what needs to be done allows me to serve the evolution and unfolding of the Divine Plan.

Spleen | Self-Actualization

Biology: Lymphatic System, Spleen, B-cells

Chakra: Solar Plexus

Resiliency Keys: Self-Trust, Courage

Quantum Purpose: To give us the intuitive impulses about right timing for survival, health and wellness, and economic action.

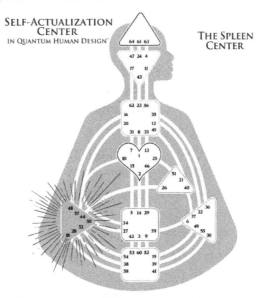

Defined: To be connected to consistent instinctual awareness around decisions related to honing skills, increasing proficiency, and excellence. Intuitive connection to a sense of timing for actions related to survival, avoiding pain, and increasing value, sustainability, and alignment with integrity.

Optimal Expression: The presence and awareness to know what you need to know when you need to know it and do what you need to do when you need to do it to be aligned with sustainability, integrity, and expansion.

Unbalanced Expression: To be hypervigilant and allow fear to run patterns of avoidance and over-preparation that keep you from being present to what actually needs to be done.

Lesson/Challenge: To learn to be present in order to interpret the awareness for right timing, survival, health and wellness, and economic action.

Contemplations:

- Do you trust yourself?
- Do you let fear keep you paralyzed in inaction?
- Do you trust that you'll know what you need to know when you need to know it?
- Are you creating in alignment with your integrity?

- Do you have patterns from the past that are keeping you trapped?

Affirmation: I have a deep connection with the pulse of Divine Timing and Wisdom that informs me when I need to take action. I am deeply aligned with the awareness necessary to cultivate and hone my skills. I integrate my experiences and allow myself to grow beyond past patterns. I stand firm in the integrity of my Authentic Self and trust that when I am wholly occupying my unique, vital and irreplaceable role in the Cosmic Plan, I completely trust that I'll know what I need to know when I need to know it. My sense of timing allows me to make aligned and informed choices around what I need to continue to become self-actualized.

Open: The awareness of other people's awareness. The ability to read the perceptions of others and gauge whether these are intuitions and perceptions that you need to follow for yourself. To sample the intuitive impulses around you and know which ones you need to follow.

Optimal Expression: To feel the alignment with courage in the room and to uplift others. To overcome fear and find presence and be centered.

Unbalanced Expression: To let fear cause you to hold on to circumstances and situations longer than is healthy. To be overcome by the complexity of intuitive information you receive from others and not know what to do or what is true. To not be present because you're too busy preparing for the worst-case scenario. Hyper-vigilant.

Lesson/Challenge: To learn to observe the intuitive impulses of others and to know which ones are aligned with your integrity and your unique timing. To not let fear keep you from self-actualizing.

Contemplations:
- What do you need to let go of?
- Does fear keep you stuck?
- Do you trust that you are safe?
- Do you trust yourself?

Affirmation: I am sensitive, present, and aware of the energy in my environment. I assess the energy of the people around me and gauge which intuitive impulses are right for me. I am careful to explore the sources of fear I may be experiencing and take careful stock of whether these fears belong to me. Because of my profound awareness and sensitivity, I carefully curate an environment that sustains my health and wellness. I release old circumstances, situations, belongings, and experiences that hold me back from fully trusting that I am safe.

Root | Divine Timing

Biology: Adrenals, hydration, ingestion, and assimilation

Chakra: Root

Resiliency Keys: Vitality, Empowerment

Quantum Purpose: To receive and respond to what the Earth needs and wants as part of the evolution of the planet.

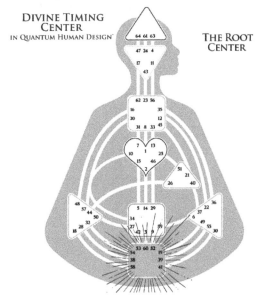

Defined: A deep inner connection with the pulse of Diving Timing. To live in the flow of action when the timing is right.

Optimal Expression: To be deeply connected to the accompanying energy flow state that is experienced when the timing for action is aligned.

Unbalanced Expression: To burn out because you're pushing against right timing. To fail to take care of circumstances, situations, and conditions that could influence timing. To fail to be ready for when the time is aligned.

Lesson/Challenge: To learn to trust your inner sense of timing. To tend to what is necessary on the material plane in order to influence time and timing.

Contemplations:

- Are there things you need to take care of in order to be ready for what you want?
- How do you navigate things you have to do when your energy isn't aligned?
- Do you trust the timing of the Universe?

Affirmation: I am deeply attuned to the pulse of the Earth and the unfolding of perfect and right timing. When the timing is right, my energy is aligned, and I am in the flow of creativity and right action.

Open: An amplified experience of the pulse of Divine Timing that can create an energy boost to take aligned action.

Optimal Expression: To use adrenaline energy in a sustainable way to ensure right action at the right time.

Unbalanced Expression: To perceive the energy of the Earth as a sense of pressure. To react to this pressure with adrenaline and feel stress and mistrust in right and aligned timing. Burnout.

Lesson/Challenge: To learn to interpret adrenaline energy in a healthy way and to use it for inspired action at the right time.

Contemplations:

- How do you relax and trust?
- Do you trust the timing of the Universe?
- How do you manage stress and pressure?
- Does pressure make you do things you don't want to do?

Affirmation: I observe the world and enjoy the electrical pulse of right timing and right action. The spark of right timing inspires in me a surge of energy that allows me to create in a flow state. I observe the actions and energy of others and carefully choose which sparks I allow to inspire right action in me. I tend to my own inner sense of timing by ensuring that I'm ready for when the timing is right. In between actions, I rest and cultivate an inner sense of trust in Divine Timing.

Planets

Sun
Outer Expression - what you're here to give the world

Earth
What Grounds You - what you need in order to be stable and grounded

North Node
Breathing Out - life theme you're moving towards after Uranus Opposition (approx. 38-42 yrs.)

South Node
Breathing In - life theme you start in, youth to midlife

Moon
What Drives You - why you do what you do

Mercury
Communication - what you're here to communicate about and share

Venus
Values - what you really value and love in your relationships

Mars
Immaturity - where you experience your youthful lessons

Jupiter
Blessings - where you receive your rewards and blessings

Saturn
The Great Teacher - what you are here to learn. Brings what you need to release or be challenged by in order to grow

Chiron
The Wounded Healer - part of your Life & Spiritual Purpose or Spiritual Challenge (Challenge if born before 1978.)

Uranus
Where You are Different - your faith teacher. Where you can expect the unexpected

Neptune
Your Spiritual Theme - your (veiled) Spiritual connection/work/purpose

Pluto
Expansion/Challenge (Generational) - where you grow, evolve and transform through a release and rebirth

The Circuitry

Three Main Circuits and Seven Sub-Circuits

There are three kinds of Circuits in Human Design, Individual (Transformation in Quantum Human Design), Tribal (Sustainability in Quantum Human Design), and Collective (Synergy in Quantum Human Design). Each Circuit plays an essential role in the evolution of humanity.

Individual Circuitry brings mutation and change. Tribal Circuitry explores and implements the ideas brought in by the Individual Circuit, and once the change has demonstrated that it's functional and adaptable, it is integrated into the Collective.

Think of it like this. Imagine that there are two caveman brothers, Bob and Tom. Bob is a little weird and strange. He tries his whole life to fit in, but no one really "gets" him. Bob moves out of his family group and makes a home on his own by the edge of a fruitful river a mile or so away from his family, where he is very happy to be free to do his own thing.

Tom is very different from his brother, Bob. Tom has a deep sense of being rooted in his family group and works tirelessly to make sure that his family has everything they need to be healthy and abundant. This includes his brother, Bob. Once a week, Tom travels to visit Bob at his home by the river to make sure Bob is okay and thriving. Both brothers enjoy their weekly meetings because, even though they are very different, they deeply love each other.

One week Tom notices that Bob is using a cool tool that he invented that makes construction and work much more manageable. Tom studies the tool and decides to make his own when he gets home to his family group.

The tool is so popular and makes work so much easier that soon all of his family group has made their own and is using the tool to make building shelters and gathering fruit easier.

In the fall, Tom travels over the hill with extra food and supplies to a gathering place with other leaders from different family groups. He brings his new tool with him. Other leaders from the different family groups see Tom using his new tool and making their own; they bring this new invention to their family groups.

Soon, the leaders of the different family groups gather and decide that this tool is incredibly valuable and that all known family groups far and wide should have access to this powerful tool because it saves so much time, energy, and effort. They create a committee to make the tools and to travel around the area delivering the tools to different family groups and increasing the quality of life everywhere they travel.

Bob represents the core theme of the Individual Circuit. He doesn't quite fit in. He has his own ideas. He stays true to those ideas and travels on his own on a journey of self-exploration and self-expression.

Bob's new ideas and insights profoundly influence Tom, who represents Tribal Circuitry. Tom is deeply occupied with exploring what would make the people he loves happy and safe. He takes great joy in nurturing others, and his contribution makes everyone around him feel loved and safe.

The leaders from the other family groups who enable new legislation for the tool represent Collective Circuitry. Their joint actions create initiatives that not only make their own family groups safer and more sustainable, but they also work to ensure that others have the same opportunities for growth and access to resources.

This is an idealized version of how all the Circuits work together. Let me remind us all that we all have all of the Gates and Circuits; just some of them are defined (colored in), and some are open (white). We all have Gates from all of the Circuits defined in our charts.

Some of us are more profoundly influenced by the themes of the different Circuits. If you have Channels in a particular Circuit defined in your chart, it will most likely give you the theme of that particular Circuit in your life story.

Ra used to teach that Individual Circuitry "doesn't care." I think this teaching gets wildly misinterpreted.

Let's start first with the definition of the verb "to care."

Essential Meanings of **care:**

1: Effort made to do something correctly, safely, or without causing damage.

She used care in selecting a doctor for her son.

A box marked "Handle with Care" [=handle carefully]

2: Things that are done to keep someone healthy, safe, etc.

The children have inadequate medical care and little formal education.

We need to provide poor people with better dental care.

3: Things that are done to keep something in good condition.

She wrote a book about car care.

With proper care, the machine should last a decade or more.

Somehow in the interpretation of the phrase, "Individuality 'doesn't care'," we concluded that people with a lot of Individual Circuitry don't have empathy or feelings for other people, have little regard for what others think or experience, and basically can wander the Earth oblivious to the impact of their choices on others.

((Sigh))

Let's be clear, this kind of not caring is the shadow expression of the Will Center (Ego), NOT individuality. The Will Center, by the way, is almost exclusively a Tribal Center, all of the Channels connected to the Will Center, except for Channel 25/51, the Channel of Initiation in Quantum Human Design, are Tribal and all about caring. The Channel of Initiation is the Channel that bridges our personal identity (Ego) to the Higher Self.

The not caring of the Individual Circuitry is not about not caring about others; it's about not caring about what other people think of your unique way of expressing yourself, your innovative ideas, and your exquisite alignment with your Authentic Self. The ability of the individual to stay true to their unique, vital, and irreplaceable role in the Cosmic Plan allows the individual to serve their essential role of bringing change and consequent evolution to the world.

When we live in alignment with our Authentic Self, and we claim our unique place in the Cosmic Plan, we live from a place of understanding of our value. That recognition of our own personal value enables us to not only claim our own value but to see the value of others.

Alignment with the Authentic Self creates a high frequency of energy and a state of physiological heart coherence, which in turn influences your electro-magnetic resonance. All of these states are contagious. When you live true to yourself, you create a wave of energy that lifts others up and encourages them to be in the same energy field of pure self-expression.

Your alignment creates a resonance field that entrains others to be in alignment too, which then spreads to other people and to more people and to other people and so on and so on.

THIS is the power of individuality.

Not only that, fully expressing your Authentic Self and the initiatives that are yours to fulfill creates phenomenal change and transformation.

Think about Bob.

What would have happened if Bob had denied his alignment with his Authentic Individual Self? What if he had sucked it up, settled down, and forced himself to fit inside the Tribal box he was born into? What might never have been born into existence if he had failed to follow his true path?

What might never be born into existence if you fail to follow your own true path? That is the question for us to explore and contemplate over the next few years.

Individual | Transformation

Optimal Expression: The ability to stay true to your authentic identity with the awareness that you are fulfilling the full expression of your identity and inspiration creates the potential of a wave of new possibilities for humanity. To serve as a global change agent by simply being the fullest expression of yourself. To know that your authentic story transforms the world.

Unbalanced Expression: To rebel in reaction to feeling uncertain and insecure. To ignore right timing and readiness and share what you know without waiting. To feel hurt, left out, and the need to compromise who you are to feel loved and accepted. To not honor the transformation, you must bring enough to value yourself and your unique contribution to the world.

Lesson/Challenge: To learn to love and value your Authentic Self. To conquer standing in your appreciation for who you are and the transformation you bring and not compromise who you are for the sake of belonging or fitting in. To trust that, at the right time, you can share what you know with the right people who your knowledge will transform. Trusting in the Divine Plan.

Resiliency Keys: Courage, Authenticity, Vitality, Empowerment, Self-Worth, Self-Trust, Emotional Wisdom

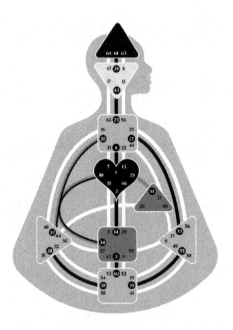

Keynotes:

- Auditory
- Timing
- Mutative
- Longs to belong but by definition can't
- Melancholy
- Creative
- Inspirational
- Source
- Wonder/awe
- Mood and integration

Individual-Integration | Transformation-Unifying

Optimal Expression: The ability to be responsively powerful in alignment with inner and outer timing and Love while serving the fulfillment of the full potential of the human condition.

Unbalanced Expression: To be reactive, depleted from pushing against right timing, and failing to fulfill potential due to a lack of self-love and Self-Trust.

Lesson/Challenge: To learn to assess, trust, wait and then respond. To become proficient at trusting in Divine Timing. To learn to love and honor yourself and your unique role in the Cosmic Plan enough to know that you are worth being supported and to claim and act on the unique and powerful role that only you can play in helping humanity fulfill its full potential.

Resiliency Keys: Lovability, Decisiveness, Courage, Authenticity, Vitality, Empowerment, Self-Trust

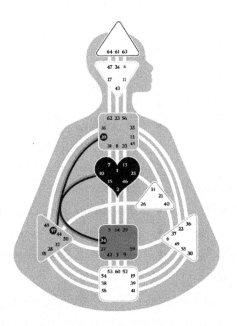

Keynotes:

- Integration
- Individual
- Takes time
- Manifest generated
- Empowering
- Intuitive life force
- Auditory
- Organizing around a common idea and giving it direction

Individual-Centering | Transformation-Calibration

Optimal Expression: The ability to embody a deep relationship and trust of Source, Higher Self, and the fulfillment of Purpose to lead others by demonstrating "The Way." To initiate others into following their own Heart by showing the world what it looks like to live from Heart.

Unbalanced Expression: Blindly following your path without respect for how it impacts others. To take actions that overcompensate for a sense of lack of lovability, low self-worth, a disconnection from Purpose and Heart, and distrust Source/God.

Lesson/Challenge: Learn to love yourself and value yourself enough to follow your convictions. Be responsible with your actions and maintain the awareness that your actions have the power to initiate others. Always be aware of where you may lead others and what you initiate them into. To learn to love yourself enough to follow your own convictions.

Resiliency Keys: Lovability, Decisiveness, Courage, Authenticity, Vitality, Empowerment, Self-Worth

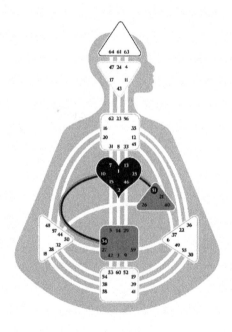

Keynotes:

- Individual
- Responsive
- Aura busting or "vortex effect"
- Gives direction to life force
- Motorizes the G-Center
- Following your convictions
- Connection to Source
- Alignment with higher purpose

Individual-Knowing | Transformation-Gnostic

Optimal Expression: The ability to trust in what you know and that you'll know what you need to know when you know it. The ability to trust in your purpose as a transformational agent on the planet and to let timing and circumstances inform you about when you need to share what you know. To sow the seeds of change with your knowledge and transform how people think, create, and connect to Source.

Unbalanced Expression: To share what you know before people are ready. To feel outcast, strange, or alienated because people aren't ready for what you know. To exhaust yourself, pushing your knowingness at the wrong time or with the wrong people.

Lesson/Challenge: Ground deeply in a faith-filled connection to Source, a deep awareness of your transformational life purpose, and trust in grace, Divine Timing, and humanity. To revel in what you know and to value it enough to not share it at the wrong time or with people who don't value your knowledge.

Resiliency Keys: Lovability, Decisiveness, Courage, Authenticity, Vitality, Empowerment, Self-Worth, Self-Trust, Emotional Wisdom

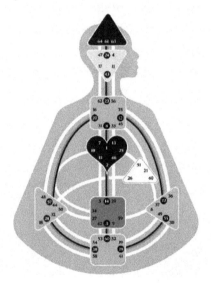

Keynotes:

- Cosmic consciousness
- Perspective
- Rationalizing
- Translating the Divine
- Right timing
- Intuitive awareness
- Challenge and adventure
- Momentum and conservatism
- Mutation
- Money and work

- Receiving and allowing
- Creativity and self-expression
- Faith and abundance
- Emotional energy
- Art, music, articulation
- Auditory
- Freaky or genius
- Loneliness
- Melancholy
- Claircognizance

Tribal | Sustainability

Optimal Expression: The ability to create sustainable resources and share them with others. The accomplishment of sharing and the embodiment of love as a verb. The ability to create peaceful agreements rooted in the possibility of win-win negotiation and justice. The management of resources which allows you to share what you have from a place of sufficiency. The ability to respond to the needs of others in a sustainable, peaceful, and just way.

Unbalanced Expression: The fear of not having enough creates hoarding, hiding, stealing, and war. The refusal to share out of fear of lack. Selfish actions or martyrdom. Depletion, exhaustion, and burnout create tension and projection. Compromising what you really want for the sake of others and feeling resentful and exhausted. The failure to take care of yourself so that you have more to give.

Lesson/Challenge: To learn to value yourself and sustain yourself as the path to creating more to share. The need to respond to the needs of others in a sustainable and just way. To learn to hold boundaries and respect the needs of others. To learn how to craft innovative and creative solutions to create enough in a sustainable way. To learn to create lasting peace by becoming great at win-win negotiations. To share without oversharing. To share without the fear of loss.

Resiliency Keys: Decisiveness, Courage, Authenticity, Vitality, Empowerment, Self-Worth, Self-Trust, Emotional Wisdom

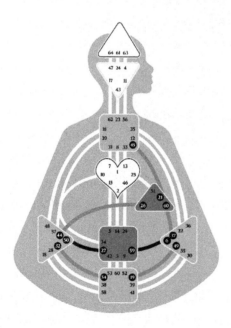

Keynotes:

- Creating sustainable resources
- Creating communities and tribes that align around the idea of sharing, contributing, aligning, and peace
- Contracts and businesses that feed the masses
- The alignment with the energy of wellbeing

Tribal-Defense | Sustainability-Nurture

Optimal Expression: The ability to respond to the need to do the work necessary to nurture and sustain resources. To educate for the sake of cultivating the right values that are rooted in nurturing, sustainable choices. Builds the foundation of love in action.

Unbalanced Expression: Codependency, over-caring, assuming responsibility for things you're not responsible for, and making impulsive, defensive choices that can lead to war and destruction.

Lesson/Challenge: To learn to respond sustainably with love to opportunities to create sustainable and nurturing choices.

Resiliency Keys: Decisiveness, Courage, Vitality, Empowerment, Self-Trust, Emotional Wisdom

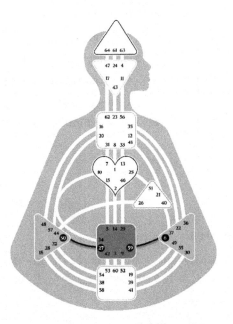

Keynotes:

- Aura busting
- Values-driven and compelling
- Food, nourishment
- Teaching, educating, transmitting information
- War and peace
- Sex and sexuality
- Resources
- Work

Tribal-Ego | Sustainability-Economic

Optimal Expression: The ability to respond to the right need at the right time to create sustainable value and shared resources.

Unbalanced Expression: Letting fear and lack create overwhelm and misuse of power and resources.

Lesson/Challenge: To learn to trust in "Enough."

Resiliency Keys: Decisiveness, Courage, Authenticity, Vitality, Empowerment, Self-Trust, Self-Worth, Emotional Wisdom

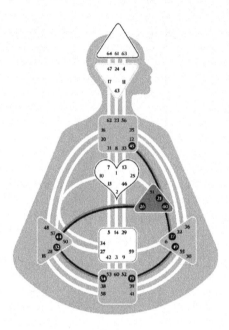

Keynotes:

- Right timing
- Resources
- Integrity
- Service
- Education
- Sharing and caring
- Community and support
- Relationships and connection
- Agreements and bonds

Two Streams in the Economic Circuit

Community (Intimacy & Relationships/Contracts) & Business
*Note: Channel 45/21 is in both streams

Community Circuit

The Rules of Engagement (*45/21, 40/37, and 19/49)

Keynotes:

- Engagement
- Agreements
- Marriage/property/resources
- Divorce/settlements
- Quid pro quo
- Willpower to keep an agreement
- Food
- Sustainability

Themes:

- Intimacy
- Relationship
- Nature
- Revolution
- Engagement
- Love and marriage/divorce
- Community
- Sustainability
- Law and regulation
- Bargains, deals, and agreements
- Legal agreements/contracts
- Allocation and management of goods

Business Circuit

(*45/21, 44/26, 32/54)

Keynotes:

- Ambition
- Enlightenment/letting go
- Sales/transmission/truth (or not)
- Intuition about creating resources/fear and lack
- Willpower to convince

Themes:

- Divine Inspiration
- Ambition
- The drive to hold on to a dream/vision
- The patterns of the past
- Beauty
- Transforming fear/pain into something of value
- Intuition/Clairolifactance (smelling a rat)
- Sales, marketing
- Transmission of truth and integrity/lying and falsehoods
- Creation of material gain in exchange for service
- Money
- Teaching
- History
- Allocation and management of resources
- Power
- Ego/sacrifice/service
- Sustainability
- Rest/endurance/will

Collective | Synergy

Optimal Expression: Understanding past experiences and patterns and using these understandings to build collective infrastructures and systems allows us to express our humanity and fully ensure the species' survival.

Unbalanced Expression: Rigidly adhering to old patterns or unproven ideas and trying to construct false systems with inaccurate information or rigidly adhering to old systems and stories that are not supported by truth.

Lesson/Challenge: To learn to embrace and respond to the flow of information and inspiration as it responds to human evolution.

Resiliency Keys: Lovability, Decisiveness, Courage, Authenticity, Vitality, Empowerment, Self-Trust, Emotional Wisdom

Circuitry Drivers:

- Spleen: Reactive
- Emotional Solar Plexus: Deliberate Conscious Creation

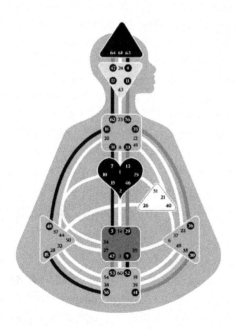

Keynotes:

- Infrastructure
- The ability to predict the future
- The need to understand the past
- The pulse for action
- The story of humanity
- Left brain

Collective-Logic | Synergy-Pattern

Optimal Expression: The ability to test and experiment with information to understand patterns. The use of patterns to predict future outcomes.

Unbalanced Expression: To adhere so rigidly to patterns that you miss the pattern interrupt. Letting fear, doubt, and suspicion keep you from changing the pattern. Discounting the wisdom of the Heart.

Lesson/Challenge: To learn to see patterns as probabilities but not to discount the exception. To learn that patterns evolve and change when people evolve and change. To realize that reasoning has its place, but without heart, it's just data.

Resiliency Keys: Lovability, Decisiveness, Courage, Authenticity, Vitality, Empowerment, Self-Trust

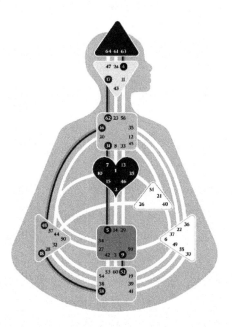

Keynotes:

- Doubt, fear, and suspicion
- The need to experiment with ideas
- Patterns
- Correcting
- Rational
- Science and democracy
- Reactive
- Data-driven/logical
- Skillful proficiency

Collective-Sensing | Synergy-Miracle

Optimal Expression: The ability to use the power of storytelling and personal narrative to break old patterns and to expand the story of what is possible.

Unbalanced Expression: To allow ungrounded fantasy and old painful experiences from the past to set the tone and the direction for life. Chaos or rigidity.

Lesson/Challenge: To learn to consciously use personal narrative as a tool to create emotional frequencies of energy that create new experiences about the human condition.

Resiliency Keys: Lovability, Decisiveness, Courage, Authenticity, Vitality, Empowerment, Self-Trust, Emotional Wisdom

Moving from Reactive Fear to Deliberate: Conscious Creation

Circuitry Drivers:

- Individuality: Self-Expression and Freedom
- Tribal: Belonging
- Collective: The Story of Humanity

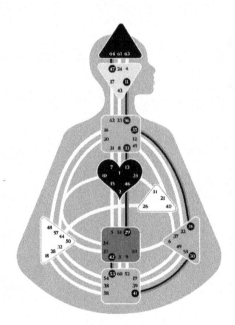

Keynotes:

- Right brain
- Teaching/storytelling
- Sensual
- Emotional
- Takes time
- Potential chaos
- Experiential

The Channels

Individual-Integration | Transformation-Unifying

57/34 - Channel of Power | Channel of Hearing

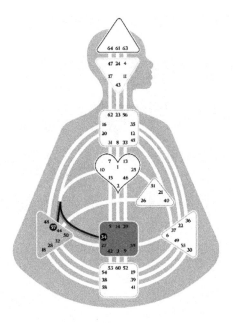

Optimal Expression: The ability to tune into the inner ear and hear whether a voice is in alignment or not. Inner auditory processing and clairaudience. Attunement with acoustical potential.

Unbalanced Expression: To ignore your inner voice. To be loud and overbearing as a strategy of getting your truth heard. Knowing the truth but feeling frustrated that you can't explain what you know.

Lesson/Challenge: To learn to trust your inner auditory process. To learn to process the awareness of a voice that is out of alignment. To learn to trust yourself. To wait for the right timing to share your insights.

Resiliency Keys: Decisiveness, Courage, Vitality, Empowerment, Self-Trust

Keynotes:

- Acoustic perfection
- Inner auditory processing
- Right ear
- Clairaudient/Claircognizant
- Auditory sensitivity
- Hears what's being said between the lines
- "Hears" the future

57/10 - Channel of Perfected Form | Channel of Human Potential

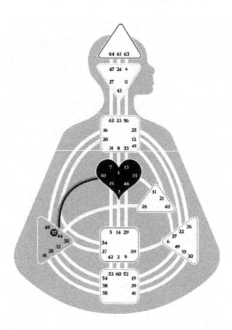

Optimal Expression: To see the perfection in everything. To learn to trust in timing for the fulfillment of potential. To recognize the right time to express the potential for love.

Unbalanced Expression: To let the fear of not being perfect stop you from moving forward in life. To stop exploring and experimenting because you might fail. To devalue imperfect attempts.

Lesson/Challenge: To learn that potential will always be fulfilled when you take responsibility and calibrate with love. There are no mistakes, only mistaken motivations.

Resiliency Keys: Lovability, Decisiveness, Courage, Authenticity, Self-Trust

Keynotes:

- Perfection
- Fear of making mistakes can sometimes create a fantasy in relationships because you can see the potential of this perfect and perfected love. Sometimes that's disappointing, and you have to work to bridge the gap between the fantasy of the potential and the reality of how you work towards the experience of creating greater love in your world.

34/20 - Channel of Charisma | Channel of Responsive Power

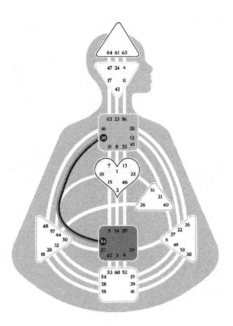

Optimal Expression: To trust that when your response and power are required, the opportunity to take the lead will show itself. To manage your energy so that it stays sustainable so that when it's time to act, you will be ready.

Unbalanced Expression: To initiate ideas without responding. To leap without waiting. To push and feel deeply frustrated and angry that nothing seems to be working out the way you thought. To let your fear of other people's judgments keep you playing small.

Lesson/Challenge: To learn to trust in the Universe's timing. To wait patiently and prepare to take action. To keep your energy occupied while you wait. To allow yourself to be powerful and not play small.

Resiliency Keys: Decisiveness, Courage, Authenticity, Vitality, Empowerment

Keynotes:

- Sustainable manifesting in response
- Archetype of Time Bender (Manifesting Generator)
- Wait, respond
- Busy-ness as energy management
- Think and act big
- Patience

10/20 - Channel of Awakening | Channel of Self-Assurance

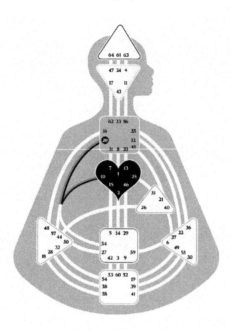

Optimal Expression: The ability to organize people around higher-order ideas and concepts rooted in the energies of self-love and self-empowerment. To speak words that change the narrative and the direction of people's lives and uplift them to higher expressions of self-love and self-empowerment.

Unbalanced Expression: The Verbal Gunslinger. Using language to disempower or hurt others as a symptom of your own lack of self-love. Defensive.

Lesson/Challenge: To learn to love yourself enough to be immune to being hurt by others' judgments and criticisms, and perceptions. To learn the power of language and to fully embody using language as a tool to transform the world. To learn to speak words of love and empowerment. To not seek revenge.

Resiliency Keys: Lovability, Decisiveness, Courage, Authenticity, Vitality, Self-Trust

Keynotes:

- The Buddha Channel
- Awakening
- Pure beingness

Individual-Centering | Transformation-Calibration

34/10 - Channel of Exploration | Channel of Courage

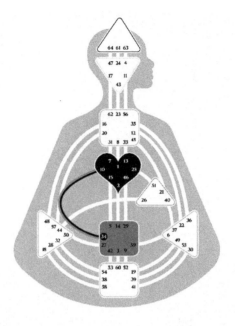

Optimal Expression: Having a deep enough connection to Self, self-love, and self-worth and an awareness of what actions need to be taken to respond to an opportunity to express a higher principle and the fulfillment of Love. The courage to respond to taking the "right" action and the more principled approach.

Unbalanced Expression: Taking reckless actions to prove your lovability and self-worth. Not acting out of fear and self-preservation.

Lesson/Challenge: To skillfully navigate the conviction and courage necessary to follow your Heart and the right thing. Remember, you are worth being true to yourself.

Resiliency Keys: Lovability, Decisiveness, Courage, Authenticity, Vitality, Empowerment

Keynotes:

- Responding with self-love, conviction & power
- Courage
- Conviction
- Self-love

- Power
- Heart
- Self-worth
- Higher principle

51/25 - Channel of Initiation | Channel of Higher Purpose

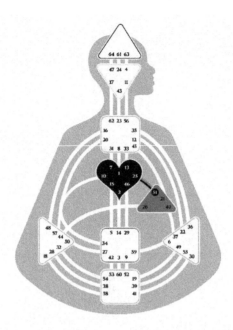

Optimal Expression: The ability to transcend personal experience and disruption and to see the higher purpose. Allowing the ego to serve the Higher Self. Using the material world's resources to serve the Heart's direction. Using wisdom and connection to Source as a way to initiate others into the power of their own Hearts.

Unbalanced Expression: Serving the self at a cost to others. Living with a Backup Plan for the Divine. Losing connection with life and soul purpose. Anger and bitterness over feeling out of control of circumstances. Using "shock" as a tool to gain attention and power.

Lesson/Challenge: To learn to trust Source. To know there is a higher purpose to all experiences. To welcome challenges as a path to growth and evolution. To use your experiences to inspire others.

Resiliency Keys: Lovability, Decisiveness, Courage, Authenticity, Vitality, Empowerment, Self-Worth

Keynotes:

- Shock/shocking (the will to survive shock)
- Surrender to Spirit
- Love of Spirit
- Healing
- Transformation
- Here to be awakened and to awaken others (initiating energy)
- Competitive (or perceived that way)
- Using material resources to implement the desires of the heart

Individual-Knowing | Transformation-Gnostic

61/24 - Channel of Awareness | Channel of Cosmic Perspective

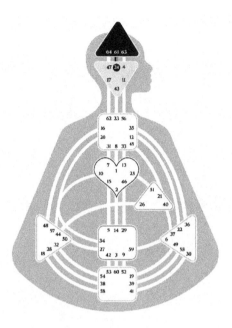

Optimal Expression: The ability to see the big picture and to find the blessings that time and perspective bring. The ability to "see" the Divine nature of experience and to receive knowing insights that have the potential to change your thinking and the way others think and perceive reality.

Unbalanced Expression: To resist bigger perspectives and lock yourself into a micro-perspective that limits possibility in your life.

Lesson/Challenge: To learn to see the bigger purpose in life experiences. To trust in your perspective even if others don't see it the same way. To release limiting perspectives and to know that there is a purpose for all of life—including the challenges.

Resiliency Keys: Decisiveness, Self-Trust

Keynotes:

- The Thinker or The Bridge between "Above" and "Below"
- Needs time to think
- Mutative epiphanies
- Reaches to know the unknowable and then rationalizes
- Melancholy (especially if they don't have time to think)
- Can seem lost in thought

43/23 - Channel of Structuring | Channel of Innovative Thinking

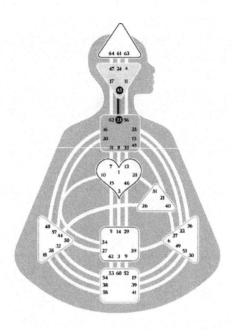

Optimal Expression: The ability to articulate what you know and to share it at the right time with the right people when you are asked. Projected. The ability to use your knowing to change the way people think.

Unbalanced Expression: Sharing what you know at the wrong time with the wrong people and feeling alienated, melancholic, and misunderstood. Missing the opportunity to transform others.

Lesson/Challenge: To know that your insights have the power to change the way people think. To value the innovation that you bring enough to be a steward of your innovative ideas. To place your ideas into the minds of others when asked, and only when asked.

Resiliency Keys: Decisiveness, Self-Trust, Authenticity, Vitality

Keynotes:

- Waiting for the right timing to change the thoughts of others
- Needs time to think
- Mutative epiphanies
- Melancholy (especially if they don't have time to think)
- Can seem lost in thought

- Brilliant insights with the right timing
- Inner auditory process—The Channel of Not Listening
- Always making "noise"
- Knowingness

38/28 - Channel of Struggle | Channel of Meaning

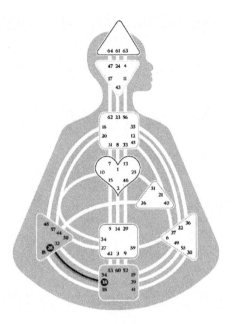

Optimal Expression: The ability to endure with an idea, possibility, or potential to explore whether it is worthy of fighting or holding a vision. The drive to envision a new possibility and to root yourself in holding true to the vision.

Unbalanced Expression: Directionless struggle and fighting. Fighting and struggling for the sake of fighting without meaning, OR not being willing to engage in exploration due to fear of the challenge.

Lesson/Challenge: To learn that all transformational ideas need the "work" of enduring the time it takes to set the stage and lay the foundation for right timing to transmit. To value an idea enough to fight for it. To redefine yourself as an explorer on the edge of human potential and to enjoy the adventure.

Resiliency Keys: Courage, Vitality, Empowerment, Self-Trust

Keynotes:

- Adrenalized
- Projected
- Be invited to live as yourself in the now
- Melancholic
- You have to be invited to struggle; otherwise, it is painful

- Immune system and health
- Potential for great bitterness
- Struggle for the meaning of life
- Struggle can be fun!
- Power struggle dynamic
- Auditory

57/20 - Channel of the Brainwave | Channel of Prediction

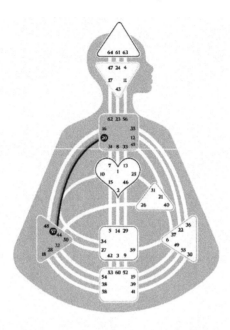

Optimal Expression: The instinctual awareness to know what is necessary to craft a vision of the future. The awareness of right timing and readiness to share what you know.

Unbalanced Expression: To share what you know without waiting for the right timing or the right audience. OR to not share what you know or fail to act from fear of the future.

Lesson/Challenge: To learn to trust your inner impulses. To cultivate patience and be in tune with the right audience to share what you know. To become proficient in self-trust.

Resiliency Keys: Courage, Authenticity, Vitality, Self-Trust

Keynotes:

- Intuitive awareness
- Presence
- Patience
- Inner knowing
- Self-trust
- Potential paralysis from the fear of the future

60/3 - Channel of Mutation | Channel of Innovation

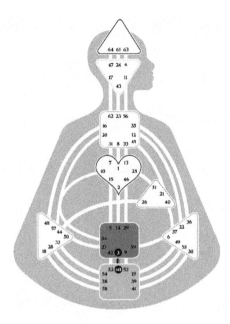

Optimal Expression: The ability to innovate by expanding on what works and transforming it through right work and with aligned timing. The ability to do the right work necessary to bring about transformation and innovation.

Unbalanced Expression: Forcing new ideas into form. Pushing with innovation without respect for what has come before. Wasting energy trying to innovate without context and respect.

Lesson/Challenge: To lay the foundation for innovation by exploring what works, taking the elements that ARE working, and innovating. To be aware of the challenge that needs innovation and to address it with respect to what has come before. To learn to wait for something to respond to before doing the work of innovation.

Resiliency Keys: Decisiveness, Courage, Vitality, Empowerment

Keynotes:

- Taking what works and expanding on it in innovative ways
- Possibility
- "Don't throw the baby out with the bathwater"
- Working within limits to create something new
- The desire to change things
- The need for right timing (adrenaline pulse) to push through and access the energy to do something different
- Working within limits to create change
- Taking stock of past, present, and future possibilities and mutating them
- Genetic mutation
- Gratitude is the impetus for Transformation

14/2 - Channel of The Beat | Channel of Progress

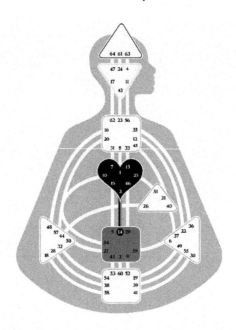

Optimal Expression: The ability to respond to innovative ways to create opportunities to create abundance and resources. Entrepreneurship.

Unbalanced Expression: The desperation for resources that pushes until depletion. The willingness to compromise for the sake of resources. The ends justify the means.

Lesson/Challenge: To learn to trust that in Divine Timing, the right idea will bear fruit and transform the economic landscape.

Resiliency Keys: Lovability, Decisiveness, Courage, Authenticity, Vitality, Empowerment

Keynotes:

- The energy to use innovative ways to generate resources
- New ways of working that access support
- Working and responding for resources
- Receiving and allocating resources
- The sustainable energy to work for resources

- The energy to innovate how we work
- Responding to the right timing to work for change
- Responding to work that creates resources and gives direction to innovation
- The only place in the chart where we work for money

1/8 - Channel of Inspiration | Channel of Self-Fulfillment

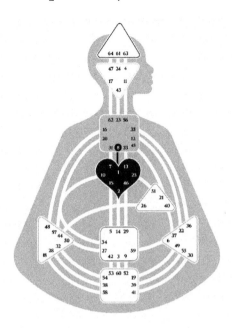

Optimal Expression: To relentlessly and without compromise express the fullness of the Authentic Self. To live, lead and transform from the Heart of Who You Are. To be able to articulate the Truth of Who You Are. In being the fulfillment of the Self, you show others how to do the same.

Unbalanced Expression: The fear of failing your life purpose.

Lesson/Challenge: To learn that expressing the Authentic Self is the fulfillment of your life purpose. YOU are the contribution you are here to give the world.

Resiliency Keys: Lovability, Decisiveness, Courage, Authenticity, Vitality

Keynotes:

- The capacity to add to the beauty in the world by being the fullest expression of who you truly are
- Self-expression AS the creative contribution you make to the world
- Being Yourself
- Pressure to find your purpose
- Here to be a role model-by BEING-but feels like DOING instead
- Innovative contribution to change the world
- Vulnerable to criticism
- Needs recognition to know when the timing is right

39/55 - Channel of Emoting | Channel of Deliberate Creation

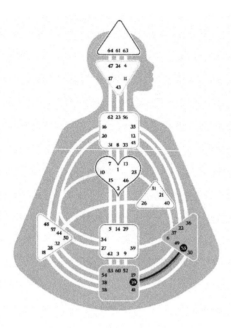

Optimal Expression: The ability to consciously harness emotional energy to stay in a state of expectation and faith as the foundation of creating in the world.

The ability to realign a situation with a higher frequency of faith and possibility by maintaining a high quality of emotional alignment. Sufficiency and Trust.

Unbalanced Expression: To create from a place of lack. To hoard, worry, be indecisive, and selfish in the face of lack. To block the flow of sufficiency because of a belief in lack and a low-quality frequency of emotional energy.

Lesson/Challenge: To learn to trust in your sufficiency and support. To learn how to sustain and maintain a high frequency of emotional alignment. To take right action in the name of sufficiency.

Resiliency Keys: Decisiveness, Courage, Vitality, Empowerment, Emotional Wisdom

Keynotes:

- Deeply emotional
- Creative
- Alchemical
- Auditory
- Mutative
- Energy and mood fluctuate

- Eating
- Provocative
- Purpose is to restore things to the flow and return us to spirit

22/12 - Channel of Openness | Channel of Grace

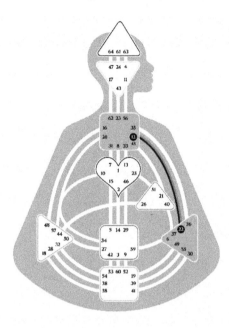

Optimal Expression: The ability to transform through self-expression and creative emotional alignment. To use language and creative expression to align people with a higher expression of possibility. The ability to create beyond limitations when the emotional alignment and timing are correct.

Unbalanced Expression: Low-frequency emotional expression that brings others down. Shyness, struggle to express when the timing or alignment is off.

Lesson/Challenge: To learn to trust in Divine Timing. To know that your creative expression has the power to transform others and the world and to use it wisely and judiciously. To be a global change agent and to serve the words that come through you.

Resiliency Keys: Decisiveness, Courage, Authenticity, Vitality, Empowerment, Emotional Wisdom

Keynotes:

- Emotional
- Creative voice for Individuality
- In the mood, or not
- Social, or not
- Articulate, or not

- Musical, poetic, and passionate in every way
- Charm/grace, or not
- Voice in the wilderness

Tribal-Defense | Sustainability-Nurture

27/50 - Channel of Preservation | Channel of Sustenance

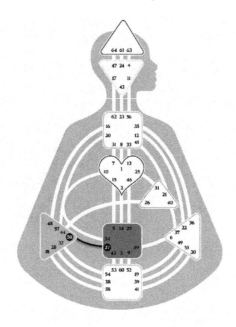

Optimal Expression: The ability, through responding, to nurture, nourish, sustain, and live aligned with values rooted in Love and sustainability. The ability to feed and nourish everyone.

Unbalanced Expression: To over-care, be rigid with values, be codependent and closed-minded. To yield unbending values and punish those who don't follow. To hold back nourishing those who don't share common values.

Lesson/Challenge: To learn that Love causes the manifestation of sufficiency and sustenance. To trust in Plenty. To allow for common ground.

Resiliency Keys: Decisiveness, Courage, Vitality, Empowerment, Self-Trust

Keynotes:

- Mother or Feminine energy
- Cooking
- Education
- Value and values transmission, rules, and law
- Nurturing

- Responsibility and obligation
- Guilt
- Codependency
- Education

59/6 - Channel of Reproduction | Channel of Provision

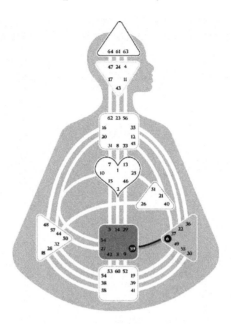

Optimal Expression: The ability to respond and align with the right emotional energy to provide and procure sustainable resources and use resources peacefully. The energy for sexual relationships is in the right energy and rooted in shared values that build a foundation for a family and a tribe.

Unbalanced Expression: Scarcity and fighting for resources. Lack which triggers war and fighting. Sexual energy that isn't matched with shared values and isn't sustainable. Feeling like a failure when you fail to provide for your family or tribe.

Lesson/Challenge: To learn to wait to respond when the energy is aligned to work for, procure and align with the right provisions. Learning to wait to respond when the energy is aligned to bond sexually. To learn to create peacefully with people who don't share your values.

Resiliency Keys: Decisiveness, Courage, Vitality, Empowerment, Emotional Wisdom

Keynotes:

- Impactful
- Penetrating
- War/peace
- Sexual or not
- Reproduction

- Provision of resources
- Hunter, Warrior, Masculine Archetype

Tribal-Ego | Sustainability-Economic

54/32 - Channel of Transformation | Channel of Revelation

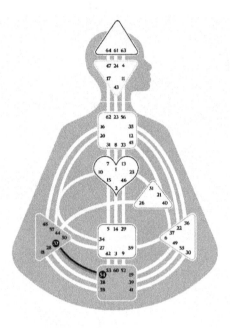

Optimal Expression: The drive to prepare and lay the foundation for the manifestation of an idea. The endurance and patience to wait for the right timing to share the idea with others.

Unbalanced Expression: The pressure to implement an idea or inspiration and to burn out pushing against right timing. To fail to do the work necessary to put an idea into action due to the fear of failure.

Lesson/Challenge: To trust in right timing. To have the confidence and faith to trust your inner knowing and the potential of an inspiration to do the work necessary to prepare for the next step.

Resiliency Keys: Courage, Vitality, Empowerment, Self-Trust

Keynotes:

- The drive to build the foundation of business from inspiration (Divine Spark) to prepare to go to market
- Timing
- Splenic
- Fear of failure

- Turning dreams into reality
- Building the foundation
- Endurance
- Starting
- Ideas
- Drive and ambition

44/26 - Channel of Surrender | Channel of Alignment

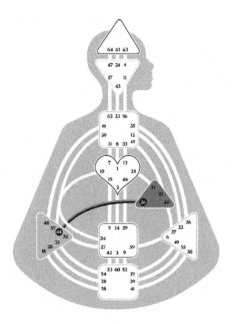

Optimal Expression: The energy to transform pain into something of greater value and to share it. The will to stay in integrity with yourself and others even if you're scared or feel "less than." The ability to transform past patterns and create something sustainable and valuable for yourself and others. The will to do the right thing even when it's hard.

Unbalanced Expression: To take, seize, lie, cheat. Or to be out of integrity with the Self as a symptom of fear and lack or low self-esteem.

Lesson/Challenge: To learn to break the patterns of the past that are rooted in pain and lack. To learn to reclaim self-worth and the role of your Higher Self. To value yourself enough to stay in integrity with yourself.

Resiliency Keys: Courage, Vitality, Empowerment, Self-Worth, Self-Trust

Keynotes:

- The will to hold to Truth and Integrity
- The will to wait to find the purpose in the pain
- The ability to transform pain into something of value (learning)

- The past
- The will to do the right thing
- Sales and marketing
- Lies and trickery
- Beauty

19/49 - Channel of Love & Marriage | Channel of Intimacy & Connection

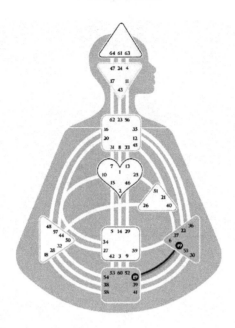

Optimal Expression: An intimate emotional connection that supports, nurtures, and expands with the right emotional frequency.

Unbalanced Expression: Codependency or lack of intimacy and awareness.

Lesson/Challenge: To learn to use emotional frequencies to maintain and sustain intimacy and connection. To learn how to commit and endure with the right emotional energy.

Resiliency Keys: Decisiveness, Courage, Vitality, Empowerment, Emotional Wisdom

Keynotes:

- Intimacy
- Engagement
- Can look or feel clingy or codependent
- Together, or not!
- Connection with the animal kingdom
- Very sensitive
- The need for a supportive environment to help with creativity

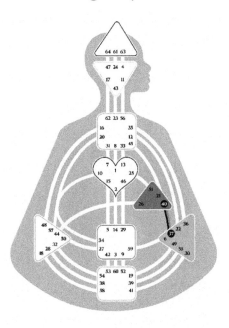

Optimal Expression: The ability to make sustainable agreements that create the peaceful administration of resources and energy. The energy stream that attunes the Heart.

Unbalanced Expression: Not making or keeping agreements because of perceived lack.

Lesson/Challenge: To learn to value yourself and others enough to create agreements that express that value. To make aligned and honest agreements and trust in the flow of abundance. To create from sufficiency and "enough-ness."

Resiliency Keys: Decisiveness, Courage, Vitality, Empowerment, Self-Worth, Emotional Wisdom

Keynotes:

- Quid Pro Quo
- The Marriage Contract
- Bargains need to be made out loud and not in fantasy
- Broken deals can lead to broken hearts and emotional pain
- The ability to sustain the agreement
- Sharing

21/45 - Channel of The Money Line | Channel of Sustainable Resources

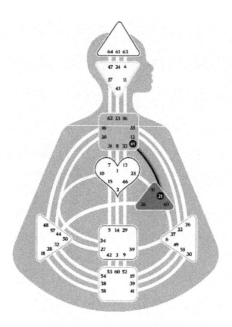

Optimal Expression: The ability to equitably, peacefully, and sustainably share resources for the betterment of others.

Unbalanced Expression: Hoarding, lack, holding back, overusing, hiding, or stealing resources for personal gain.

Lesson/Challenge: To learn to cultivate "enoughness" sustainably. To be aligned with Authentic Value. To establish sustainable, enduring ways to share.

Resiliency Keys: Authenticity, Vitality, Empowerment, Self-Worth

Keynotes:

- Management and distribution of resources
- Including money, material goods, information
- Teaching energy
- Built-in power struggle
- Money or not
- Sustainability is created from endurance and planning
- Leadership
- Ego
- Sharing

Collective-Logic | Synergy-Pattern

63/4 - Channel of Logic | Channel of Potentiality

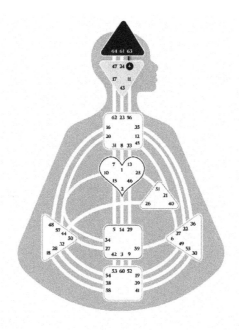

Optimal Expression: The ability to use the power of thinking to explore the possibility of new ideas and inspirations. The ability, by virtue of contemplation, to explore whether an idea has validity or not.

Unbalanced Expression: To have a closed mind that is doubtful, suspicious, or displays invalid certainty. To refuse to explore possibilities.

Lesson/Challenge: To learn to use the power of thinking (or questioning) to generate new possibilities and be open-minded to the possibility of change.

Resiliency Keys: Decisiveness, Self-Trust

Keynotes:

- Doubt and suspicion
- Questioning
- Can this be proven to be true?
- Experimental answers that may or may not be true
- Scientific question

- Right eye
- Visual learner
- Left brain
- Projected
- Linear thinking

17/62 - Channel of Acceptance | Channel of Formulation

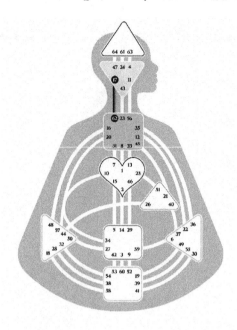

Optimal Expression: The ability to gather information and details necessary to explore the validity of an idea or to begin the process of becoming accomplished. The formation of a hypothesis and the beginning of an experiment.

Unbalanced Expression: To be afraid that you won't be ready. Panic. To overcompensate for not knowing by being overly prepared.

Lesson/Challenge: To learn to plan with confidence and the awareness that all of life is an experiment. To learn to trust that you'll still be okay even if you're not prepared.

Resiliency Keys: Decisiveness, Authenticity, Self-Trust, Vitality

Keynotes:

- Planning and preparing
- Organized
- Struggles with trusting
- The need to organize others
- Ideas about what "should" be done
- Projected "What should we do?"

16/48 - Channel of Talent | Channel of Excellence

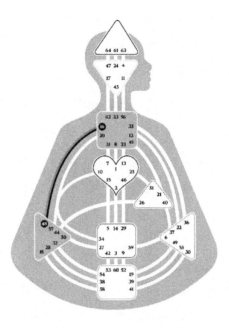

Optimal Expression: The ability to sense the right timing and share wisdom accumulated from practice, revision, and improvement.

Unbalanced Expression: Talent is only cultivated with practice. To rely on talent without practice and to share without the wisdom of experience.

Lesson/Challenge: Practice makes perfect. Skillful accomplishment is only achieved through trying, experimenting, and preparing.

Resiliency Keys: Courage, Authenticity, Vitality, Self-Trust

Keynotes:

- Practice
- Depth from study and learning
- Natural talent
- The desire to share wisdom gained from practice when the timing is right
- The need for experimenting as a path to wisdom
- The "scientific experiment" and the collection of data

18/58 - Channel of Judgment | Channel of Improvement

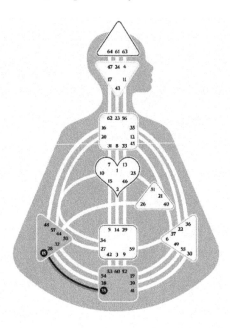

Optimal Expression: The ability to sense when practiced patterns need correction, realignment, and improvement. The joyous drive is constantly growing in the expression of full understanding.

Unbalanced Expression: Offering unsolicited corrections and judgments. The fear of imperfection and lack of joy over the imperfect expression of knowledge.

Lesson/Challenge: To learn that perfection is a constantly evolving state, not an endpoint. To value your insights enough to wait to be asked to share them. To appreciate the effort, not the outcome.

Resiliency Keys: Courage, Vitality, Empowerment, Self-Trust

Keynotes:

- Projected
- Criticism when the timing is off
- Potential for joy
- Driven to practice and improve for the sake of the joy of genius
- The ability to see imperfections
- The fear of imperfection
- Often hurt and confused when people don't understand original intention
- The drive to skillfully conquer something because you love it

52/9 - Channel of Focus | Channel of Clarity

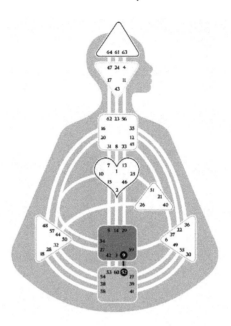

Optimal Expression: The ability to see the big picture and to know where to focus your attention and energy for the sake of maximizing creative potential.

Unbalanced Expression: Adrenalized or pressurized action that precedes the right clarity. Wasted efforts. Attention deficit.

Lesson/Challenge: To trust in Divine Timing and know that with clarity comes the energy for focus, perspective, and, ultimately, right action.

Resiliency Keys: Decisiveness, Courage, Vitality, Empowerment

Keynotes:

- Focus
- Concentration
- Format energy
- The pulse to concentrate and focus and get things done

5/15 - Channel of Rhythm | Channel of Natural Order

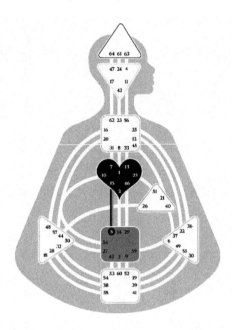

Optimal Expression: The ability to respond to being in the flow and alignment of the natural order. The ability to know when to align or abandon the pattern for the sake of growing in compassion.

Unbalanced Expression: Struggling to find the right rhythm and flow. Longing for consistency and bored with regularity.

Lesson/Challenge: To learn to respond to being in the flow. To learn to cultivate patterns and habits but to know that all patterns must change as part of growth.

Resiliency Keys: Lovability, Decisiveness, Courage, Authenticity, Vitality, Empowerment

Keynotes:

- In the flow
- Contributes to humanity
- The natural rhythm of life
- Tantric
- Can have a built-in conflict
- Deeply elemental

7/31 - Channel of The Alpha | Channel of Egalitarianism

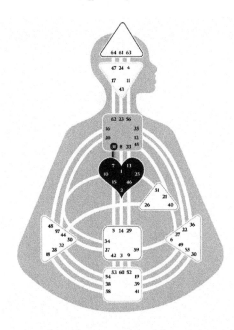

Optimal Expression: The ability to take leadership when recognized. A leadership style that incorporates collaboration, wisdom, experience, and proficiency. To lead with resiliency and stability even during cycles of pattern disruption. The ability to lead with Heart.

Unbalanced Expression: The need to be recognized for being a leader. Letting the need for recognition overshadow the path of service.

Lesson/Challenge: To learn to lead from Heart with the desire to serve the highest good of all. The ability to learn to lead even when the patterns are disrupted and when there is uncertainty. To learn the best ways to administer the patterns.

Resilience Keys: Lovability, Decisiveness, Courage, Authenticity, Vitality

Keynotes:

- Democratic leadership
- Leadership that is supported
- Leadership based on its demonstration over time of its effectiveness
- When it's not logical, it's not supported

Collective-Sensing | Synergy-Miracle

64/47 - Channel of Abstraction | Channel of Divine Potential

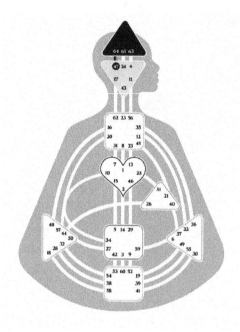

Optimal Expression: The ability to receive inspiration and to cultivate it in deep alignment with the awareness that, at the right time, in the right way, the inspiration will manifest. To serve as the steward for inspiration by giving it energy through thought.

Unbalanced Expression: Trying to force an idea into action. Figuring out how to do something and then trying to do it without waiting for right timing.

Lesson/Challenge: To learn to trust in right timing. To prepare for the outer manifestation of the next step or the inner epiphany.

Resiliency Keys: Decisiveness, Self-Trust

Keynotes:

- Gate of dreaming
- Highly visual—left eye
- Confusion followed by an epiphany
- The pressure to figure out HOW?!

- Right brain dominant
- Clairvoyant
- Mindset
- The initiation of inspiration

11/56 - Channel of Curiosity | Channel of The Framework

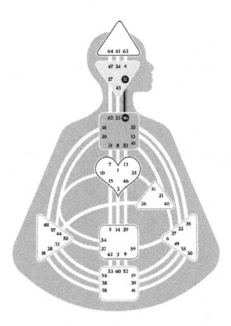

Optimal Expression: Using the power of storytelling and metaphors to create the framework of something new. Using language to explore potential and possibility. Transmitting ideas that can inspire.

Unbalanced Expression: Sharing ideas without waiting for right timing. Over-telling and ignoring the sacredness of the inspiration you carry. The need to share for the sake of attention and recognition.

Lesson/Challenge: To learn to become a steward of inspiration. To recognize the transformative power of language and use words to transmit the seeds of potential. To use the power of storytelling to leap over the conditioning of old patterns and break people free from previous limitations.

Resilience Keys: Decisiveness, Authenticity, Vitality, Self-Trust

Keynotes:

- Seeking but not necessarily finding
- Possibility thinking
- Abundant ideas and inspirations
- Projected channel
- Teach
- Inspire
- Storytelling

41/30 - Channel of Fantasy & Desire | Channel of Intention

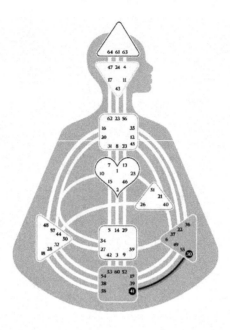

Optimal Expression: The ability to envision an intention/dream and hold the emotional frequency of the intention until the timing is right to act on it.

Unbalanced Expression: Acting on a desire-based impulse without waiting for right timing or lack of dreams and desire that blocks momentum.

Lesson/Challenge: To learn to use the power of imagination to begin the creative process. To adroit use of imagination and the ability to sustain a vision as a key element to manifesting and changing the patterns of your life and Life.

Resiliency Keys: Decisiveness, Courage, Vitality, Empowerment, Emotional Wisdom

Keynotes:

- The drive to hold onto a vision until the timing and vibration is right to take action to bring it into form
- Delusion
- Projection
- Intensity

- Creativity
- Response to what is in the tangible world
- Initiating
- All things start first in mind
- What would happen if...?

36/35 - Channel of Transitoriness | Channel of The Threshold

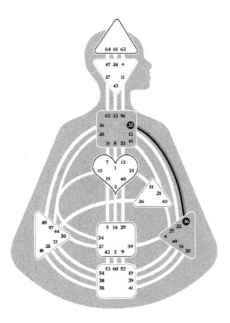

Optimal Expression: The ability to incorporate new experiences and push the boundaries of the limits of the human story.

Unbalanced Expression: To act recklessly out of boredom. To fail to explore the boundaries and edges of human potential.

Lesson/Challenge: To learn to wait for the right timing and emotional alignment to test the threshold of human potential.

Resiliency Keys: Decisiveness, Courage, Authenticity, Vitality, Empowerment, Emotional Wisdom

Keynotes:

- Timing
- Emotional alignment
- Boredom
- Jaded
- Stretching the boundaries of human potential
- Prepare for the right experience

53/42 - Channel of Maturation | Channel of Executive Function

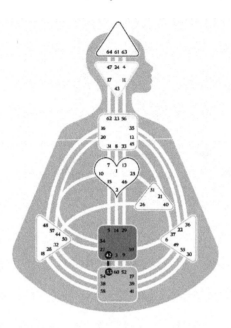

Optimal Expression: The ability to initiate and complete an experience for the sake of the fulfillment of the potential of humanity.

Unbalanced Expression: The struggle to know what to start or finish, or both. Stuckness.

Lesson/Challenge: To wait for the right timing to prepare for the fulfillment of potential. To do the work necessary to push forward and expand potential.

Resiliency Keys: Decisiveness, Courage, Vitality, Empowerment

Keynotes:

- Responsive
- Right timing
- Starting and letting go
- Being in the flow of fulfillment

29/46 - Channel of Discovery | Channel of Dedication

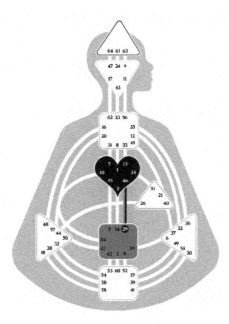

Optimal Expression: The ability, through responding, to dedicate yourself to fulfilling the potential of the human story on the physical plane. Success through commitment and devotion. The embodiment of the fulfillment of potential.

Unbalanced Expression: The failure to commit and succeed results in burnout and physical dysfunction. Overcommitment and burnout.

Lesson/Challenge: To learn to respond to the right opportunities. To avoid devoting yourself to the wrong thing to prove your love-worthiness. To use the body to express the fulfillment of human potential. To explore through dedication the limits of human potential.

Resiliency Keys: Lovability, Decisiveness, Courage, Authenticity, Vitality, Empowerment

Keynotes:

- Commitment
- "YES!"
- Embodiment
- Succeeding where others fail and failing where others succeed
- Fake willpower
- Spirit in physical form
- The endurance to make it happen
- Body is a barometer
- Often fascinated with the physical
- Hides out
- Olympic athletes

13/33 - Channel of the Prodigal | Channel of Collective Consciousness

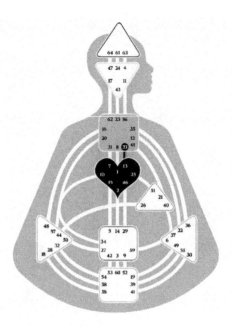

Optimal Expression: The ability to share a narrative that sets the stage, the tone, and the direction for the expansion of love and the fulfillment of human potential. The transmission of the stories of what has come before, to glean the lessons and move forward from the past with clear intention. The use of narrative as a template for the expansion of possibility.

Unbalanced Expression: To get stuck in old stories that limit potential and possibility.

Lesson/Challenge: To learn to take the blessings of past events and the stories of what has come before to craft a deliberate narrative that influences the fulfillment of the potential of the human story.

Resiliency Keys: Lovability, Decisiveness, Courage, Authenticity, Vitality

Keynotes:

- Telling the stories of the past
- The story you tell defines who you are and what direction your life takes
- Forgiveness
- Secret keeper, bears witness
- The historian
- Aloneness

The Gates

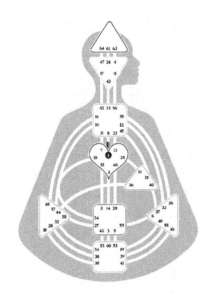

Gate 1: Purpose

I Ching: The Creative
Traditional Human Design: Self-Expression
Astrological Sign: Scorpio
Biology: Liver

Optimal Expression: The ability to know the Authentic Self and experience a deep connection with a Life Purpose.

Unbalanced Expression: An erratic or purposeless life, panic and a feeling of failing at a life mission, pressure to create something unique in the world, struggle to find purpose, hiding because the purpose feels too big, too much, or egotistical.

Lesson/Challenge: To discover a personal, meaningful, and world-changing narrative that aligns with a sense of purpose and mission. "I am…" To learn to love yourself enough to honor the idea that your life is the canvas, and you are the artist. What you create with your life IS the contribution you give the world.

Center: The Calibration Center

Resiliency Keys: Lovability, Decisiveness, Courage, Authenticity

Contemplations:

- Are you fully expressing your Authentic Self?
- What needs to be healed, released, aligned, or brought to your awareness for you to more deeply express your Authentic Self?
- Where are you already expressing who you are?
- Where have you settled or compromised? What needs to change?
- Do you feel connected to your life purpose? What do you need to do to deepen that connection?

Keynotes:

- Yang/Yang
- Pressure to fulfill your purpose
- Deep quest for meaning
- Vulnerable
- Creative force
- Authenticity
- Heart

Affirmation: My life is an integral part of the Cosmos and the Divine Plan. I honor my life and know that the full expression of who I am is the purpose of my life. The more I am who I am, the more I create a frequency of energy that supports others in doing the same. I commit to exploring all of who I am.

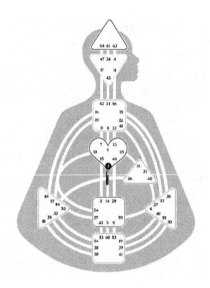

Gate 2: Allowing

I Ching: The Receptive
Traditional Human Design: Keeper of the Keys
Astrological Sign: Taurus
Biology: Liver

Optimal Expression: To set intentions and move solidly towards the fulfillment of the Authentic Self with complete trust that you are supported in being the full expression of who you are and your life purpose, even if you don't know how or what the support will look like. Trust in Source. Living in a state of gratitude.

Unbalanced Expression: To experience stress, fear, and ultimately compromise on what you want and who you are because you don't trust that you are supported. To be valiantly self-sufficient to the point of burning yourself out. To never ask for help.

Lesson/Challenge: To love yourself enough to open to the flow of support, love, and abundance. To incrementally increase over the course of your life what you're willing to allow yourself to receive. To learn to know that you are valuable and lovable simply because you exist.

Center: The Calibration Center

Resiliency Keys: Lovability, Decisiveness, Courage, Authenticity

Contemplations:

- Do you ask for help when you need it? Why or why not?
- Do you trust the Universe/God/Spirit/Source to support you in fulfilling your intentions?
- Are you grateful for what you have? Make a list of everything you're grateful for.
- Can you transform your worry into trust?
- Do you believe that you deserve to be supported?

Keynotes:
- Self-worth
- Gratitude
- Faith
- Authenticity
- Trust
- Yin/Yin

Affirmation: I allow myself to receive the full flow of resources and abundance I need to fully express all of who I am. I recognize that my life is a vital, irreplaceable part of the Cosmic Tapestry, and I receive all that I need because it helps me contribute to all that I am.

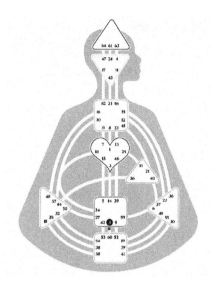

Gate 3: Innovation

I Ching: Difficulty at the Beginning
Traditional Human Design: Ordering
Astrological Sign: Aries/Taurus
Biology: Ovaries and Testes

Optimal Expression: The ability to embrace and integrate new ideas and ways of doing things. To learn to stay in appreciation for your unique way of thinking and being and to trust that, as an innovator on the leading edge of consciousness, your time to transmit what you're here to bring forth will come, so you wait and cultivate your ideas with patience.

Unbalanced Expression: To feel pressured and panicked about the need to share an idea or innovation. To burn yourself out trying to override Divine Timing.

Lesson/Challenge: To learn to trust in Divine Timing and to know that your ideas and insights will be transmitted to the world when the world is ready.

Center: The Evolution Center

Resiliency Keys: Vitality, Decisiveness, Courage, Empowerment

Contemplations:

- Where has Divine Timing worked out in your life? What has waiting taught you?
- Do you trust in Divine Timing?
- If the opportunity to share your ideas with the world presented itself today, would you be ready?
- If not, what do you need to prepare to be ready?

Keynotes:
- The pressure to be different
- The willingness/unwillingness to explore what has come before
- Weird for no reason
- Genetic mutation

Affirmation: I am here to bring change to the world. My natural ability to see what else is possible to create something new is my strength and my gift. I patiently cultivate my inspiration and use my understanding of what is needed to help evolve the world.

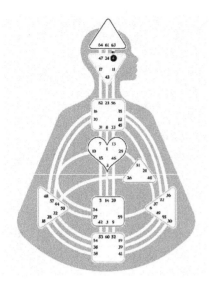

Gate 4: Possibility

I Ching: Youthful Folly
Traditional Human Design: Answers
Astrological Sign: Leo
Biology: Anterior and Posterior Pituitary Glands

Optimal Expression: The ability to experience an idea as a possibility. To learn to use that idea as a "seed" for the imagination and use the imagination to create an emotional response that calibrates the Heart and attracts experiences and opportunities that match the possibility into your life.

Unbalanced Expression: Self-doubt and fear that you have an idea that you can't figure out. The pressure to try to share or implement the idea before it has had time to seed the manifestation. Acting too soon without waiting for the right timing.

Lesson/Challenge: To learn to embrace ideas as possibilities, not answers, and to let the power of the possibility stimulate the imagination as a way of calibrating the emotions and the Heart. This Gate teaches us the power of learning to wait to see which possibility manifests in the physical world and to experiment with options in response. This Gate also teaches us not to be doubtful if the idea isn't manifesting immediately or to turn doubt inward if we can't figure out how to make this idea a reality.

Center: The Divine Translator Center

Resiliency Keys: Self-Trust, Decisiveness

Contemplations:

- What ideas do I have right now that need me to nurture and activate them?
- What possibilities do these ideas stimulate right now?
- Take some time to write or visualize these possibilities.
- Are you comfortable with waiting?
- What can you do to increase your patience and curiosity?

Keynotes:

- The pressure to have the answer
- Possibility, not truth
- The need to wait for the truth to be proven over time
- The fear of not knowing or being judged for not knowing

Affirmation: I am tuned into the Cosmic Flow of Possibility. I am inspired to explore new possibilities and potentials. I use the power of my thoughts to stretch the limits of what is known and engage my imagination to explore the potential of the unknown.

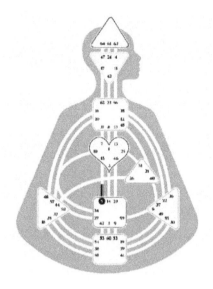

Gate 5: Consistency

I Ching: Waiting
Traditional Human Design: Patterns
Astrological Sign: Sagittarius
Biology: Ovaries and Testes

Optimal Expression: The ability to stay consistent with habits and choices that bring you closer to living true to who you are through alignment and not overusing willpower.

Unbalanced Expression: Life will seem like a constant struggle to stay connected and live habitually in a way that creates stability, sustainability, and a fulfilled expression.

Lesson/Challenge: To learn to craft order, habits, and rhythm that support alignment, connection, and the flow of life force energy and the fulfillment of purpose. To become skilled at staying in tune with consistent habits and alignment that support your growth and evolution no matter what is happening around you. Aligning with natural order and staying attuned to unfolding the flow of the natural world.

Center: The Evolution Center

Resiliency Keys: Vitality, Decisiveness, Courage, Empowerment

Contemplations:

- What do you need to do to create habits that fuel your energy and keep you vital and feeling connected to yourself and Source?
- What habits do you have that might not be serving your highest expression?
- How can you change those habits?
- What kind of environment do you need to cultivate to support your rhythmic nature?

Keynotes:

- Aligned with natural rhythm (gives direction)
- Fixed pattern
- Highly rhythmic
- Needs consistency
- Connected with the natural world
- Pattern makes effective

Affirmation: Consistency gives me power. When I am aligned with my own natural rhythm and the rhythm of life around me, I cultivate strength and connection with Source and am a beacon of stability and order. The order I hold is the touchstone, the returning point of love, that is sustained through cycles of change. The rhythms I maintain set the standard for compassionate action in the world.

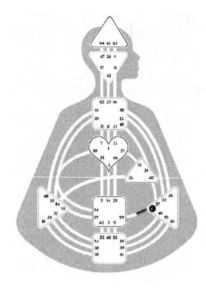

Gate 6: Impact

I Ching: Conflict
Traditional Human Design: Friction
Astrological Sign: Virgo
Biology: Kidneys and Pancreas

Optimal Expression: Maintaining a high frequency of emotional energy that supports equitability, sustainability, and peace. Using your emotional alignment to influence others and to serve as an energetic beacon of peace.

Unbalanced Expression: Feeling desperate, emotionally reactive, lacking, invisible, and willing to do whatever it takes to gather resources and energy for your own good, regardless of the means. Fear you'll never be seen or heard.

Lesson/Challenge: To become proficient in using emotional energy and learn to trust that your impact is in service to the world. When you understand that your life is a vehicle for service and your energy is being used to influence and impact those around you, you assume a greater obligation and responsibility to maintain a high frequency of energy. The quality of the emotional energy you cultivate influences others to come together in an equitable, sustainable, and peaceful way. Learning to trust that your words and impact will have an effect when the timing is correct and not overriding Divine Timing.

Center: The Creative Center

Resiliency Keys: Courage, Emotional Wisdom, Empowerment, Decisiveness

Contemplations:

- What do you need to do to deepen your trust in Divine Timing?
- What do you need to do to prepare yourself to be seen and to have influence?
- What do you need to do to sustain your emotional energy to align with peaceful and sustainable solutions?
- How do you feel about lack? How do you feel about abundance?
- How can you create a greater degree of emotional abundance in your life and daily practice?

Keynotes:
- Impactful
- Can create tension
- Needs to wait for emotional alignment
- War/peace
- Sexual energy or not
- Seeks to align others around common values or find a path to peace with differing values

Affirmation: My emotional energy influences the world around me. I am rooted in the energy of equity, sustainability, and peace. When aligned with abundance, I am an energetic source of influence that facilitates elegant solutions to creating peace and wellbeing. I am deliberate and aligned with values that create peace in my life, in my community, and in the world.

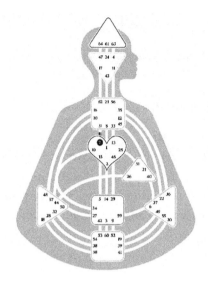

Gate 7: Collaboration

I Ching: The Army
Traditional Human Design:
Role of the Self in Interaction
Astrological Sign: Leo
Biology: Liver

Optimal Expression: To embrace the idea that power comes from supporting, influencing, and collaborating with leadership. To recognize that you don't have to be the figurehead to influence the direction that leadership assumes. The chief of staff is often more powerful than the president. The energy to unify people around an idea that influences the direction of leadership.

Unbalanced Expression: To struggle and fight to be seen and recognized as *the* leader at a cost to your energy and the fulfillment of your purpose.

Lesson/Challenge: To understand the need to be in front and allow yourself to serve through building teams, collaborating, and influencing the figurehead of leadership. To be at peace with serving the leader through support and collaboration. To recognize that the voice of the leader is only as strong and powerful as the support they receive.

Center: The Calibration Center

Resiliency Keys: Lovability, Decisiveness, Courage, Authenticity

Contemplations:

- What are your gifts and strengths? How do you use those gifts to influence and lead others?
- How do you feel about not being the figurehead of leadership?
- What happens when you *only* support leadership?
- Do you still feel powerful? Influential?
- Make a list of the times when your influence has positively directed leadership.

Keynotes:
- Provides direction for leadership
- Support that needs to be recognized (projected)

Affirmation: I am an agent of peace who influences the direction and organization of leadership. I unify people around ideas. I influence with my wisdom, my knowledge, and my connections. I am a team builder, a collaborator, and I organize people in ways that empower them and support them in creating a collective direction rooted in compassion.

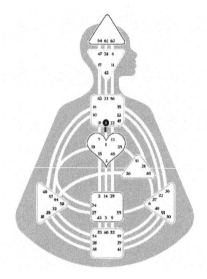

Gate 8: Fulfillment

I Ching: Holding Together
Traditional Human Design: Contribution
Astrological Sign: Taurus/Gemini
Biology: Thyroid/Parathyroid, Throat

Optimal Expression: To push the edges and boundaries of authentic self-expression and realize that being the full expression of your Authentic Self IS your life purpose. To use your authentic expression to inspire others to fulfill themselves.

Unbalanced Expression: Feeling panicked and disconnected from your Life Purpose. Thinking that your Life Purpose is something you have to "do" versus someone you have to "be." To try to be someone you're not in an attempt to serve as a role model.

Lesson/Challenge: To learn to express yourself authentically. To wait for the right people to see the value of who you are and to share yourself with them with vulnerability and all of your heart. To learn to trust that you are a unique expression of the Divine with a purpose and a path. To find that path and walk it without self-judgment or holding back.

Center: The Activation Center

Resiliency Keys: Authenticity, Vitality

Contemplations:

- Do you feel safe being vulnerable?
- What experiences have caused you to feel unsafe expressing your true self?
- Can you rewrite those stories?
- What would an uncompromising life look like for you?
- What do you need to remove from your current life to make your life more authentic?
- What is one bold action you can take right now that would allow you to express who you are more authentically in the world?
- What is your true passion?
- What do you dream of?

Keynotes:
- Vulnerable
- Meaningful
- Timing
- Expressive
- Contributes by showing what authentic alignment looks like

Affirmation: I am devoted to the full expression of who I am. I defend and protect the story of my life. I know that when I am expressing myself, without hesitation or limitation, I AM the contribution that I am here to give the world. Being myself IS my life purpose, and my direction flows from my authentic alignment.

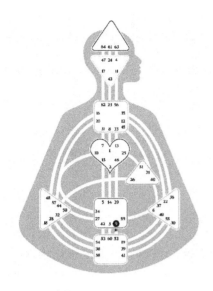

Gate 9: Convergence

I Ching: The Taming Power of the Small
Traditional Human Design: Focus
Astrological Sign: Sagittarius
Biology: Ovaries and Testes

Optimal Expression: The ability to see the big picture and prioritize where to focus your energy.

Unbalanced Expression: Feeling pressured to figure out where to place your focus. Feeling overwhelmed and confused by too many options and choices. Not being able to see the relationship between ideas and actions and missing the essential details.

Lesson/Challenge: The energy is about learning where to place your focus. When we work with the energy of this Gate, we have to learn to see the trees AND the forest. This Gate can make us seem blind to the big picture and we can lose our focus by getting stuck going down a rabbit hole.

Center: The Evolution Center

Resiliency Keys: Vitality, Decisiveness, Courage, Empowerment

Contemplations:

- Where am I putting my energy and attention?
- Is it creating the growth that I'm seeking?
- What do I need to focus on?
- Is your physical environment supporting you in staying focused?
- Do you have a practice that supports you in sustaining your focus?
- What can you do to increase your focus?

Keynotes:
- Focused
- Lack of focus or obsession (hyper-focused)
- The pulse to focus energy

Affirmation: I place my focus and attention on the details that support my creative manifestation. I am clear. I quickly see the parts of the whole, and I know exactly what to focus on to support my evolution and the evolution of the world.

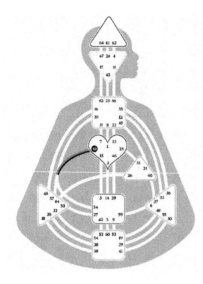

Gate 10: Self-Love

I Ching: Treading
Traditional Human Design: Love of Self
Astrological Sign:
Sagittarius on the Cusp of Capricorn
Biology: Liver

Optimal Expression: To see your love for yourself as the source of your true creative power.

Unbalanced Expression: To question your lovability, struggle to prove your love-worthiness, give up and settle for less than what you deserve, and blame others for your circumstances and situations. Victim consciousness.

Lesson/Challenge: To learn to love yourself. To learn to take responsibility for your own creations.

Center: The Calibration Center

Resiliency Keys: Lovability, Courage, Empowerment, Decisiveness

Contemplations:

- Do you love yourself?
- What can you do to deepen your self-love?
- Where can you find evidence of your lovability in your life right now?
- What do you need to do to take responsibility for situations you hate in your life right now? What needs to change?
- Where are you holding blame or victimhood in your life? How could you turn that energy around?

> **Keynotes:**
> - Self-empowerment/empowerment
> - Blaming/victimhood
> - Self-love
> - Self-loathing

Affirmation: I am an individuated aspect of the Divine. I am born of Love. My nature is to Love and be Loved. I am in the full flow of giving and receiving Love. I know that the quality of Love that I have for myself sets the direction for what I attract into my life. I am constantly increasing the quality of love I experience and share with the world.

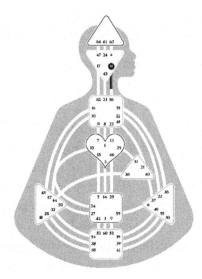

Gate 11: The Conceptualist

I Ching: Peace
Traditional Human Design: Ideas
Astrological Sign: Sagittarius
Biology: Anterior and Posterior Pituitary Glands

Optimal Expression: The awareness that you are a vessel for ideas. To understand that those ideas are for you to hold and protect until the right person comes along for you to share them with. To let go and serve as the vessel and know that not all ideas are yours to build upon. To use the power of your inspiration to stimulate the imagination of yourself and others.

Unbalanced Expression: Desperately trying to force every idea you have into manifestation.

Lesson/Challenge: To sort through and manage all the ideas and inspiration you hold. To trust that the ideas that are yours will show up for you in an actionable way. To value yourself enough to value the ideas you have and to wait for the right people to share those ideas with.

Center: The Divine Translator Center

Resiliency Keys: Decisiveness, Self-Trust

Contemplations:

- What do you do with inspiration when you receive it?
- Do you know how to serve as a steward for your ideas?
- Or do you feel pressure to try to force them into form?
- How much do you value yourself?
- Are you valuing your ideas?
- Do you trust the Universe?
- Do you trust that the ideas that are yours to take action on will manifest in your life according to your Human Design Type and Strategy?
- What can you do to manage the pressure you feel to manifest your ideas?
- Are you trying to prove your value with your ideas?

Keynotes:

- Inspired ideas
- Waiting for the right time/person/activation
- "Idea Book"
- Steward for possibility thinking
- Transmission

Affirmation: I am a Divine Vessel of Inspiration. Ideas flow to me constantly. I protect and nurture these ideas knowing that my purpose in life is to share ideas and inspiration with others. I use the power of these ideas to stimulate my imagination and the imagination of others. I trust the infinite abundance and alignment of the Universe and wait for signs to know which ideas are mine to manifest.

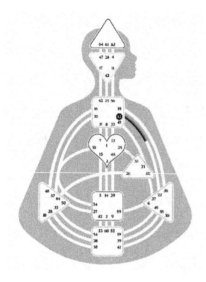

Gate 12: The Channel

I Ching: Caution
Human Design: Caution
Astrology: Gemini
Biology: Thyroid and parathyroid

Optimal Expression: To know that your voice is an expression of transformation and a vehicle for Divine Insight. The words you speak, the insights and creativity you share have the power to change others and the world. This energy is so powerful that people have to be ready to receive it. When you are articulate, then the timing is correct. If you struggle to find the words, have the courage to wait until it feels more aligned. A powerful ability to craft language and creative expressions that changes people's perceptions.

Unbalanced Expression: The struggle to try to speak ideas into form when it's not the right time. Letting hesitancy and caution paralyze you. Trying to force ideas and words.

Lesson/Challenge: To honor the Self enough to wait for the right time and *mood* to speak. To know that *shyness* is actually a signal that the timing is not right to share transformational insights and expressions. When the timing IS right, to have the courage to share what you feel and sense. To honor the fact that your voice and the words you offer are a direct connection to Source and you channel the potential for transformation. To own your creative power.

Center: The Activation Center

Resiliency Keys: Authenticity, Vitality

Contemplations:

- How has shyness caused you to judge yourself?
- What do you need to do to cultivate a deeper connection with Source?
- What do you need to do to connect more deeply with your creative power?

Affirmation: I am a creative being. My words, self-expression, and creative offerings have the power to change the way people see and understand the world. I am a vessel of Divine Transformation and I serve Source through the words that I share. I wait for the right timing and when I am aligned with timing and flow, my creativity creates beauty and grace in the world. I am a Divine Channel and I trust that the words that I speak will open the hearts of others.

Keynotes:

- Articulate or not
- Shy or bold
- Creative
- Expressive
- Auditory
- Mutative
- Individual
- Connects to Super Consciousness
- Mood as a regulator

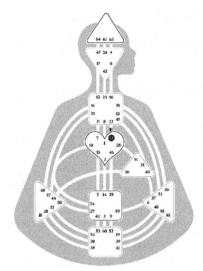

Gate 13: Narrative

I Ching: The Fellowship of Man
Traditional Human Design: The Listener
Astrological Sign: Aquarius
Biology: Liver

Optimal Expression: The ability to use the power of personal narrative to create with power and intention.

Unbalanced Expression: Staying stuck in old stories. Holding on to old past pains. Staying the victim in a story that repeats itself because your personal narrative is stuck in an old story.

Lesson/Challenge: To forgive the past and redefine who you are each and every day. To tell a personal narrative that is empowering, self-loving, and reflecting of your value and your Authentic Self. To bear witness to the pain and narrative of others and offer them a better story that allows them to expand on their abundance and blessings.

Center: The Calibration Center

Resiliency Keys: Lovability, Decisiveness, Courage, and Authenticity

Contemplations:

- What stories about your life are you holding on to?
- Do these stories reflect who you really are and what you want to be creating with your life?
- What or who do you need to forgive to liberate yourself to tell a new story?
- What secrets or stories for others are you holding?
- Do you need to release them?
- Write the true story of who you really are...

> **Keynotes:**
> - Listening and hearing
> - Not getting stuck in old stories
> - Consciously crafting an empowered narrative
> - Using narrative to create a new possibility

Affirmation: The story that I tell myself and the one I tell the world sets the tone and the direction for my life. I am the artist and creator of my story. I have the power to rewrite my story every day. The true story I tell from my Heart allows me to serve my right place in the Cosmic Plan.

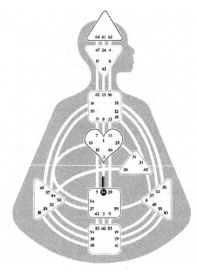

Gate 14: Creation

I Ching: Power Skills
Traditional Human Design:
Possession in Great Measure
Astrological Sign: Scorpio/Sagittarius
Biology: Ovaries and Testes

Optimal Expression: The ability to be at peace about having resources. To be in a constant state of trust that everything you need will show up in your outer reality in accordance with your alignment with Source. The resources you have allow you to increase the resources for others. To change the definition of work. To no longer work for material gain but work for the sake of transforming the world and being in the flow of life. To know that support flows from alignment with your Heart.

Unbalanced Expression: Fear and worry about money. Being willing to compromise your right work to do whatever you have to do for material gain.

Lesson/Challenge: To learn to trust to respond to opportunities that bring resources instead of forcing them or overworking. To learn to value resources and to appreciate how easily they can be created when you are aligned. To be gracious and grateful and not take for granted the resources you have.

Center: The Evolution Center

Resiliency Keys: Decisiveness, Courage, Vitality, Empowerment

Contemplations:

- Do you trust that you are supported?
- Are you doing your right work?
- What is the work that feels aligned with your purpose?
- How is that work showing up in your life right now?
- What resources do you have right now that you need to be grateful for?
- What work would you be doing if you didn't need the money?

Keynotes:
- Money
- Luck
- Entrepreneurship
- Work
- Responsive
- Transformational work

Affirmation: I am in the flow of Divine Support. When I trust the generous nature of the Divine and I cultivate a state of faith, I receive all the opportunities and support that I need to evolve my life and transform the world. I know that the right work shows up for me and I am fulfilled in the expression of my life force energy.

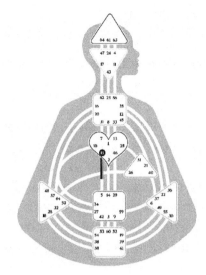

Gate 15: Compassion

I Ching: Modesty
Traditional Human Design: Extremes
Astrological Sign: Gemini
Biology: Liver

Optimal Expression: The ability to trust your own flow and rhythm, to trust that you will have cycles that disrupt old patterns and force you to recreate your direction and flow. To learn to set parameters for your creativity and work within the parameters when it feels right and then rest in between. Nature has rhythm AND extremes. You are here to change old rhythms and patterns to align them with greater compassion.

Unbalanced Expression: Self-judgment and extreme habits that are frenetic and non-productive. Trying to force your natural waves of rhythm into the daily practices and habits that society defines as successful and struggling with follow-through. Denying your own Heart. Being too afraid to do what feels right.

Lesson/Challenge: To learn to allow yourself to be in the flow of your own rhythm. To not beat yourself up because you don't have daily habits. To have the courage to do the right thing even if you are worried about not having enough. To share from the Heart without giving up your Heart and serving as a martyr.

Center: The Calibration Center

Resiliency Keys: Courage, Lovability, Decisiveness, Authenticity

Contemplations:

- Do you trust your own rhythm?
- Do you share from the Heart?
- Do you overshare?
- Does your sharing compromise your own Heart?
- Do you judge your own rhythm?
- Can you find peace in aligning with your own rhythm?
- What old patterns do you need to break?

Keynotes:
- Love of Humanity
- Extreme rhythms (no direction)
- Huge aura
- Gives direction to Life Force (sacral)
- The pattern interrupt

Affirmation: Like the power of a hurricane to transform the shoreline, my unique rhythm brings change to the landscape of my life and the world around me. I embrace my own rhythm and acknowledge the power of my own Heart. I share with ease, and I serve my own Heart as the foundation of all I have to give the world.

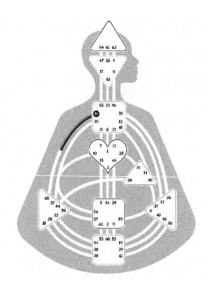

Gate 16: Zest

I Ching: Enthusiasm
Traditional Human Design: Skills
Astrological Sign: Gemini
Biology: Thyroid and Parathyroid

Optimal Expression: The courage to leap into action and inspire others to act, even if you don't know all the details. The courage to trust your own intuition that the timing is right, and you are ready enough even if you don't know exactly how your journey will unfold. Faith in the outcome.

Unbalanced Expression: Having a pattern of leaping into the unknown without sufficient preparation. Not assessing whether an idea or inspiration is actually an expression of skillful accomplishment. Leaping without looking. Holding yourself back when you know the time is right because others tell you you're not ready.

Lesson/Challenge: To learn to temper your enthusiasm through making sure you are prepared enough for whatever it is you are trying to do or create.

Center: The Activation Center

Resiliency Keys: Authenticity, Vitality

Contemplations:

- Do you trust your gut?
- Do you need to slow down and make sure you've done your homework before you take action?
- Have you sidelined your enthusiasm because other people have told you that you can't do what you're dreaming of doing?

Keynotes:

- Enthusiasm
- Sometimes needs to do their "homework"
- Contagious force

Affirmation: I am a Faith-Filled Contagious Force. I take guided actions and I trust my intuition and awareness to let me know when I am prepared and ready to leap into expanding my experience and genius. My enthusiasm inspires others to trust in themselves and to take their own giant leaps of growth.

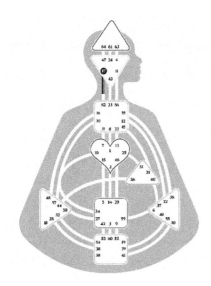

Gate 17: Anticipation

I Ching: Following
Traditional Human Design: Opinions
Astrological Sign: Aries
Biology: Anterior and Posterior Pituitary Glands

Optimal Expression: To use the power of your mind to explore potentials and possibilities that stretch our ideas about what else is possible in the human condition. To use your thoughts to inspire others to think bigger and bolder. To use your words to inspire and set the stage for creating energy that expands potential.

Unbalanced Expression: To share opinions that degrade options. To embrace opinions as truth and act on them. To create personal and collective narratives that are negative and filled with doubt.

Lesson/Challenge: To learn to share your thoughts about possibilities only when people ask for them. To not let doubt and suspicion keep you from seeing the potential of positive outcomes.

Center: The Divine Translator Center

Resiliency Keys: Decisiveness, Self-Trust

Contemplations:

- What do you need to do to manage your insights and ideas so that they increase the options and potential of others?
- How do you feel about holding back from sharing your insights until the timing is right?
- What can you do to manage your need to share without waiting for the right timing?
- What routines and strategies do you need to cultivate to keep your perspectives expanding and possibility oriented?
- How can you improve your ability to manage doubt and fear?

Keynotes:
- Opinions
- Influential
- Exploratory
- Projected
- Possible option

Affirmation: I use the power of my mind to explore possibilities and potential. I know the inspirations and insights I have create exploration and experimentation that can inspire the elegant solutions necessary to skillfully control the challenges facing humanity.

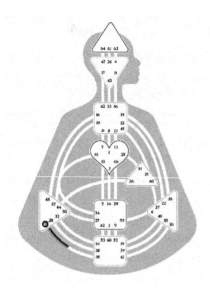

Gate 18: Re-Alignment

I Ching: Work on What Has Been Spoiled
Traditional Human Design: Correction
Astrological Sign: Libra
Biology: Spleen and Lymphatic System

Optimal Expression: To see a pattern that needs correcting and to wait for the right timing and circumstances to correct and align it. To serve joy.

Unbalanced Expression: To be critical. To share criticism without respect to the impact. To be concerned with your own "rightness" than to assess whether your insight is actually adding more joy to the world.

Lesson/Challenge: To learn to wait for the right timing and right circumstances to offer your intuitive insights into how to fix or correct a pattern. To wait for right timing and the right reason to share your critique. To understand the purpose of realignment is to create more joy, not to be right.

Center: The Self-Actualization Center

Resiliency Keys: Self-Trust, Courage

Contemplations:

- What does joy mean to you?
- How do you serve it?
- How do you cultivate joy in your own life?
- How does it feel to be right about something and keep it to yourself?
- Do you need to release any old stories about needing to be right?
- Do you trust your own insights?
- Do you have the courage to share them when it's necessary?

Keynotes:

- Instinctual sense of patterns and alignment
- The ability to know when the pattern is off or not working
- Can feel critical
- The corrections that create joy

Affirmation: I am a powerful force that re-aligns patterns. My insights and awareness give people the information they need to deepen their expertise and to experience greater joy. I serve joy and I align the patterns of the world to increase the world's potential for living in the flow of joy.

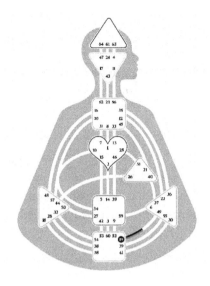

Gate 19: Attunement

I Ching: Approach
Traditional Human Design: Wanting
Astrological Sign: Aquarius
Biology: Adrenal Glands

Optimal Expression: The ability to sense the emotional needs of others and your community and to know how to bring the emotional energy back into alignment with sufficiency and sustainability. The ability to be emotionally vulnerable and present to increase Heart to Heart connections.

Unbalanced Expression: Being overly sensitive and shutting down or compromising your own needs and wants. Feeling disconnected from others as a way of coping with being overly sensitive. Being emotionally clingy or needy as a way of forcing your natural desire for intimacy.

Lesson/Challenge: To learn how to manage being a highly sensitive person and not let your sensitivity cause you to compromise what you want and who you are. To learn to keep your own resources in a sustainable state in order so that you have more to give. To not martyr yourself to the needs of others. To learn how to become emotionally intimate without being shut down or codependent.

Center: The Divine Timing Center

Resiliency Keys: Vitality, Empowerment

Contemplations:

- How do you manage your sensitivity?
- What coping mechanism do you have that keeps you emotionally connected in a healthy way?
- Are you emotionally present in your relationships?

Keynotes:
- Highly sensitive
- Wants to belong or be close
- Can feel clingy
- Deeply connected to the animal kingdom

- Do you need to become more attuned to your own emotional needs and ask for more of what you want and need?
- What emotional patterns do you have that may be causing you to give up what you need and want to fulfill other people's emotional needs?
- Are you able to be present to the emotional energy around you to help calibrate in a creative, intimate and sustainable way?

Affirmation: I am deeply aware of the emotional needs and energy of others. My sensitivity and awareness give me insights that allow me to create intimacy and vulnerability in my relationships. I am aware and attuned to the emotional frequency around me and I make adjustments to help support a high frequency of emotional alignment. I honor my own emotional needs as the foundation of what I share with others.

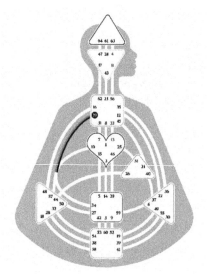

Gate 20: Patience

I Ching: Contemplation
Traditional Human Design: Metamorphosis
Astrological Sign: Gemini
Biology: Thyroid and Parathyroid

Optimal Expression: The ability to trust your intuition, to know what needs to be set in place, what people need to be gathered, what skills need to be accomplished, and to be ready when the time is right. To trust in the right timing and to heed the intuition to get ready.

Unbalanced Expression: To act before the time is right. To fail to listen to your inner guidance and prepare. To feel pressure to act before the time is right and to feel frustrated or to quit.

Lesson/Challenge: To be patient and conquer the ability to wait. To be prepared and watchful but resist the urge to act if the timing isn't right or if there are details that still need to be readied.

Center: The Activation Center

Resiliency Keys: Authenticity, Vitality

Contemplations:

- How do you manage your need for action?
- Are you patient?
- Do you trust in Divine Timing?
- Do you trust your intuition?
- What needs to be healed, released, aligned and brought to your awareness for you to trust your intuition?

Affirmation: I am in the flow of perfect timing. I listen to my intuition. I prepare. I gather the experience, resources, and people I need to support my ideas and my principles. When I am

Keynotes:

- Awareness to know when to manifest power
- True power lies in sharing it with others
- Inspires and connects
- Hesitates
- Does not share leadership with others
- Collective leadership is learned, making it a life lesson

ready, I wait patiently, knowing that right timing is the key to transforming the world. My alignment with right timing increases my influence and my power.

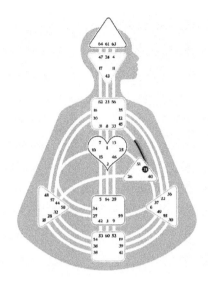

Gate 21: Self-Regulation

I Ching: Biting Through
Traditional Human Design: The Treasurer
Astrological Sign: Aries
Biology: Thymus

Optimal Expression: The ability to regulate your inner and outer environment in order to sustain a vibrational frequency that reflects your true value. The ability to be self-generous and to set boundaries that maintain your value and support you in being sustainable in the world. To take the actions necessary to honor your unique role in the Cosmic Plan.

Unbalanced Expression: To feel the need to control life, others, resources, etc. out of fear that you aren't worthy of being supported.

Lesson/Challenge: To learn to let go. To become proficient at self-regulation. To release the need to control others and circumstances. To trust in the Divine and to know that you are supported. Knowing that you are worthy of support, and you don't have to overcompensate.

Center: The Resource Center

Resiliency Keys: Self-Worth, Vitality, Empowerment

Contemplations:

- Where do you need to release control in your life?
- Do you trust the Universe?
- Do you value yourself?
- Do you trust that you'll be supported in accordance with your value?
- What do you need to do to create an internal and external environment of self-generosity?
- What needs to be healed, released, aligned, and brought to your awareness for you to embrace your true value?

Keynotes:

- Controls resources for the greater good of the whole
- Materialistic
- Controlling
- Loves to budget

Affirmation: I am worthy of claiming, protecting, and defending my rightful place in the world. I create an inner and outer environment that is self-generous, and I regulate my environment to sustain a high frequency of alignment with my true value. I know that I am an irreplaceable and precious part of the Cosmic Plan and I create my life to reflect the importance of my right place in the world.

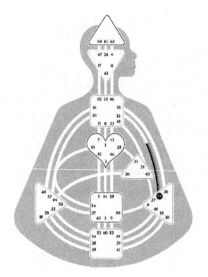

Gate 22: Surrender

I Ching: Grace
Traditional Human Design: Grace
Astrological Sign: Pisces
Biology: Kidney and Pancreas

Optimal Expression: The grace to know that you are fully supported by the Universal flow of abundance and to pursue your passion and your unique contribution to the world no matter what. To trust that you will be given what you need when you need it in order to make your unique contribution to the world.

Unbalanced Expression: Fear that you are not supported. Holding back or stifling your passion because you think you can't afford to pursue it. Compromising, settling, or letting despair regulate your emotional energy causing the creative process to feel shut down or stuck.

Lesson/Challenge: To trust that your passions and deepest desires are supported by the Universal flow of abundance. To have the courage to follow your passion and know you will be supported. To learn to regulate your emotional energy so you have faith that everything will unfold perfectly.

Center: The Creative Center

Resiliency Keys: Courage, Emotional Wisdom, Empowerment, Decisiveness

Contemplations:

- Where are you denying passion in your life?
- Where have you settled for less than what you want because you're afraid you can't get what you want?
- What do you need to do to fully activate your passion?
- What is one bold step towards your genius that you could take right now?
- Do you trust the Universe?
- What do you need to do to deepen trust?
- Do you have a regular practice that supports you in sustaining a high frequency of emotional energy and alignment?
- What needs to be healed, released, aligned and brought to your awareness for you to deepen your faith?

Keynotes:
- Grace/charm, or not
- Moody/emotional
- Individual
- Auditory
- Creative
- Trust
- Self-expression
- Alignment with support

Affirmation: I am a global change agent. I am inspired with passions that serve the purpose of transforming the world. I trust my emotions and my passions will align me with faith and the flow of resources I need to fulfill my life purpose. When I let go and follow my passion, I am given everything I need to change the world.

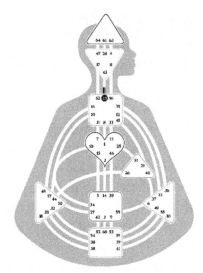

Gate 23: Transmission

I Ching: Splitting Apart
Traditional Human Design: Assimilation
Astrological Sign: Taurus
Biology: Thyroid and Parathyroid

Optimal Expression: The ability to translate transformative insights with people that offers them a way to transform the way they think. To share what you know with awareness of right timing and to trust your knowingness as an expression of your connection to Source.

Unbalanced Expression: The need to be right. An anxiety or pressure to share what you know with people who aren't ready and then to feel despair or bitterness that they don't understand things the way that you do.

Lesson/Challenge: To recognize that change and transformation are inevitable. To know what needs to happen next, to wait for the right timing and the right people to share your insights with. To not jump the gun and try to convince people to understand what you know. To not let yourself slip into negativity and despair when people aren't ready.

Center: The Activation Center

Resiliency Keys: Authenticity, Vitality

Contemplations:

- How can you strengthen your connection to Source?
- Do you trust what you know?
- What comes up for you when you know something, but you don't know how you know what you know?
- How do you handle yourself when you know something but the people around you aren't ready to hear it?

Affirmation: I change the world with what I know. My insights and awarenesses have the ability to transform the way people think and perceive the world. I know that my words are powerful and transformative. I trust that the people who are ready for the change that I bring, will ask me for what I know. I am a vessel for my knowingness, and I nurture myself while I wait to share what I know.

Keynotes:

- Can see which next, new awareness/knowledge/ inspiration is worthy of pursuing or assimilating into the world
- Does not listen
- Visionary or freak
- Has to trust in correct timing
- The ability to structure transformation ideas into language
- Teaching
- Right timing
- Feeling heard
- Great ideas
- Innovation

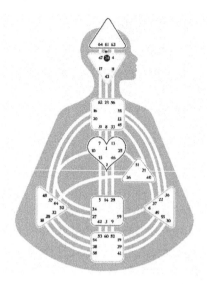

Gate 24: Blessings

I Ching: Returning
Traditional Human Design: Rationalization
Astrological Sign: Taurus
Biology: Anterior and Posterior Pituitary Glands

Optimal Expression: To recognize all experiences have the potential for growth and expansion. To redefine the stories of your experiences to reflect what you learned and how you grew. To be grateful for all of your life experiences and to liberate yourself from stories that no longer serve you.

Unbalanced Expression: To protect yourself by staying stuck in old patterns. To refuse to transform. To rationalize allowing less than what you deserve.

Lesson/Challenge: To learn to allow what you truly deserve in your life. To not rationalize an experience that allowed for less than you deserve. To find the blessings and power from painful experiences and to use them as catalysts for transformation.

Center: The Divine Translator Center

Resiliency Keys: Self-Trust, Decisiveness

Contemplations:

- What are the blessings you learned from your greatest painful experiences?
- Can you see how these experiences served to teach you?
- What did you learn?
- What are you grateful for from the past?
- Where might you be rationalizing staying stuck or settling for less than what you really want or deserve?
- What do you need to do to break out of this pattern?

Affirmation: I embrace the Mystery of Life with the awareness that the infinite generosity of the Universe gives me blessings in every event in my life. I find the blessings from the pain. I grow and expand beyond the limitations of my experiences and stories. I use what I have learned to create a life and circumstances that reflect the miracle that I am.

Keynotes:

- Settling for less
- Rationalizing
- One of the places where gratitude lives in the chart
- The ability to begin to translate knowingness
- Tries to answer "why?"
- Can rationalize anything including the good and the bad
- Has the ability to determine whether a transformative idea is rational

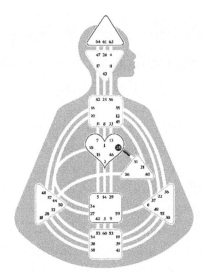

Gate 25: Spirit

I Ching: Innocence
Traditional Human Design: Love of Spirit
Astrological Sign: Pisces
Biology: Liver

Optimal Expression: To connect with Source with consistency and diligence so as to fulfill your Divine Purpose and fulfill the true story of who you are and the role you play in the Cosmic Plan. To use your alignment with Source as a way of healing the world.

Unbalanced Expression: Fear and mistrust of Spirit. Using your life strictly for personal gains regardless of the impact on others. Ego in its lowest expression. Not feeling worthy of being loved by Source and using your will power to create instead of alignment.

Lesson/Challenge: To trust the Divine Order in all areas of your life. To learn to connect with Source as the path to creating wellbeing in your life. To remember that your life serves an irreplaceable role in the Cosmic Plan and to honor that role and to live from it. To trust Source.

Center: The Calibration Center

Resiliency Keys: Lovability, Decisiveness, Courage, Authenticity

Contemplations:

- Do you trust Source?
- Do you have a regular practice that connects you to Source?
- Do you know your life purpose?
- Are you living true to your Purpose?
- How can you deepen your connection to your Purpose?

Affirmation: I am an agent of the Divine. My life is the fulfillment of Divine Order and the Cosmic Plan. When I am connected to Source, I serve my right place. I take up no more than my space and no less than my place in the world. I serve and through serving, I am supported.

Keynotes:
- Everything is rooted in the love of Spirit
- Great healers
- Transcends the Self/ Self-less
- Healing energy
- Divine Order
- Surrender and trust
- Spirit as source of direction

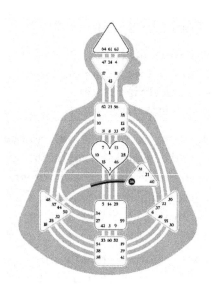

Gate 26: Integrity

I Ching: The Taming Power of the Great
Traditional Human Design: The Trickster
Astrological Sign: Sagittarius
Biology: Thymus

Optimal Expression: To live in physical, resource, identity, moral, and energetic integrity with courage and trust. To set clear boundaries and take the actions necessary to preserve the integrity of your right place.

Unbalanced Expression: To compromise your integrity because you feel or are afraid that you can't afford to fulfill your right place.

Lesson/Challenge: To learn to value your right place and your value enough to act as if you are precious. To heal past traumas and elevate your self-worth. To trust in support enough to do the right thing and to nurture yourself so that you have more to give.

Center: The Resource Center

Resiliency Keys: Self-Worth, Vitality, Empowerment

Contemplations:

- Where might you be experiencing a breach in your physical, resource, identity, moral, or energetic integrity?
- What do you need to do to bring yourself back into integrity?
- What trauma do you have that you need to heal?
- How can you rewrite the story of your trauma as an initiation back into your true value?
- What do you need to do right now to nurture yourself and to replenish your value?

> **Keynotes:**
> - Alignment and integrity
> - The self-worth to stay in integrity
> - Trauma
> - The Closer
> - Truth or lies
> - Sustainability

Affirmation: I am a unique, valuable, and irreplaceable part of the Cosmic Plan. I am always supported in fulfilling my right place. I take care of my body, my energy, my values, and my resources so that I have more to share with the world. I claim and defend my value and fully live in the story of who I am with courage.

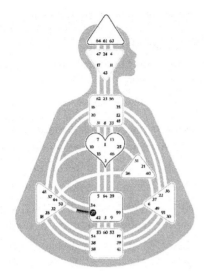

Gate 27: Accountability

I Ching: Nourishment
Traditional Human Design: Responsibility
Astrological Sign: Taurus
Biology: Ovaries and Testes

Optimal Expression: The ability to support, nurture and lift others up. To sense and to act on what is necessary to increase the wellbeing of others and the world. To feed people with healthy food and healthy nourishment to ensure that they thrive. To hold others accountable for their own self-love and self-empowerment.

Unbalanced Expression: Codependency. Guilt. Over-caring. Martyrdom.

Lesson/Challenge: To care without over-caring. To allow others to assume responsibility for their own challenges and choices. To learn to accept other people's values. To not let guilt cause you to compromise what is good and right for you.

Center: The Evolution Center

Resiliency Keys: Decisiveness, Courage, Vitality, Empowerment

Contemplations:

- Are you taking responsibility for things that aren't yours to be responsible for?
- Whose problem is it?
- Can you return the responsibility for the problem back to its rightful owner?
- What role does guilt play in motivating you?
- Can you let go of the guilt?
- What different choices might you make if you didn't feel guilty?
- What obligations do you need to set down, in order for you to take better care of yourself?
- Are there places where you need to soften your judgments on other people's values?

Keynotes:
- Deeply responsible, sometimes to a fault
- Teaching gate
- Transmits values
- Cooking, nurturing, nourishing
- Obligated
- Martyrdom
- Needs to be reminded to care for themselves first

Affirmation: I have a nurturing and loving nature. It is my gift to be able to love and care for others. I know that the greatest expression of my love is to treat others as capable and powerful. I support when necessary, and I let go with love so that my loved ones can discover their own strength and power.

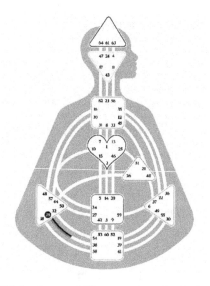

Gate 28: Adventure/Challenge

I Ching: Preponderance of the Great
Traditional Human Design: Struggle
Astrological Sign: Scorpio
Biology: Spleen and Lymph

Optimal Expression: To learn to share from your personal experience, your struggles, and your triumphs. To persevere and to know that the adventures in your life deepen your ability to transform life into a meaningful journey. To understand that your struggles help deepen the collective ideas about what is truly valuable and worthy of creating.

Unbalanced Expression: Refusing to act out of fear that the journey will be too painful, wrought with struggle, or fail. To feel like a failure. To fall into victim consciousness.

Lesson/Challenge: To not let struggle and challenge leave you feeling defeated and despairing. To learn to face life as an adventure. Do not let challenge and struggle cause you to feel as if you have failed.

Center: The Self-Actualization Center

Resiliency Keys: Self-Trust, Courage

Contemplations:

- How can you turn your challenge into adventure?
- Where do you need to cultivate a sense of adventure in your life?
- What do you need to do to rewrite the story of your failures?
- What meanings, blessings, lessons have you learned from your challenges?
- What needs to be healed, released, aligned, and brought to your awareness for you to trust yourself and your choices?

Keynotes:

- Struggles to discover the meaning of life
- Loves to take the hard way/be challenged
- Planetary influence can tell history of struggles in family of origin
- In Neptune, often associated with addictions
- Life can feel exhausting if struggles are not engaged in properly
- Here to teach from experience

- What do you need to do to forgive yourself for your perceived past failures?

Affirmation: I am here to push the boundaries of life and what is possible. I thrive in situations that challenge me. I am an explorer on the leading edge of consciousness and my job is to test how far I can go. I embrace challenges. I am an adventurer. I share all that I have learned from my challenges with the world. My stories help give people greater meaning, they teach that the world is truly worthy of creating, and inspire people to transform.

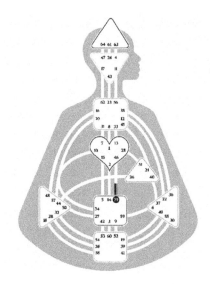

Gate 29: Devotion

I Ching: The Abysmal
Traditional Human Design: Perseverance
Astrological Sign: Leo/Virgo
Biology: Ovaries and Testes

Optimal Expression: The ability to respond to committing to the right thing. To know that your perseverance and determination change the narrative of the world and shows people what is possible. Your devotion sets the tone for the direction life takes you.

Unbalanced Expression: To over-commit. To not know when to let go and when enough is enough. To fail to commit to the right thing. To burnout and deplete yourself because you don't say yes to yourself. To do something just because you can, not because you want to.

Lesson/Challenge: To discover what and who you need to devote yourself to. To sustain yourself so that you can sustain your devotion. To learn to say no to what you need to say no to and to learn to yes to what you want to say yes to.

Center: The Evolution Center

Resiliency Keys: Decisiveness, Courage, Vitality, Empowerment

Contemplations:

- What devotion do you have right now that drives you?
- Is this a devotion that inspires you, or do you feel overly obligated to it?
- Who would you be, and what would you choose, if you gave yourself permission to say no more often?
- What would you like to say *no* to that you are saying *yes* to right now?
- What obligations do you need to take off your plate right now?
- What would you like to devote yourself to?

> **Keynotes:**
> - Commit/over-commit
> - Devotion as a path to awakening
> - "Yes"
> - Devotion to the embodiment of Spirit

Affirmation: I have an extraordinary ability to devote myself to the manifestation of an idea. My commitment to my story and to the fulfillment of my intention changes the story of what's possible in my own life and for humanity. I choose my commitments with great care. I devote myself to what's vital for the evolution of the world and I nurture myself first because my wellbeing is the foundation of what I create.

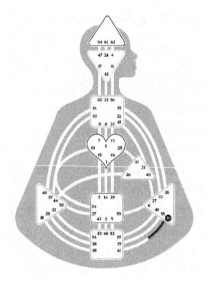

Gate 30: Passion

I Ching: The Clinging Fire
Traditional Human Design: Desire
Astrological Sign: Aquarius/Pisces
Biology: Pancreas

Optimal Expression: The ability to sustain a dream, intention, and a vision until you bring it into form. To inspire others with the power of your dream. To inspire passion in others.

Unbalanced Expression: Burnout. Impatience and not waiting for the right timing. Misdirected passion that is perceived as too much intensity. Leaping into chaos.

Lesson/Challenge: To be able to sustain a dream or a vision without burning out. To know which dream to be passionate about. To not let passion overwhelm you and to wait for the right timing to share your passion with the world.

Center: The Creative Center

Resiliency Keys: Courage, Emotional Wisdom, Empowerment, Decisiveness, Vitality

Contemplations:

- What are you passionate about?
- Have you lost your passion?
- How is your energy?
- Are you physically burned out?
- Are you burned out on your idea?
- What do you need to do to sustain your vision or dream about what you are inspired to create in your life?
- Do you have a dream or vision you are avoiding because you're afraid it won't come true?

Keynotes:
- Potential for burnout
- Intensity
- Contagious passion
- Needs passion as drive to create

Affirmation: I am a passionate creator. I use the intensity of my passion to increase my emotional energy and sustain the power of my dream and what I imagine for Life. I trust in the Divine flow, and I wait for the right timing and the right circumstances to act on my dream.

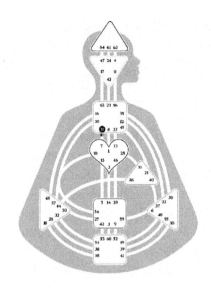

Gate 31: The Leader

I Ching: Influence
Traditional Human Design: Democracy
Astrological Sign: Leo
Biology: Thyroid and Parathyroid

Optimal Expression: The ability to listen, learn, hear, and serve the people you lead and to assume and value your right leadership position as the voice for the people you lead.

Unbalanced Expression: To push and seize leadership for the sake of personal gain or to be afraid to lead and not feel worthy of serving as a leader.

Lesson/Challenge: To learn to lead as a representative of the people you are leading. To cultivate a leadership agenda of service. To not let your fear of not being seen, heard, or accepted get in the way of healthy leadership. To learn to take your right place as a leader and not hide out.

Center: The Activation Center

Resiliency Keys: Authenticity, Vitality

Contemplations:

- How do you feel about being a leader?
- Are you comfortable leading?
- Do you shrink from taking leadership?
- What is your place of service?
- Who do you serve?

Keynotes:
- Expresses supported leadership
- Leadership that needs recognition (projected)
- The highest potential for Human unity

Affirmation: I am a natural born leader. I serve at my highest potential when I am empowering others by giving them a voice and then serving their needs. I use my power to lead people to a greater expansion of who they are and to support them in increasing their abundance, sustainability, and peace.

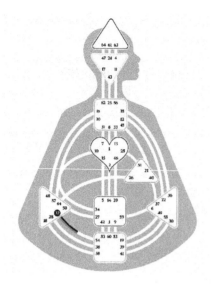

Gate 32: Endurance

I Ching: Duration
Traditional Human Design: Continuity
Astrological Sign: Libra
Biology: Spleen and Lymphatic System

Optimal Expression: The awareness of what needs to be done to make a dream a manifested reality. Setting the stage, preparation, being ready. The patience to trust that once the stage is set, the timing will unfold as needed to serve the highest good of all. To translate Divine Inspiration into readiness.

Unbalanced Expression: Letting the fear of failure cause you to avoid preparing what you need to do. To not be ready when the timing is right. To push too hard, too fast, too long against right timing.

Lesson/Challenge: To trust in Divine Timing. To prepare for the next step of manifestation and to align with the unfolding of the process. To be patient.

Center: The Self-Actualization Center

Resiliency Keys: Self-Trust, Courage

Contemplations:

- What do you need to do to be prepared to manifest your vision?
- What actionable steps need to be completed for you to be ready when the timing is right?
- What do you need to do to cultivate patience?
- Do you have a fear of failing that is causing you to avoid being prepared?
- Are you overdoing it and being overly prepared?
- Are you pushing too hard?
- What can you let go of?

Keynotes:
- Fear of failure
- Tenacity
- The ability to hold on to an idea and cultivate it
- Impatience
- Right timing

Affirmation: I am a Divine Translator for Divine Inspiration. I sense and know what needs to be prepared on the earthly plane in order to be ready for right timing. I am aligned with right timing, and I prepare and wait patiently knowing that when the time is right, I am ready to do the work to help transform pain into power.

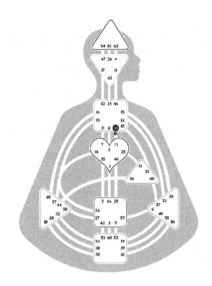

Gate 33: Retelling

I Ching: Retreat
Traditional Human Design: Privacy
Astrological Sign: Leo
Biology: Thyroid and Parathyroid

Optimal Expression: The ability to translate a personal experience into an empowering narrative that teaches and gives direction to others. Finding the power from the pain. Waiting for the right timing to transform or share a narrative so that it has the greatest impact on the Heart of another.

Unbalanced Expression: Staying stuck and sharing a personal narrative rooted in pain, disempowerment, and victimhood.

Lesson/Challenge: To learn to share a personal narrative that reflects your true value and your worth. To share a personal narrative when it serves the intention to serve, improving the direction of others. To share history in an empowering way.

Center: The Activation Center

Resiliency Keys: Authenticity, Vitality

Contemplations:

- What personal narratives are you telling that might be keeping you stuck, feeling like a victim, or feeling unlovable?
- How can you rewrite these stories?
- What listening practices do you have?
- What can you do to listen better so you can gauge when it is the right time to share in a powerful way?

Affirmation: I am a processor of stories. My gift is my ability to help others find the blessings, the love, and the power from stories of pain. I hold people's secrets and stories and transform them to share when the time is right. The stories I tell change the direction of people's lives. I use the power of stories to increase the power of Heart in the world and to help build a world of Love.

Keynotes:

- Stuck in the re-telling
- The possibility of sharing stories that expand the potential of humanity
- The stories that embody the current level of consciousness
- Retelling the stories of what has come before and transmitting the potential of what will be

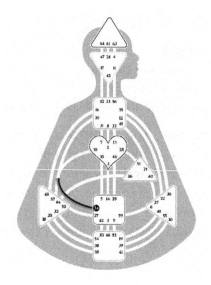

Gate 34: Power

I Ching: The Power of The Great
Traditional Human Design: Power
Astrological Sign: Sagittarius
Biology: Ovaries and Testes

Optimal Expression: The ability to respond to opportunities to unify the right people around a transformative and powerful idea when the timing and circumstances are correct.

Unbalanced Expression: Being too busy to tune into the right timing and the right people. Feeling frustrated with pushing and trying to make things happen. Forcing manifestation with little results. Depleting yourself because you're pushing too hard.

Lesson/Challenge: To learn to measure out energy in order to stay occupied and busy but to not burn yourself out trying to force the timing or the "rightness" of a project. To wait to know which project or creation to implement based on when you get something to respond to.

Center: The Evolution Center

Resiliency Keys: Decisiveness, Courage, Vitality, Empowerment

Contemplations:

- Do you trust in Divine Timing?
- What do you need to do to deepen your trust?
- How do you cultivate greater patience in your life?
- What fears come up for you when you think of waiting?
- How can you learn to wait with greater faith and ease?
- What do you do to occupy yourself while you're waiting?

Keynotes:

- Busy, busy, busy
- Can be asexual or very sexual
- Generated power or otherwise is powerless
- A lightning bolt in a jar
- Responsive
- Power when responding
- Right timing
- Multi-tasking

Affirmation: I am a powerful servant of Divine Timing. When the timing is right, I unify the right people around the right idea and create transformation on the planet. My power is more active when I allow the Universe to set the timing. I wait. I am patient. I trust.

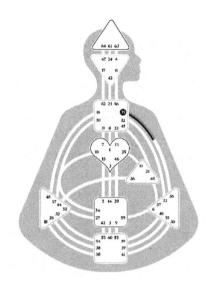

Gate 35: Experience

I Ching: Progress
Traditional Human Design: Change
Astrological Sign: Gemini
Biology: Thyroid and Parathyroid

Optimal Expression: The ability to know which experiences are worthy and worthwhile. To partake in the right experience and to share your knowledge from the experience for the sake of changing the story of what's possible in the world.

Unbalanced Expression: To be bored with life. To let the boredom of life cause you to settle for a life that never challenges the status quo.

Lesson/Challenge: To not let experience lead to feeling jaded or bored. To have the courage to share what you know from your experience. To know which experiences are worth participating in. To let your natural ability to become accomplished at anything keep you from being enthusiastic about learning something new. To embrace that even though you know how to know, you don't know everything.

Center: The Activation Center

Resiliency Keys: Authenticity, Vitality

Contemplations:

- Where are you finding passion in your life?
- Do you need to create or discover more passion in your life right now?
- Do you share your knowledge and the stories of your experiences?
- Do you see the value of what you must share?
- What are you curious about?
- How can you expand on that curiosity?

Keynotes:
- The potential for wisdom
- The potential for being jaded
- The ability to share the knowledge gleaned from experience

Affirmation: I am an experienced, wise, and knowledgeable resource for others. My experiences in life have added to the rich tapestry that is the story of humanity. I share my stories with others because my experiences open doorways of possibility for others. My stories help others create miracles in their lives.

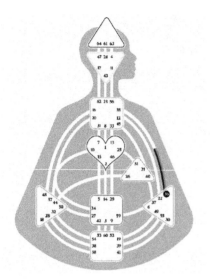

Gate 36: Exploration

I Ching: The Darkening of the Light
Traditional Human Design: Crisis
Astrological Sign: Pisces
Biology: Kidneys and Pancreas

Optimal Expression: The ability to hold a vision and sustain it with an aligned frequency of emotional energy and to bring the vision into form when the timing is right. The ability to stretch the boundaries of the story of Humanity by breaking patterns. Creating miracles through emotional alignment.

Unbalanced Expression: Not waiting for the right timing and leaping into new opportunities without waiting for alignment, causing chaos. To leap from opportunity to opportunity without waiting to see how the story will play out and never getting to experience the full fruition of the experience.

Lesson/Challenge: To not let boredom cause you to leap into chaos. To learn to stick with something long enough to become skillfully proficient and to bear the fruits of your experience.

Center: The Creative Center

Resiliency Keys: Courage, Emotional Wisdom, Empowerment, Decisiveness

Contemplations:

- How does boredom impact your life?
- What do you do when you feel bored?
- What can you do to keep yourself aligned even when you're bored?
- What stories have you experienced that have shattered old patterns and expectations?
- How have your stories changed or inspired others?
- What do you do to maintain or sustain emotional alignment?

Keynotes:
- Boredom
- Leaping out of the frying pan into the fire
- With preparation and alignment comes the next right new experience
- Pushing the threshold of human capacity

- What do you need to add to your daily practice to amp up your emotional energy around your intentions?

Affirmation: My experiences and stories break old patterns and push the boundaries of the edge of what is possible for humanity. I defy the patterns and I create miracles through my emotional alignment with possibility. I hold my vision and maintain my emotional energy as I wait to bear the fruit of my intentions and visions.

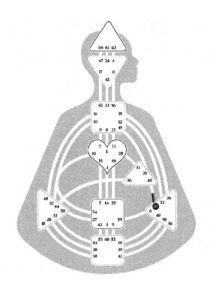

Gate 37: Peace

I Ching: The Family
Traditional Human Design: Friendship
Astrological Sign: Pisces
Biology: Kidneys and Pancreas

Optimal Expression: The ability to stay connected to sustainable peace and to respond to life by generating peace no matter what is happening in your reality. Creating the emotional alignment to make peaceful choices no matter what's happening in the outer world.

Unbalanced Expression: Desperately struggling to find peace outside of yourself. Trying to control the outer world to create inner peace.

Lesson/Challenge: To find inner peace as the true source of outer peace. To not let chaos and outer circumstances knock you off your center and disrupt your peace.

Center: The Creative Center

Resiliency Keys: Courage, Emotional Wisdom, Empowerment, Decisiveness

Contemplations:

- What habits, practices, and routines do you have that cultivate your inner alignment with sustainable peace?
- How do you cultivate inner peace when you feel that your outer world is chaotic and disrupted?
- What do you need to do to cultivate a peaceful emotional frequency?

Keynotes:
- Just wants peace, or not
- The emotional alignment with peace
- The need to be at peace

Affirmation: I am an agent of peace. My being, aligned with peace, creates an energy of contagious peace around me. I practice holding a peaceful frequency of energy, and I respond to the world with the intention of creating sustainable peace.

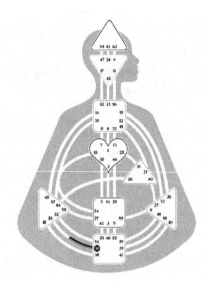

Gate 38: The Visionary

I Ching: Opposition
Traditional Human Design: The Fighter
Astrological Sign: Capricorn
Biology: Adrenal Glands

Optimal Expression: The ability to know what's worth committing to and fighting for. To use your experiences to craft a vision that anchors the possibility of something truly meaningful and worthy in the world. Serving the world as a visionary.

Unbalanced Expression: To struggle and fight for the sake of fighting. To not engage in meaningless fights. Aggression and struggle.

Lesson/Challenge: To experience challenges as a way of knowing what is worth fighting for. To turn the story of struggle into a discovery of meaning and to let the power of what you discover serve as the foundation for a strong vision of transformation that brings dreams into manifested form.

Center: The Divine Timing Center

Resiliency Keys: Vitality, Empowerment

Contemplations:

- Do you know what's worth committing to and fighting for in your life?
- Do you have a dream that you are sharing with the world?
- Do you know how to use your struggles and challenges as the catalyst for creating deeper meaning in the world and in your life?

Affirmation: My challenges, struggles, and adventures have taught me what is truly valuable in life. I use my understandings to hold a vision of what else is possible for the world. I am aligned with the values that reflect the preciousness of life, and I sustain a vision for a world that is

Keynotes:

- Knows what's worth fighting for
- Projected
- Mutative
- Auditory
- A design of stubbornness
- Preserve individual integrity through opposition
- Melancholic
- Auditory

aligned with Heart. My steadfast commitment to my vision inspires others to join me in creating a world of equitable, sustainable peace.

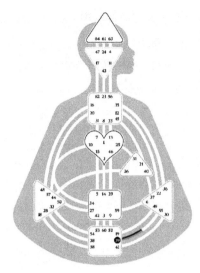

Gate 39: Recalibration

I Ching: Obstruction
Traditional Human Design: Provocation
Astrological Sign: Cancer
Biology: Adrenal Glands

Optimal Expression: The ability to transform an experience into an opportunity to shift to greater abundance. To see and experience internal or external lack and to use your awareness of lack to recalibrate your energy towards sufficiency and abundance.

Unbalanced Expression: Feeling overwhelmed by lack and panicking. Hoarding and over-shopping as a result of fear of scarcity. Provoking and challenging others and holding others responsible for your inner alignment with sufficiency.

Lesson/Challenge: To challenge and tease out energies that are not in alignment with faith and abundance. To bring them to awareness and to use them as pushing off points to deepen faith and trust in Source.

Center: The Divine Timing Center

Resiliency Keys: Vitality, Empowerment

Contemplations:

- Do you trust Source?
- What do you need to do to deepen your trust in Source?
- Do you feel like you are enough?
- Do you feel like you have enough?
- Take stock of everything you have and everything you've been given.
- Do you have enough?
- Have you ever really not been supported?
- What do you have that you're grateful for?
- Have you abdicated your own power to create?
- What needs to be healed, released, aligned, or brought to your awareness to reactivate your power to create your own abundance?

Keynotes:

- Provocative
- Eating
- The Shopping Gate
- Hoarding
- Diabetes/weight issues
- Individual
- Auditory
- Mutative

Affirmation: I am deeply calibrated with my faith. I trust that I am fully supported. I use experiences that create desire and wanting in me as opportunities to deepen my faith that I will receive and create all I need to fulfill my mind, body, and spirit. I am in the perfect flow of abundance, and I am deeply aligned with Source.

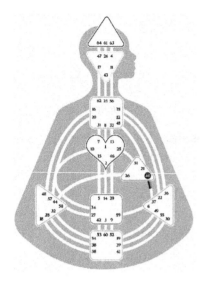

Gate 40: Restoration

I Ching: Deliverance
Traditional Human Design: Loneliness
Astrological Sign: Virgo
Biology: Stomach

Optimal Expression: The ability to retreat as a way of replenishing your inner and outer resources and to bring your renewed Self back into the community when you are ready so that you have more to give.

Unbalanced Expression: Martyrdom. Loneliness and blaming that causes you to compromise what you need and to try to prove your value by overdoing and over-giving.

Lesson/Challenge: To learn to value yourself enough to retreat from the community and the energy of those you love to restore, restock, and replenish your inner resources. To learn to interpret the signal of loneliness correctly. To take responsibility for your own care and resources and not abdicate your own power to take care of yourself.

Center: The Resource Center

Resiliency Keys: Self-Worth, Vitality, Empowerment

Contemplations:

- What role does loneliness play in your life?
- Has loneliness caused you to doubt your value?
- What do you need to do to restore your energy?
- Are you doing enough to take care of yourself?
- What agreements are you making in your relationships that might be causing you to compromise your value?
- How can you rewrite these agreements?
- Are you abdicating responsibility for your self-care?
- Are you living a martyr model?

Keynotes:
- Loneliness, but it's not personal
- Stomach
- Defined Sacral with open Will Center, will forget to eat
- The drive to connect with others
- The need for rest and restoration in order to create and maintain healthy relationships
- Introvert Gate

- What needs to be healed, released, aligned, and brought to your awareness for you to take responsibility for cultivating your own sense of value and self-worth?

Affirmation: I am a powerful resource for my community. The energy that I hold impacts others deeply and brings them to deeper states of alignment and sustainability. I take care of my body, mind, and soul because I know the more that I am and the more I have, the more I can give to others. I take care of myself first because I know that good things flow from me. I am valuable and powerful, and I claim and defend the true story of Who I Truly Am.

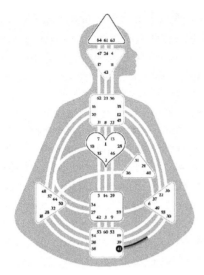

Gate 41: Imagination

I Ching: Decrease
Traditional Human Design: Fantasy
Astrological Sign: Aquarius
Biology: Adrenal Glands

Optimal Expression: The ability to use your creative imagination to generate ideas about new abundant opportunities in the world. To sustain these abundant visions, share them when necessary and to use your imagination to break old patterns and limiting beliefs. To be able to hold the vision of a miracle that transcends expectations.

Unbalanced Expression: To imagine worst-case scenarios and fixate on them. Denying your creative capacity and abdicating your creative power. Being afraid to share other options because they defy the current expectations or patterns. Being fearful of being judged by others for being a dreamer.

Lesson/Challenge: To learn to use your imagination as a source of creative inspiration and manifestation. To experience the world and imagine more abundant possibilities. To stay connected to your creative fire.

Center: The Divine Timing Center

Resiliency Keys: Vitality, Empowerment

Contemplations:

- Do you own your creative power?
- How can you deepen the self-honoring of your creative power?
- What do you do to express your creative abilities?
- What do you do to hold on to your dreams and visions?
- Are you sustaining them, or do you give up?
- What can you do to deepen your sustainability?
- Do you allow yourself to dream of good things?
- Do you believe in miracles?
- How can you deepen your faith in the goodness of the world?

Keynotes:

- Imagination
- Envisioning
- Fantasy
- Projection
- Initiating Gate of the Human Design year

Affirmation: I am a creative nexus of inspiration for the world. My ideas and imaginings inspire people to think beyond their limitations. My ideas stimulate new possibilities in the world. I am a powerful creator, and my creative thoughts, ideas, and inspirations set the stage for miracles and possibilities that will change the story of humanity.

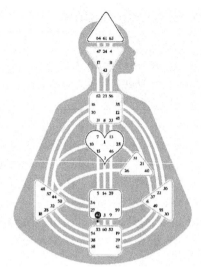

Gate 42: Conclusion

I Ching: Increase
Traditional Human Design: Finishing Things
Astrological Sign: Aries
Biology: Ovaries and Testes

Optimal Expression: The ability to respond to being inserted into opportunities, experiences, and events that you have the wisdom to facilitate and complete. To know exactly what needs to be completed to create the space for something new.

Unbalanced Expression: Pressure, confusion, and self-judgment for being unable to get things started. Avoiding or putting off things that need to be completed, creating a backlog of projects that can lead to paralysis and overwhelm. Finishing things prematurely due to pressure.

Lesson/Challenge: To learn to bring things to completion. To allow yourself to be led to where you need to be to finish things. To value your ability to know how to finish and to learn to give up your need to try to start everything. To finish things in order to create space for something new.

Center: The Evolution Center

Resiliency Keys: Decisiveness, Courage, Vitality, Empowerment

Contemplations:

- Do you own and value your natural gift of knowing how to bring things to completion?
- What things in your life do you need to finish to make room for something new?
- Are you holding on to old circumstances and patterns because you're afraid to let them go?
- Do you judge yourself for not starting things?
- How can you learn to be more gentle with yourself?

Keynotes:
- To wait for the right time to finish
- Finishing up to create space
- Holding on for too long
- People who need people

Affirmation: I am gifted at knowing when and how to finish things. I respond by bringing events, experiences, and relationships to a conclusion in order to create space for something new and more abundant. I can untangle the Cosmic Entanglements that keep people stuck in old patterns. My ability to realign and complete things helps others create space for transformation and expansion.

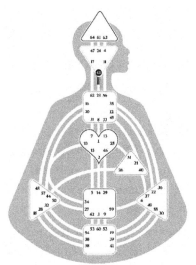

Gate 43: Insight

I Ching: Breakthrough
Traditional Human Design: Insight
Astrological Sign: Scorpio
Biology: Anterior and Posterior Pituitary Glands

Optimal Expression: The ability to tap into new knowledge, understandings, and insights that expand people's understanding of the world. To align with the right timing and trust that you'll know how to share what you know when you need to share it.

Unbalanced Expression: Feeling despair or frustration related to having knowledge but struggling to share what you know. Experiencing lightning bolts of knowingness and clarity but feeling overwhelmed by your inability to articulate what you understand. Not waiting for the right time to share what you know and feeling alone with your wisdom.

Lesson/Challenge: To be comfortable with and to trust epiphanies and deep inner knowing without doubting what you know. To trust that when the timing is right you will know how to share what you know and serve your role as a transformative messenger who has insights that can change the way people think and what they know.

Center: The Divine Translator Center

Resiliency Keys: Decisiveness, Self-Trust

Contemplations:

- Do you trust in Divine Timing?
- Do you trust yourself and your own Inner Knowing?
- What can you do to deepen your connection with your Source of Knowing?

Keynotes:

- Unique thinker with new ideas that can transform the old
- Has to wait to be recognized otherwise the timing is wrong
- Freak or genius depending on timing
- Likes to think
- Does not always listen or hear, so make physical contact to get their attention
- Epiphanies that lead to deep insights
- Need to wait for right words, right time, right people
- Inner auditory processing
- The need to talk it out sometimes

- What needs to be healed, released, aligned, or brought to your awareness for you to trust your own Inner Knowing?

Affirmation: I am a vessel of knowledge and wisdom that has the ability to transform the way people think. I share my knowledge with others when they are ready and vibrationally aligned with what I have to share. When the time is right, I have the right words, and the right insights to help others expand their thinking, recalibrate their mindset, and discover elegant solutions to the challenges facing humanity.

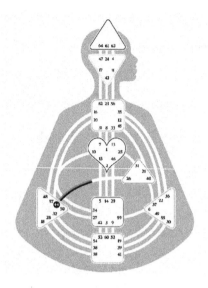

Gate 44: Truth

I Ching: Coming to Meet
Traditional Human Design: Energy
Astrological Sign: Scorpio
Biology: Spleen and Lymphatic System

Optimal Expression: The ability to see patterns that have created pain and to bring awareness to help yourself and others break old patterns and transform pain into an increased sense of value and alignment with purpose.

Unbalanced Expression: Fear and paralysis that the past patterns are insurmountable and doomed to repeat themselves.

Lesson/Challenge: To not get stuck in past patterns. To cultivate the courage to go forward without being stuck in fear of the past. To learn how to transform pain into power and to have the courage to express your Authentic Self without compromising or settling.

Center: The Self-Actualization Center

Resiliency Keys: Self-Trust, Courage

Contemplations:

- What patterns from the past are holding you back from moving forward with courage?
- Do you see how your experiences from the past have helped you learn more about Who You Truly Are?
- What have you learned about your value and your power?
- What needs to be healed, released, aligned, and brought to your awareness to fully activate your power?
- What needs to be healed, released, aligned, and brought to your awareness for you to step bolding into your aligned and authentic path?

Keynotes:
- Fear of the past
- Clairolifactant
- Smell
- Beauty
- The Greeter
- Intuitive awareness of patterns

Affirmation: I am powerfully intuitive and can sense the patterns that keep others stuck in limiting beliefs and constricted action. Through my insights and awareness, I help others break free from past limiting patterns and learn to find the power in their pain, find the blessings in their challenges and help them align more deeply with an authentic awareness of their true value and purpose.

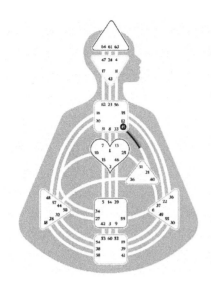

Gate 45: Distribution

I Ching: Gathering Together
Traditional Human Design: The King or Queen
Astrological Sign: Gemini
Biology: Thyroid and Parathyroid

Optimal Expression: The ability to understand that knowledge and material resources are powerful, and to know how to use both as a path of service that sustains others and helps others grow their own abundant foundation.

Unbalanced Expression: Diva energy. Selfish leadership rooted in lack and showing off. Holding back. Overcompensating for lack of self-worth with narcissism. Fear of not being seen as a leader and reacting by being controlling or bombastic.

Lesson/Challenge: To share and use your resources for the greater good of the whole. To learn to manage resources judiciously so that they benefit the greatest number of people. To teach, as a pathway of sharing.

Center: The Activation Center

Resiliency Keys: Authenticity, Vitality

Contemplations:

- Do you like to share?
- What do you have to give the world?
- How do you own your right leadership?
- Are you comfortable as a leader?
- Do you shrink from leadership?
- Do you overcompensate by pushing too hard with your leadership?
- Do you trust that when the right people are ready, you will be pressed into action as a leader and a teacher?
- What do you need to heal, release, align or bring to your awareness to trust your leadership energy more?

Keynotes:
• Teaching
• Sharing
• Ego
• Natural leadership
• Generous or selfish
• Self-less

Affirmation: I am a teacher and a leader. I use my resources, my knowledge, and my experience to expand the resources, knowledge, and experiences of others. I use my blessings of abundance to increase the blessings of others. I know that I am a vehicle of wisdom and knowledge. I sense when it's right for me to share who I am and what I know, with others.

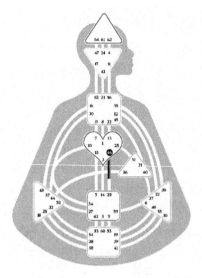

Gate 46: Embodiment

I Ching: Pushing Upward
Traditional Human Design: Love of the Body
Astrological Sign: Virgo
Biology: Liver

Optimal Expression: To recognize that the body is the vehicle for the soul and to love the body as a vital element of the soul's expression in life. To nurture, be grounded in, and fully care for the body. To savor the physicality of the human experience. To explore how to embody the Spirit in your body fully and to be committed and devoted to seeing how much life force you can embody into your physical form.

Unbalanced Expression: To disconnect from the body. To hate the body. To avoid nurturing or taking care of the body. To avoid the commitments and consistency necessary to embody life forcefully. To hide or disfigure the body.

Lesson/Challenge: To learn to love your body. To learn to fully be in your body. To learn to love the sensual nature of your physical form and to move it with love and awareness.

Center: The Calibration Center

Resiliency Keys: Lovability, Decisiveness, Courage, Authenticity

Contemplations:

- Do you love your body?
- What can you do to deepen your love for your body?
- What parts of your body do you love and appreciate?
- Make a list of every part of your body that you love.
- What do you need to do to amplify the life force you are experiencing in your body?

Keynotes:
- Body image
- Physical fulfillment
- The body as a barometer for alignment
- Using the body to carry out the job of the soul

- What kinds of devotion and commitment do you experience that help you harness greater amounts of life force in your body?
- How can you deepen your commitment and devotion to your body?

Affirmation: My body is the vehicle for my soul. My ability to fully express who I am (and my life and soul purpose) is deeply rooted in my body's ability to carry my soul. I love, nurture, and commit to my body. I appreciate its form and all of its miraculous abilities. Every day I love my body more.

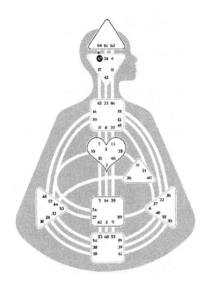

Gate 47: Mindset

I Ching: Oppression
Traditional Human Design: Realization
Astrological Sign: Virgo
Biology: Anterior and Posterior Pituitary Glands

Optimal Expression: To engage in hopeful, inspired thoughts no matter what is happening around you. To use inspiration as a catalyst for calibrating emotional frequency and the Heart.

Unbalanced Expression: To quit or give up an inspiration because you can't figure out how to make it happen. To feel defeated and broken because you think you have ideas that you can't manifest.

Lesson/Challenge: To become skilled at a mindset of open-ness and possibility. To not let inspiration die because you don't know how to fulfill it.

Center: The Divine Translator Center

Resiliency Keys: Self-Trust, Decisiveness

Contemplations:

- What thoughts do you have when you receive an idea or inspiration?
- Are you hopeful or despairing?
- How does it feel to let go of figuring out how you're going to make your idea a reality?
- What do you do to regulate your mindset?
- What practices do you need to cultivate, to increase the power of your thoughts?

Keynotes:
- The need to regulate the mind
- Epiphany
- Trust opens the mind
- The pressure to figure out "How?"
- Expansion or contraction depending on attitude

Affirmation: My mindset is the source of my inspired actions and attitude. I know that when I receive an idea and inspiration it is my job to nurture the idea by using the power of my imagination to increase the potential and emotional frequency of the idea. I consistently keep my inner and outer environment aligned with the energy of possibility and potential. I know that it is my job to create by virtue of my alignment, and I relax knowing that it is the job of the Universe to fulfill my inspirations.

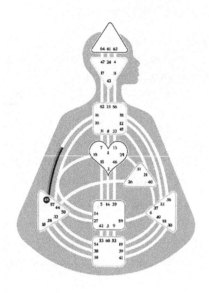

Gate 48: Wisdom

I Ching: The Well
Traditional Human Design: Depth
Astrological Sign: Libra
Biology: Spleen and Lymphatic System

Optimal Expression: The wisdom to explore and learn the depth of knowledge necessary to create a strong foundation for action and expertise. The self-trust to trust your ability to know *how* to know and your connection to Source as the true source of your knowledge.

Unbalanced Expression: Paralysis in inadequacy. To be afraid to try something new or go beyond your comfort zone because you think you don't know or are not ready.

Lesson/Challenge: To allow yourself to trust that you will know what you need to know when you need to know it. To not let the fear of not knowing stop you from creating. To not let not knowing hold you back.

Center: The Self-Actualization Center

Resiliency Keys: Self-Trust, Courage

Contemplations:

- Do you trust your own knowing?
- What needs to be healed, released, aligned, and brought to your awareness for you to deepen your self-trust?
- What practice do you have that keeps you connected to the wisdom of Source?
- How can you deepen your connection to Source?

Keynotes:
- Depth of knowledge
- Fear of inadequacy
- Sometimes needs to push through fear to get to confident proficiency
- Needs a foundation of information to feel safe

Affirmation: I am a depth of wisdom and knowledge. My studies and experiences have taught me everything I need to know. I push beyond the limits of my earthly knowledge and take great leaps of faith as a function of my deep connection to Source knowing that I'll always know what I need to know when I need to know it.

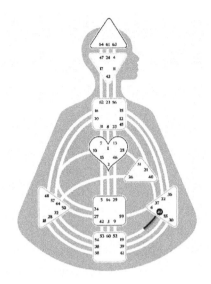

Gate 49: The Catalyst

I Ching: Revolution
Traditional Human Design: Principles
Astrological Sign: Aquarius
Biology: Kidneys and Pancreas

Optimal Expression: The ability to sense when it's time to hold to a value that supports your value. The ability to inspire others to make expansive changes that embrace higher principles and a deeper alignment with peace and sustainability. The willingness to align with a higher value.

Unbalanced Expression: Quitting too soon as a way of avoiding intimacy. Compromising on your value and upholding agreements that no longer serve you. Creating drama and fighting for outdated values that no longer serve the higher good.

Lesson/Challenge: To not quit prematurely, failing to start a necessary revolution in your life, to not hold on to unhealthy situations, relationships, or agreements that may compromise your value and worth. To hold on for longer than is healthy and to settle or compromise your value in situations, relationships, and with agreements that aren't worthy of you.

Center: The Creative Center

Resiliency Keys: Courage, Emotional Wisdom, Empowerment, Decisiveness

Contemplations:

- Are you holding on too long?
- Is there a circumstance and condition you are allowing because you fear the emotional energy associated with change?
- Do you have a habit of quitting too soon?
- Do you fail to do the work associated with creating genuine intimacy?
- What do you need to let go of right now to create room for you to align with higher principles?

Keynotes:

- Principled
- Black or white
- Can be a revolutionary rooted in principles
- Needs to wait before it quits (emotional)
- The ability to consciously cultivate the right emotional frequency to maintain and sustain intimacy

Affirmation: I am a Cosmic Revolutionary. I am aligned with higher principles that support the evolution of humanity. I stand for peace, equity, and sustainability. I align with these principles, and I stand my ground. I do the work to create the intimacy necessary to share my values with others. I value myself and my work enough to only align with relationships that support my vital role.

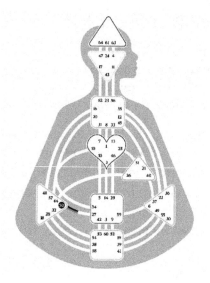

Gate 50: Nurturing

I Ching: The Cauldron
Traditional Human Design: Values
Astrological Sign: Libra/Scorpio
Biology: Spleen and Lymphatic System

Optimal Expression: The ability to nurture yourself so that you have more to give others. The intuition to know what others need to bring them into greater alignment with Love. To teach and share what you have, to increase the wellbeing of others.

Unbalanced Expression: To over-care. To let guilt stop you from sustaining yourself. To hold to rigid principles and to struggle to allow others the consequences of their choices.

Lesson/Challenge: To transcend guilt and unhealthy obligation and do what you need to take care of yourself in order to better serve others. To hold rigid principles to judge others.

Center: The Self-Actualization Center

Resiliency Keys: Self-Trust, Courage

Contemplations:

- How do you feel about taking care of yourself first?
- How do you sustain your nurturing energy?
- What role does guilt play in driving and/or motivating you?
- What would you choose if you could remove the guilt?
- Do you have non-negotiable values?
- What are they?
- How do you handle people who share different values from you?

Keynotes:
- Values
- To sense what other people need to feel loved
- Guilt or freedom
- Self-care
- Rigidity
- Fear of failing others

Affirmation: My presence brings Love into the room. I nurture and love others. I take care of myself first in order to be better able to serve Love. I intuitively know what people need, and I facilitate for them a state of self-love and self-empowerment by helping them align more deeply with the power of Love. I let go and I allow others to learn from what I model and teach. I am a deep well of love that sustains the planet.

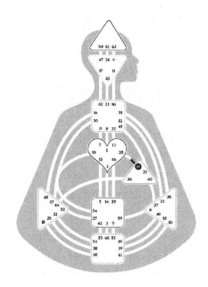

Gate 51: Initiation

I Ching: The Arousing
Traditional Human Design: Shock
Astrological Sign: Aries
Biology: Thymus

Optimal Expression: The ability to consciously use cycles of disruption and unexpected twists and turns of faith as catalysts that deepen your connection to Source and to your life and soul purpose.

Unbalanced Expression: To let the shock of disruption cause you to lose connection with your true purpose and with Source. To become bitter or angry with God. To try to control life and deplete yourself from the energy necessary to hold yourself back.

Lesson/Challenge: To not let the unexpected cause you to lose your faith. To not let a pattern of unexpected events cause you to lose your connection with your purpose and Source. To learn to use the power of your own story of initiation to initiate others into fulfilling their right place in the Cosmic Plan.

Center: The Resource Center

Resiliency Keys: Self-Worth, Vitality, Empowerment

Contemplations:

- What has shock and the unexpected taught you in your life?
- How can you deepen your connection to Source?
- How can your experiences of initiation be shared with others?
- What are you here to wake people up to?

Keynotes:

- Can have shocking life experiences that wake them up to the Love of Spirit
- Can be shocking (and kind of enjoy it)
- Can be perceived as competitive/or is competitive
- The place in the chart where the Higher Self can transcend the ego
- Initiates others

Affirmation: I navigate change and transformation with grace. I know that when my life takes a twist or a turn, it is my soul calling me out to serve at a higher level. I use disruption as a catalyst for my own growth and expansion. I am a teacher and an initiator. I use my ability to transform pain into growth and power to help others navigate through crisis and emerge on the other side of the crisis empowered and aligned.

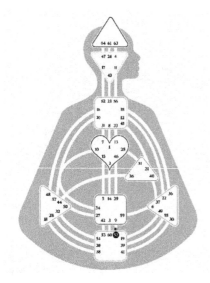

Gate 52: Perspective

I Ching: Keeping Still Mountain
Traditional Human Design: Stillness
Astrological Sign: Cancer
Biology: Adrenal Glands

Optimal Expression: The ability to see the bigger perspective and purpose of what is happening around you and to know exactly where to focus your energy and attention to facilitate the unfolding of what's next.

Unbalanced Expression: Attention deficit. To let overwhelm paralyze you and cause you to fail to act. To put your energy and attention in the wrong place and to spend your energy focused on something that bears no fruit.

Lesson/Challenge: To learn to stay focused even when you're overwhelmed by a bigger perspective. To see the big picture and not let the massive nature of what you know confuse you and cause you to struggle with where to put your energy and attention.

Center: The Divine Timing Center

Resiliency Keys: Vitality, Empowerment

Contemplations:

- What do you do to maintain and sustain your focus?
- Is there anything in your environment or your life that you need to move out of the way for you to deepen your focus?
- How do you manage overwhelm?
- What things are you avoiding because you feel overwhelmed by them?
- What is one bold action you can take to begin clearing the path for action?
- How does overwhelm affect your self-worth?
- How can you love yourself more deeply despite the overwhelm?

Keynotes:
- Stopping for guidance
- Stopping and doing nothing
- Waits for right timing to concentrate
- May feel ADD

Affirmation: I am like the eagle soaring above the land. I see the entirety of what needs to happen to facilitate the evolution of the world. I use my perspective to see my unique and irreplaceable role in the Cosmic Plan. I see relationships and patterns that others don't always see. My perspective helps us all to build a peaceful world more effectively and in a consciously directed way.

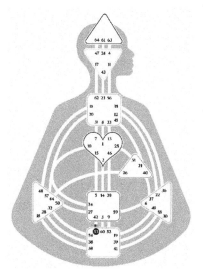

Gate 53: Starting

I Ching: Development
Traditional Human Design: Starting Things
Astrological Sign: Cancer
Biology: Adrenal Glands

Optimal Expression: The ability to sit with inspiration and be attuned to what the Inspiration wants and needs. To launch the initiation sequence for an idea and initiate it and then let the idea follow its right course with trust in the flow.

Unbalanced Expression: Reacting to the pressure to get an idea started. To feel like a failure because everything you start against right timing fails. To be afraid to start anything because of the trauma of your past failures. Starting everything and never reaping the rewards of what you start.

Lesson/Challenge: To respond in alignment with your energy blueprint to opportunities to get things started. To initiate the process of preparing or setting the state for the manifestation of a dream before it becomes a reality. To learn to trust in the timing of the Universe and not take charge and try to implement your own ideas while working against Divine Timing. To not burn out trying to complete things. To find peace as a starter, not a finisher.

Center: The Divine Timing Center

Resiliency Keys: Vitality, Empowerment

Contemplations:

- How do you feel about yourself when you have an idea and can't get it initiated?
- How do you feel when someone takes your initial idea and builds on it?
- Do you value what you started?
- What identities and attachments do you have, to be the one who starts and finishes something?
- Do you judge yourself for not finishing something?
- How can you be more gentle with yourself?
- Do you trust Divine Timing?
- How can you deepen your trust in right timing?

Keynotes:

- Starting—not finishing
- The energy to start is enough
- People who need people
- Trusting in timing and the Divine Plan

Affirmation: I am a servant to Divine Inspiration. My thoughts, inspirations, and ideas set the stage for creative expansion and the potential for evolution. I act on the ideas that present themselves to me in an aligned way. I honor all other ideas knowing that my gift is in the spark of energy that gets things rolling when the timing is right. While I wait for right timing, I guard my energy and charge my battery so that I am sustainable when the time is right for action.

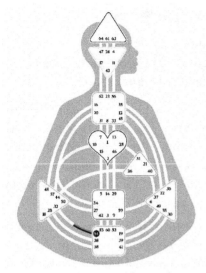

Gate 54: Divine Inspiration

I Ching: Marrying Maiden
Traditional Human Design: Drive
Astrological Sign: Capricorn
Biology: Adrenal Glands

Optimal Expression: The ability to cultivate a deep relationship with the Divine Muse, nurture the inspirational fruits of the muse, and serve as a steward for inspiration by aligning the idea energetically and preparing the way by laying foundational action and building.

Unbalanced Expression: To react to the pressure that you have to fulfill an inspiration and use force to push the inspiration into form even though it might not be your idea/dream to manifest or the right time to bring it forth.

Lesson/Challenge: To learn to be a conduit for Divine Inspiration. To be patient and to wait for alignment and right timing before taking action. To be at peace with stewardship for ideas and to learn to trust the divine trajectory of an inspiration.

Center: The Divine Timing Center

Resiliency Keys: Vitality, Empowerment

Contemplations:

- What do you do to get inspired?
- How do you interface with your creative muse?
- Is there anything you need to do or prepare to be ready for the next step in manifesting your dream or inspiration?

Keynotes:
- Inspiration
- Ideas
- Divine connection
- Dreams
- Pressure to make ideas come true

Affirmation: I am a Divine Conduit for inspiration. Through me, new ideas about creating sustainability and peace on the planet are born. I tend to my inspirations, give them love and energy, and prepare the way for their manifestations in the material world.

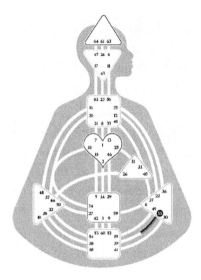

Gate 55: Faith

I Ching: Abundance
Traditional Human Design: Spirit
Astrological Sign: Pisces
Biology: Kidney and Pancreas

Optimal Expression: The ability to hold the emotional frequency of energy and the vision for a creation. To trust in sufficiency so profoundly that you're able to create without limitation.

Unbalanced Expression: Indecisiveness. Fear and lack. Hoarding, keeping from others, fighting to take more than your share. Not trusting Source and drawing on Will to create.

Lesson/Challenge: To learn to trust Source. To know that you are fully supported. To become proficient in the art of emotional alignment *as* your most creative power.

Center: The Creative Center

Resiliency Keys: Courage, Emotional Wisdom, Empowerment, Decisiveness

Contemplations:

- Do you trust that you are fully supported?
- What do you need to do to deepen that trust?
- How can you align yourself with abundant emotional energy?
- What practices or shifts do you need to make in your life to live and create in a more aligned way?
- Do you surround yourself with beauty?
- How can you deepen the experience of beauty in your life?
- What do you have faith in now?
- What old gods of limitation do you need to stop worshipping?
- Go on a miracle hunt. Take stock of everything good in your life.
- How much magic have you been blessed with?

> **Keynotes:**
> - Indecisive and fearful
> - Deeply mystical, has to learn about Abundance of Spirit and trusting the Universe
> - Restores themselves and others to flow
> - Emotional
> - Auditory
> - Mutative
> - Individual

Affirmation: I am perfectly and Divinely supported. I know that all my needs and desires are being fulfilled. My trust in my support allows me to create beyond the limitation of what others think is possible and my faith shows them the way. I use my emotional energy as the source of my creative power. My frequency of faith lifts others up and opens up a greater world of potential and possibility.

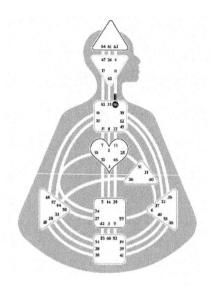

Gate 56: Expansion

I Ching: The Wanderer
Traditional Human Design: The Storyteller
Astrological Sign: Cancer/Leo
Biology: Thyroid and Parathyroid

Optimal Expression: The ability to share stories and inspirations that stimulate expansive and possibility-oriented thinking in others to stimulate powerful emotional energy that creates evolution and growth.

Unbalanced Expression: To get lost or stuck in limiting stories and narratives. To tell stories that contract and deplete the energy of others.

Lesson/Challenge: To learn. To share stories and inspirations with the right people at the right time. To learn to tell stories of expansion and not depletion and contraction.

Center: The Activation Center

Resiliency Keys: Authenticity, Vitality

Contemplations:

- What stories do you repeatedly share with others?
- Do they lift people up or cause them to contract?
- What stories do you tell about yourself and your voice, that causes you to expand or contract?
- What are you here to inspire others to do or be?

Keynotes:
- Talking/talking too much
- Storyteller
- Teacher
- Metaphors
- Possibilities
- Recognition/attention
- Uses stories as templates for transmission

Affirmation: I am a Divine Storyteller. The stories of possibility that I share have the power to inspire others to grow and expand. I use my words as a template for possibility and expansion for the world. I inspire the world with my words.

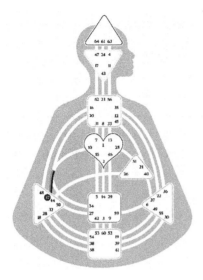

Gate 57: Instinct

I Ching: The Gentle
Traditional Human Design: Intuition
Astrological Sign: Libra
Biology: Spleen and Lymph

Optimal Expression: The ability to sense when it is the right time to act. To intuitively know what needs to be made ready to be prepared for the future and to follow through on it.

Unbalanced Expression: To be so afraid of the future that you are paralyzed. To not trust yourself and your own instinct. To know what needs to be done to prepare for the future and to fail to act on it.

Lesson/Challenge: To learn to trust your own insights and gut. To learn to tell the difference between an instinctive response versus a fear of the future. To fully grasp and conquer your connection to your sense of right timing.

Center: The Self-Actualization Center

Resiliency Keys: Self-Trust, Courage

Contemplations:

- Do you trust your intuition?
- What does your intuition feel like to you?
- Sometimes doing a retrospective analysis of your intuition/instinct makes it more clear how your intuitive signal works.
- What experiences in the past have you had that you knew you should or shouldn't do?
- How have you experienced your intuition in the past?
- When you think about moving forward in your life, do you feel afraid?
- What are you afraid of?
- What can you do to mitigate the fear?
- What impulses are you experiencing that are telling you to prepare for what's next in your life?
- Are you acting on your impulses? Why or why not?

Keynotes:
- Most intuitive energy in the chart
- Fear of the future or unknown
- Intuition is in the now and knows. It is not logical, so it can doubt itself a lot
- Often feels like it's not intuitive because the intuition here is so integrated into the rest of the chart
- Intuition in the now (clairaudient)
- Intuitive sense of right timing

Affirmation: My Inner Wisdom is deeply connected to the pulse of Divine Timing. I listen to my Inner Wisdom and follow my instinct. I know when and how to prepare the way for the future. I take guided action and I trust myself and Source.

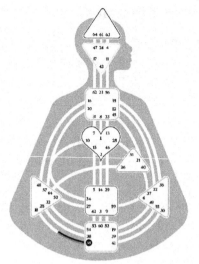

Gate 58: Joy

I Ching: Joy
Traditional Human Design: Joy of Life
Astrological Sign: Capricorn
Biology: Adrenal Glands

Optimal Expression: To harness the joy of virtuosity and refine your practice until you fulfill your potential. To live in the flow of Joy.

Unbalanced Expression: To deny joy. To avoid the practice of seeking expertise. To feel guilty or ashamed to do what you love. To disbelieve in joy.

Lesson/Challenge: To follow the drive to create the fulfillment of your potential. To learn to craft a talent and make it consummate through joyful learning and repetition. To learn to embrace joy as a vital force of creative power without guilt or denial.

Center: The Divine Timing Center

Resiliency Keys: Vitality, Empowerment

Contemplations:

- What brings you the greatest joy?
- How can you deepen your practice of joy?
- How can you create more joy in your life?
- What keeps you from fulfilling your potential and your talent?
- What are you afraid of?

Keynotes:
- Joy
- The potential for the loss of joy
- Must have a life rooted in joy
- The drive to pursue joy

Affirmation: I am a consummate curator of my own talent. I use my joy to drive me to embody the fun expression of all that I am. I practice as my path to excellency. I know that from repetition and consistency comes a more skillful expression of my talent. I embrace learning and growing, and I commit to the full expression of my joy.

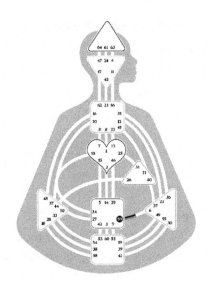

Gate 59: Sustainability

I Ching: Dispersion
Traditional Human Design: Sexuality
Astrological Sign: Virgo
Biology: Ovaries and Testes

Optimal Expression: To trust in sufficiency and to know that when you create abundance, there is great fulfillment in sharing. To craft partnerships and relationships that sustain you and the foundation of your lives.

Unbalanced Expression: To feel like you have to fight or struggle to survive. To feel the need to penetrate others and force your "rightness" on them. To let fear of lack cause you to craft relationships and agreements that are unsustainable.

Lesson/Challenge: To learn to make abundant choices that sustain you and, at the same time, others. To collaborate and initiate others into sustainable relationships from a place of sufficiency. To learn to share what you have in a sustainable way.

Center: The Evolution Center

Resiliency Keys: Decisiveness, Courage, Vitality, Empowerment

Contemplations:

- Do you trust in your own abundance?
- How do you feel about sharing what you have with others?
- Are you creating relationship and partnership agreements that honor your work?
- Do you have relationships and agreements that are draining you?
- What needs to change?
- How do you feel about being right?
- Are you open to other ways of thinking or being?
- Do you believe in creating agreements and alignments with people who have different values and perspectives?

Keynotes:

- Penetrating
- Desire for impact
- Sexual
- Responds to creating connection
- Responds to creating resources
- Perceived as seductive
- The power to influence peace

Affirmation: The energy I carry has the power to create sufficiency and sustainability for all. I craft valuable alliances and agreements that support me in expanding abundance for everyone. I hold to higher principles and values rooted in my trust in sufficiency and the all-providing Source. Through my work and alignments, my blessings serve to increase the blessings of myself and others.

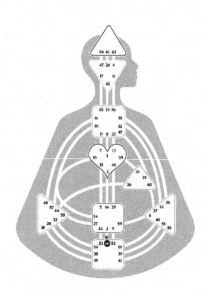

Gate 60: Conservation

I Ching: Limitation
Traditional Human Design: Acceptance
Astrological Sign: Capricorn
Biology: Adrenal glands

Optimal Expression: The ability to find the blessings in transformation. Optimism. To know how to focus on what is working instead of what's not.

Unbalanced Expression: To hold on and not allow for growth. To fight for the old and rebuke change. To let the overwhelm of change and disruption create paralysis and resistance.

Lesson/Challenge: To not let the fear of loss overwhelm your resourcefulness. To learn to find what is working and focus on it instead of looking at the loss and disruption.

Center: The Divine Timing Center

Resiliency Keys: Vitality, Empowerment

Contemplations:

- What change are you resisting?
- What are you afraid of?
- What are the things in your life that are working that you need to focus on?
- Is your fear of loss holding you back?

Keynotes:
- Gratitude
- Letting go
- Right timing
- Solution orientation
- Exploring what works with an open mind

Affirmation: I am grateful for all the transformation and change in my life. I know that disruption is the catalyst for my growth. I am able to find the blessings of the past and incorporate them into my innovative vision for the future. I am optimistic about the future, and I transform the world by growing what works.

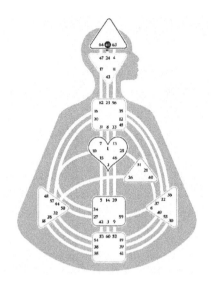

Gate 61: Wonder

I Ching: Inner Truth
Traditional Human Design: Mystery
Astrological Sign: Capricorn
Biology: Pineal Gland

Optimal Expression: The ability to see purpose in a bigger perspective that transcends the smaller details of an experience or event. The ability to stay in a state of innocence and delusional confidence as a way of sustaining powerful creativity.

Unbalanced Expression: Allowing the pressure to know "why" to create bitterness or victimhood that is often perpetuated in a rationalized pattern.

Lesson/Challenge: To not get lost in trying to answer or figure out why. To maintain a state of wonder and awe. To not let the pressure of trying to know keep you from being present.

Center: The Quantum Interface Center

Resiliency Keys: Decisiveness, Self-Trust

Contemplations:

- What do you do to maintain your sense of wonder?
- How can you deepen your awe of the magnificence of the Universe?
- What old thoughts, patterns, and beliefs do you need to release in order to align with your knowingness and to trust "delusional confidence" as a powerful creative state?
- What greater perspectives on the events of your life can you see?
- What are the greatest lessons you've learned from your pain?
- How do you use these lessons to expand your self-expression?

Keynotes:
- Why?
- Curious
- Perspective
- Dreaming
- Difficulty translating 'knowing'
- Articulation
- Thinking

Affirmation: I have a direct connection to a Cosmic Perspective that gives me an expanded view of the meaning of the events in my life and the lives of others. I see the wonder and innocence of life and stay present in a constant state of awe. I am innocent and pure in my understanding of the world and my innocence is the source of my creative alignment.

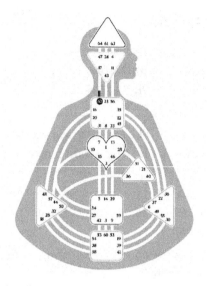

Gate 62: Preparation

I Ching: The Preponderance of the Small
Traditional Human Design: Details
Astrological Sign: Cancer
Biology: Thyroid and Parathyroid

Optimal Expression: The ability to be attuned to what is necessary to be prepared, and trust that your alignment will inform you of everything you need. Being able to relax and trusting that you'll know what you need to know when you need to know it.

Unbalanced Expression: Fear and worry. Over-preparation. Allowing the plan to override the flow.

Lesson/Challenge: To trust that you will be prepared for the next step. To not let worry and over-preparation detract you from being present to the moment. To let the fear of not being ready keep you trapped.

Center: The Activation Center

Resiliency Keys: Authenticity, Vitality

Contemplations:

- Do you worry?
- What do you do to manage your worry?
- What can you do to trust that you know what you need to know?
- What proof do you have that you are in the flow of preparation?
- Is there anything you need to plan for in your life right now?
- Are you over-planning?
- Does your need for contingency plans keep you stuck?

> **Keynotes:**
> - Organized
> - Prepared
> - Worry and overwhelm
> - Projected
> - Feels comfortable with a plan or the details
> - Learning to trust

Affirmation: I create the foundation for the practice of excellence by engineering a plan of action that creates growth. I am in the flow of my understanding, and I use my knowledge and experience to be prepared for the evolution of what's next. I am ready and I am prepared. I trust my own preparation and allow myself to be in the flow of what's next, knowing that I'll know what I need to know when I need to know it.

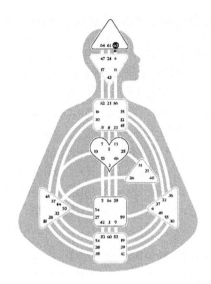

Gate 63: Curiosity

I Ching: After Completion
Traditional Human Design: Doubt
Astrological Sign: Pisces
Biology: Pineal Gland

Optimal Expression: The ability to use questioning and curiosity to stimulate dreams of new possibilities and potentials. Thoughts that inspire the question of what needs to happen to make an idea a reality.

Unbalanced Expression: Doubt (especially self-doubt) that leads to suspicion and the struggle for certainty. The unwillingness to question an old idea. The loss of curiosity.

Lesson/Challenge: To not let self-doubt and suspicion cause you to stop being curious.

Center: The Quantum Interface Center

Resiliency Keys: Decisiveness, Self-Trust

Contemplations:

- Are you curious about life?
- Do you regularly allow yourself to be curious about what else is possible in the world? In your life?
- Do you doubt yourself and your ideas?
- What needs to happen to unlock your need to be right about an idea and allow yourself to dream of possibilities again?

Keynotes:

- Doubt, suspicion and inadequacy
- The pressure for answers
- What else is possible? Is this true? What?
- Right eye
- Visual
- Left brain
- Neurotransmitter production
- Trust

Affirmation: My curiosity makes me a conduit of possibility thinking. I ask questions that stimulate imaginations. I allow the questions of my mind to seed dreams that stimulate my imagination and the imagination of others. I share my questions as an opening to the fulfillment of potential in the world.

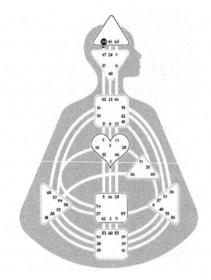

Gate 64: Divine Transference

I Ching: Before Completion
Traditional Human Design: Confusion
Astrological Sign: Virgo
Biology: Pineal Gland

Optimal Expression: The ability to receive a big idea and to serve the idea by giving it your imagination and dreaming. To trust that you'll know how to implement the idea if it is yours to make manifest. To hold the energy of an idea for the world.

Unbalanced Expression: To feel pressure to try to manifest a big idea. To feel despairing or inadequate or ungrounded if you don't know how to make an idea a reality. To feel deep mental pressure to figure out an idea. To give up dreaming.

Lesson/Challenge: To not let the power of your big ideas overwhelm you and shut down dreaming and creating. To get lost in the pressure of answering the how question.

Center: The Quantum Interface Center

Resiliency Keys: Decisiveness, Self-Trust

Contemplations:

- What do you do to take care of your Big Ideas?
- How do you feel about having dreams but not always the solutions?
- How can you stop judging the gift of your dreams?
- Do you trust that the "how" of your ideas will be revealed?
- How can you deepen this trust?

Keynotes:

- Inspiration
- Pressure
- Big ideas
- Overwhelm
- How?

Affirmation: I am a conduit for expansive thinking. My inspirations and ideas create the seeds of possibility in my mind and the mind of others. I honor the dreams that pass through my mind and allow my big ideas to stimulate my imagination and the imagination of others. I trust the Universe to reveal the details of my dreams when the time is right. I use the power of my dreams to stimulate a world of possibility and expansion.

The Four Quarters

The Human Design year is divided into four Creative Quarters. Each quarter represents the work that needs to be done to manifest the fulfillment of our goals for the annual solar cycle. The Quarters invite us to explore key themes and what we need to focus on to complete our goals and intentions for the year.

Each quarter begins when the Sun highlights one of the four Gates of the Incarnation Cross of the Sphinx.

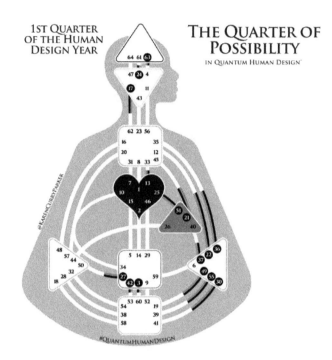

1ST QUARTER OF THE HUMAN DESIGN YEAR

THE QUARTER OF POSSIBILITY
IN QUANTUM HUMAN DESIGN

Quarter 1

The Quarter of Initiation | The Quarter of Possibility

The Quarter of Possibility is highlighted by the Gates of the Emotional Solar Plexus, the Gates of the Will and G-Center that represent self-regulation and higher purpose, Gates in the Sacral, which represent obligation, completion, and innovation, and mental Gates that invoke possibility thinking.

I am a gardener. The rhythm of my year is dictated by planting cycles. As a resident of the Northern Hemisphere, this time of year is the planning part of my garden. I spend weekends studying heirloom seed catalogs and plotting my garden beds.

The Quarter of Possibility is similar to studying seed catalogs. We've been contemplating last year and evaluating what worked and what didn't. Now we're preparing the soil to receive the seeds of our creativity and clarity. We're planning. We're setting intentions and cultivating the faith to do the work to bring into form the dreams we nurtured all winter.

We start this quarter with the Sun highlighting the Gate 13, the Gate of Narrative. This start position for this quarter gives us an overarching theme of exploring the stories we tell about ourselves and each other so that we can rewrite our narrative so that it supports us in creating what we truly desire for our lives. We're cultivating the ability to use the power of personal narrative to create with power and intention.

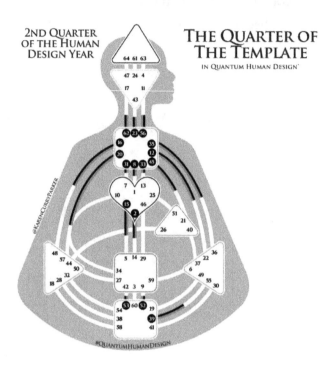

Quarter 2

The Quarter of Civilization | The Quarter of The Template

The second quarter of the year, the Quarter of the Template, begins with the Sun in the Gate 2, the Gate of Allowing. We are exploring the question of how much good we are willing to receive and allow in our lives.

The Sun travels through all the Gates of the Activation Center during the Quarter of the Template, encouraging us to put words to our dreams and intentions. Our words activate our intentions and either set them into motion or invite others to join us and support us.

We are learning to honor our voices, and the words we offer are a direct transmission from Source. The words we speak have the potential to transform the world, so we use our words carefully and with high regard for right timing, and also the receptivity of others.

Words create. We are learning to use words as a key element of our creative power. Words allow for Unity. They transmit. They are the interface between the Divine and the Human. Words are Power. They translate the infinite to the finite. Words are a code for a story. Words carry frequencies of energy, and our DNA responds to that language.

This quarter we are tasked with finding the words that build the template for who we are becoming and what we want to create.

Returning to the garden metaphor, the Quarter of the Template is analogous to planting the seeds and doing the actual work of initiating the garden. We are tilling the soil, making sure we've placed the right plants next to each other, and made sure that the plants are receiving the right light and nutrients for optimal growth.

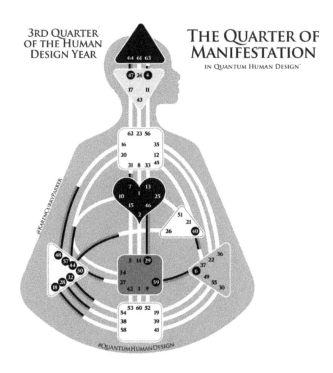

Quarter 3

The Quarter of Duality | The Quarter of Manifestation

The third Creative Quarter of the year begins with the Sun highlighting the Gate 7, the Gate of Collaboration. We are invited to explore our place of service to the greater good, our relationships with each other, and the theme of influence and empowerment.

This quarter highlights all the Gates of the Self-Actualization Center, highlighting the theme of courage and acting when the internal or external timing is aligned.

We aren't going to arrive on the threshold of an equitable, sustainable, just, abundant, and peaceful world by ourselves—rugged individuals staking our claim. We've tried that model of creating, and it really isn't increasing the wellbeing of the world.

The only way we're going to create the world that so many of us have been dreaming of and holding in our hearts for our whole lives is if we collaborate. We will arrive into this world together, holding hands and calling each other forward.

If we look at the Gates highlighted in the Creative Quarter of Manifestation, we see the story of collaboration unfolding.

Collaboration has the power to override fear, to instill patience and trust in right timing. Collaboration harnesses the power of perseverance, determination, and devotion because the results are no longer tied up in the messiness of our egos and our sense of worth. We are driven by compassion, not by winning. Collaboration makes us more sustainable. Collaboration is expansive and cracks us open to new and bigger possibilities and reminds us that we are all in this together.

Collaboration doesn't have to be complicated. Sometimes it can be as simple as thousands of people holding the energy of the idea that we can create an equitable, just, peaceful, sustainable, and abundant world even if we don't know how yet. We amplify our power when we unify our vision.

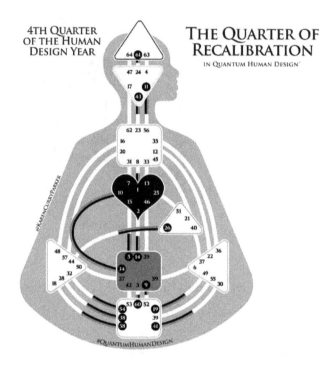

Quarter 4

The Quarter of Mutation | The Quarter of Recalibration

The final Creative Quarter of the Human Design year invites us to look back to see how close (or far) we are from where we started. We review what we grew in our metaphorical garden, thinking about our intentions and goals and exploring whether we hit the mark and how we can expand on what we accomplished.

The Sun initiates this quarter by highlighting the Gate 1, the Gate of Purpose. This Gate is the most *yang* of all the Gates and a part of Transformation Circuitry. Transformation Circuitry brings mutation and change and the theme of individuality.

At the heart of individuality is the need to follow your own conviction, not because it's selfish, but because it blazes a path forward for others to follow. Individuality creates waves of change, and when we follow our own convictions, it gives others to do the same.

Following your own conviction isn't selfish, but if you're not taking action that is deeply rooted in self-love and a high sense of self-worth, your conviction has the potential to actually be a rebellious attempt to prove your lovability or your value.

True conviction initiates a new direction that is rooted in Love, which expands the capacity of love's expression in the world. It's not selfish to follow these kinds of convictions. It's a radical stand for truth.

This quarter invites us to, first and foremost, explore the narratives we tell about who we are and to assess whether our creations this year have been an expression of our Authentic Selves. Remember, this isn't so much about what we've done, but rather, are we being honest about who we are? Your life purpose ISN'T about what you do. It's about being who you ARE.

How to Interpret the Incarnation Cross

The position of the Conscious and Unconscious Sun and Earth create a vital configuration that constitutes 70% of the energy of your being. This configuration, called the Incarnation Cross, represents the energy frequency and the storyline of the life purpose in the chart. 192 basic Incarnation Crosses are configured from this combination of Earth and Sun positions.

HUMAN DESIGN CHART
INCARNATION CROSS 35/5 | 63/64

Design

☉ 63.4	
⊕ 64.4	SUN GATE
☊ 33.4	EARTH GATE
☋ 19.4	
☽ 55.3	
☿ 49.2	
♀ 37.1	
♂ 22.5	
♃ 18.5	
♄ 18.5	
♇ 14.6	
♅ 11.3	
♇ 32.4	
☊ 2.2	

Personality

☉ 35.2	SUN GATE
⊕ 5.2	EARTH GATE
☊ 31.1	
☋ 41.1	
☽ 12.6	
☿ 15.6	
♀ 12.6	
♂ 8.5	
♃ 46.3	
♄ 46.6	
♇ 14.4	
♅ 11.2	
♇ 32.2	
☊ 23.1	

@KARENCURRYPARKER

#QUANTUMHUMANDESIGN

The Incarnation Cross does NOT give specific details about your employment or career path. You can fulfill your Incarnation Cross no matter what work you do.

The Incarnation Cross gives specific details that tell you what you're here to give the world and what you need to have in place to feel stable and supported in the fulfillment of your gifts.

The most important position in the Cross to explore is the Conscious Sun. Every element in the entire chart is expressed through the theme of the Conscious Sun. Even if you only tell clients you are working with about the position of their Conscious Sun, they will know a lot more about who they are and what they're here to do.

The Unconscious Sun is also vital but often feels more hidden or elusive compared to the Conscious Sun. When the theme of the Unconscious Sun is not fulfilled, it can feel like pressure or an unspoken, hidden desire that pushes to emerge.

The Earth positions both represent what it is you need to feel grounded and what you need to receive in the way of support to fulfill the highest expression of the Sun Gates in the Cross. You can often look to the Earth Gates to find vital information to stimulate motivation and drive if someone is struggling. The Earth Gates represent a code that can often heal the feminine nature of a client and can help reveal what needs to be restored in order to improve lovability and self-worth.

The fulfillment of the purpose of the Incarnation Cross happens in combination with the deconditioning process. The more a person de-conditions, the easier it is for them to create a life that fulfills the intention of the Incarnation Cross.

The Relationship between the Incarnation Cross Variations and the Quarters

There are 192 basic Incarnation Crosses. Many Crosses have multiple variations indicated by the small number following the name of the Cross. This number indicates which quarter the variation of the Cross occurs in. The variation and the consequent theme of the quarter it appears in influences how the theme of the Cross is experienced but, the purpose of the base Cross stays the same. Because of this, you will see that Crosses with variations will have the same description.

For example, the Incarnation Cross of Contagion has four variations. A variation of the Cross occurs during each of the four Creative Quarters. The Incarnation Cross of Contagion 3 occurs during the third Creative Quarter. This gives the Incarnation Cross of Contagion 3 the added dimension of spreading ideas that increase collaboration and align with the right timing to implement these ideas, the themes of quarter three, the Quarter of Manifestation.

If you want to go into greater detail with a client and explore the theme of the Cross, look at the Conscious Sun position. (Remember, to express the highest potential of the Incarnation Cross, a certain degree of deconditioning has to happen.)

There are three different types of Crosses for each Conscious Sun/Earth combination: the Right Angle Cross, the Juxtaposition Cross, and the Left Angle Cross. These Cross types are determined by the Profile. Right Angle Crosses always have Right Angle Profiles. Juxtaposition Crosses are always Juxtaposition Profiles. Left Angle Crosses always have Left Angle Profiles.

Right Angle Incarnation Crosses model and help others by sharing their own experiences and inner process. Juxtaposition Incarnation Crosses bring information and a depth of expression of their Cross, that they learn from studying and carefully exploring their theme over the course of their life. Left Angles Incarnation Crosses are here to lead, teach and inspire and have a purpose of living out the theme of the Cross through leadership and relationships.

Right Angle Crosses have a different Unconscious Sun/Earth combination than the Juxtaposition and Left Angle Cross with the same Conscious Sun and Earth. Juxtaposition and Left Angle Crosses in the same Conscious Sun and Earth theme have the same Gates but are expressed differently because the Profile is different.

The Incarnation Crosses

RAX Quantum Alignment 4
Conscious Sun Gate: 1
Conscious Earth Gate: 2
Unconscious Sun Gate: 7
Unconscious Earth Gate: 13

Traditional HD IC Name: Right Angle Cross of The Sphinx 4
Quantum HD IC Name: Right Angle Cross of Quantum Alignment 4

Quantum Description:

To model and help others live aligned with their authentic purpose in a relentlessly authentic way. To teach and model leadership that comes from the Heart. To help heal others by reconnecting them to their inherent value and remembering their worth, and to teach them how to reframe and take back control of their personal narrative so that they are open and receptive to all the good and support that the Universe has in store for them. To use your life experience to show others the way.

Resiliency Keys:

Lovability, Decisiveness, Courage, Authenticity

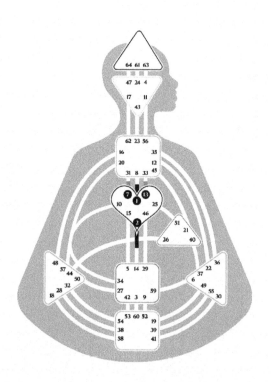

Traditional HD IC Name: Juxtaposition Cross of Self-Expression
Quantum HD IC Name: Juxtaposition Cross of The Way Shower

Quantum Description:

To model and help others live aligned with their authentic purpose in a relentlessly authentic way. To help people find the depth of information necessary for them to discover revolutionary and catalytic answers that help them heal their self-worth so that they can be open and receptive to all the good and support that the Universe has in store for them. To have a depth of knowledge and understanding about living aligned with purpose that you share with others.

Resiliency Keys:

Lovability, Decisiveness, Courage, Authenticity, Self-Trust, Emotional Wisdom, Empowerment

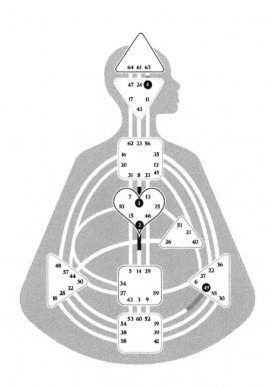

LAX The Creative Catalyst 2
Conscious Sun Gate: 1
Conscious Earth Gate: 2
Unconscious Sun Gate: 4
Unconscious Earth Gate: 49

Traditional HD IC Name: Left Angle Cross of Defiance 2
Quantum HD IC Name: Left Angle Cross of The Creative Catalyst 2

Quantum Description:

To model and help others live aligned with their authentic purpose in a relentlessly authentic way. To see the potential in others and to teach and lead them by giving them revolutionary answers that transform and heal their self-worth so that they can be open and receptive to all the good and support that the Universe has in store for them. To teach, lead and embody ways to live in alignment with your authentic purpose.

Resiliency Keys:

Lovability, Decisiveness, Courage, Authenticity, Self-Trust, Emotional Wisdom, Empowerment

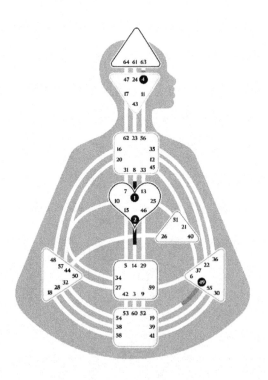

Traditional HD IC Name: Right Angle Cross of The Sphinx 2

Quantum HD IC Name: Right Angle Cross of Quantum Alignment 2

Quantum Description:

To model and help others live aligned with their authentic purpose in a relentlessly authentic way. To teach and model leadership that comes from the Heart. To help heal others by reconnecting them to their inherent value and remembering their worth, and to teach them how to reframe and take back control of their personal narrative so that they are open and receptive to all the good and support that the Universe has in store for them. To use your life experience to show others the way.

Resiliency Keys:

Lovability, Decisiveness, Courage, Authenticity

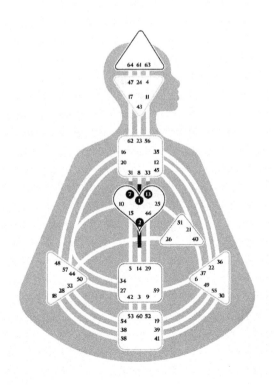

JUX Allowing
Conscious Sun Gate: 2
Conscious Earth Gate: 1
Unconscious Sun Gate: 49
Unconscious Earth Gate: 4

Traditional HD IC Name: Juxtaposition Cross of The Driver
Quantum HD IC Name: Juxtaposition Cross of Allowing

Quantum Description:

To model and help others live aligned with their authentic purpose and in a relentlessly authentic way. To teach and model leadership that comes from the Heart. To help heal others by reconnecting them to their inherent value and remembering their worth, teaching them how to reframe and take back control of their personal narrative so that they are open and receptive to all the good and support that the Universe has in store for them. To help others remember the generous nature of the Universe and how to be receptive to the support necessary to fulfill your true purpose. To use your life experience to show others the way. To build a foundation of understanding about living aligned with purpose to share with others.

Resiliency Keys:

Lovability, Decisiveness, Courage, Authenticity, Self-Trust, Emotional Wisdom, Empowerment

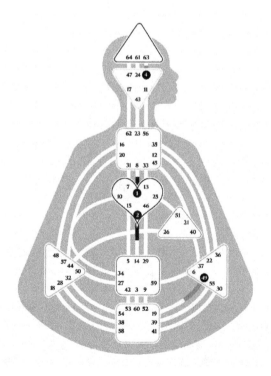

Traditional HD IC Name: Left Angle Cross of Defiance
Quantum HD IC Name: Left Angle Cross of The Creative Catalyst

Quantum Description:

To model and help others live aligned with their authentic purpose in a relentlessly authentic way. To see the potential in others and to teach and lead them by giving them revolutionary answers that transform and heal their self-worth so that they can be open and receptive to all the good and support that the Universe has in store for them. To teach, lead and embody ways to live in alignment with your authentic purpose.

Resiliency Keys:

Lovability, Decisiveness, Courage, Authenticity, Self-Trust, Emotional Wisdom, Empowerment

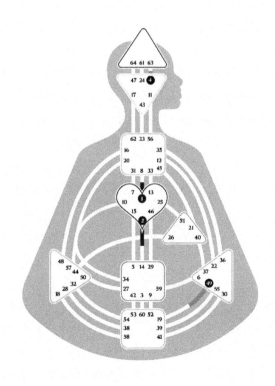

RAX Evolution
Conscious Sun Gate: 3
Conscious Earth Gate: 50
Unconscious Sun Gate: 60
Unconscious Earth Gate: 56

Traditional HD IC Name: Right Angle Cross of Laws
Quantum HD IC Name: Right Angle Cross of Evolution

Quantum Description:

To bring innovation and new possibilities to the world by using gratitude to expand on what already works. To learn to use the power of narrative, metaphor, and storytelling to transform the story of what is possible and to shift the collective definition of value. To bring innovative ideas to the world that increase our ability to support, nurture, feed, and care for each other.

Resiliency Keys:

Vitality, Decisiveness, Courage, Empowerment, Self-Trust, Authenticity

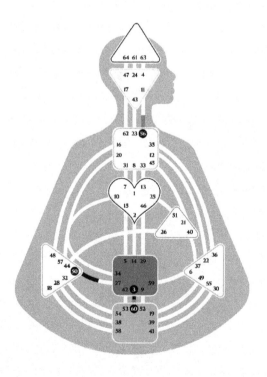

Traditional HD IC Name: Juxtaposition Cross of Mutation

Quantum HD IC Name: Juxtaposition Cross of Momentum

Quantum Description:

To build a foundation of creativity that harnesses the power of imagination to create innovation. To establish practices that foster creativity and the integration of new values. To lead others in integrating innovative ideas, creative possibilities and establishing new laws and values that support growth and transformation.

Resiliency Keys:

Vitality, Decisiveness, Courage, Empowerment, Self-Trust, Emotional Wisdom, Authenticity

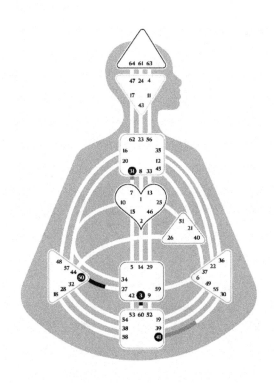

LAX Transformation
Conscious Sun Gate: 3
Conscious Earth Gate: 50
Unconscious Sun Gate: 41
Unconscious Earth Gate: 31

Traditional HD IC Name: Left Angle Cross of Wishes
Quantum HD IC Name: Left Angle Cross of Transformation

Quantum Description:

To lead, teach, and inspire others in adopting and adapting to new values that include the importance and the power of creativity and imagination as keystones to innovation. To lead others in integrating innovative ideas and creative possibilities. To begin establishing new laws and values that support growth and transformation. To usher in innovation and new ideas by establishing the value of creativity and imagination in the collective.

Resiliency Keys:

Vitality, Decisiveness, Courage, Empowerment, Self-Trust, Emotional Wisdom, Authenticity

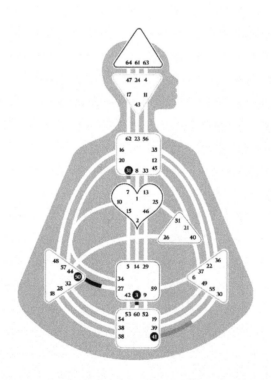

Traditional HD IC Name: Right Angle Cross of Explanation 3
Quantum HD IC Name: Right Angle Cross of The Divine Translator 3

Quantum Description:

To share revolutionary ideas and possibilities that have the power to transform the way people think. To teach and transmit new ideas and possibilities that change the way people understand and perceive the world. To transform old ideas into new possibilities when the timing and the energy is aligned. To serve the world by sharing new ideas that awaken planetary consciousness.

Resiliency Keys:

Self-Trust, Decisiveness, Courage, Emotional Wisdom, Empowerment, Authenticity, Vitality

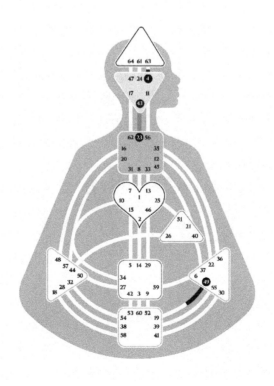

JUX Reframing
Conscious Sun Gate: 4
Conscious Earth Gate: 49
Unconscious Sun Gate: 8
Unconscious Earth Gate: 14

Traditional HD IC Name: Juxtaposition Cross of Formulization
Quantum HD IC Name: Juxtaposition Cross of Reframing

Quantum Description:

To build a foundation of knowledge that supports people in catalyzing transformation in the ways in which they work. To help people align with the answers that help them create greater abundance when they express their true and authentic voice. To change the economic landscape so that right work includes authentic self-expression. To help people break free from the idea that they have to compromise who they are to create abundance.

Resiliency Keys:

Self-Trust, Decisiveness, Courage, Emotional Wisdom, Empowerment, Authenticity, Vitality

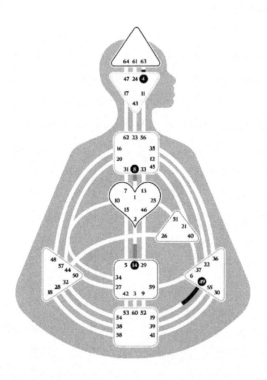

Traditional HD IC Name: Left Angle Cross of Revolution 2
Quantum HD IC Name: Left Angle Cross of Revelation 2

Quantum Description:

To lead, teach, and inspire people to catalyze transformation in their work. To help people align with the answers that help them create greater abundance when they express their true and authentic voice. To change the economic landscape, so that right work includes authentic self-expression. To help people break free from the idea that they have to compromise who they are to create abundance.

Resiliency Keys:

Self-Trust, Decisiveness, Courage, Emotional Wisdom, Empowerment, Authenticity, Vitality

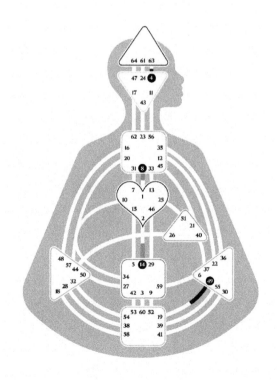

RAX The Quantum Pulse 4
Conscious Sun Gate: 5
Conscious Earth Gate: 35
Unconscious Sun Gate: 64
Unconscious Earth Gate: 63

Traditional HD IC Name: Right Angle Cross of Consciousness 4
Quantum HD IC Name: Right Angle Cross of The Quantum Pulse 4

Quantum Description:

To explore, experiment with, and experience the habits and rhythms necessary to implement new ideas and possibilities. To share and demonstrate the habits and consistency born of experience that set the stage for the exploration of new ideas. To embody and teach others how to be consistent and habitual. To teach from experience and to use your experience to know which new ideas to explore and experiment with. To lay the foundation of rhythm and consistency as the medium for exponential growth and compassionate expansion.

Resiliency Keys:

Vitality, Decisiveness, Courage, Empowerment, Authenticity, Self-Trust

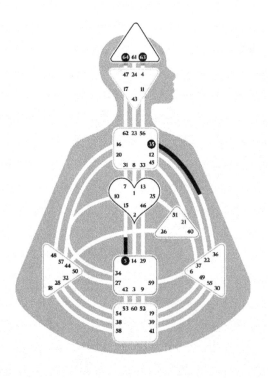

Traditional HD IC Name: Juxtaposition Cross of Habits
Quantum HD IC Name: Juxtaposition Cross of Ordering

Quantum Description:

To embody and create a foundation of consistent habits and actions that support cultivating a healthy mindset and deep alignment with a trusting relationship with Source and abundance. To model and hold the knowledge necessary to teach others the power and importance of a healthy mindset in creating abundance and finding elegant solutions to challenges.

Resiliency Keys:

Vitality, Decisiveness, Courage, Empowerment, Authenticity, Self-Trust, Emotional Wisdom

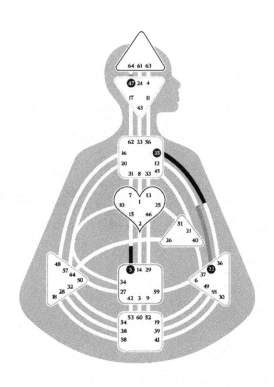

LAX Coherence 2
Conscious Sun Gate: 5
Conscious Earth Gate: 35
Unconscious Sun Gate: 47
Unconscious Earth Gate: 22

Traditional HD IC Name: Left Angle Cross of Separation 2
Quantum HD IC Name: Left Angle Cross of Coherence 2

Quantum Description:

To lead, teach, and inspire others to build a deliberate and intentional practice that supports the maintenance and the ability to sustain a constructive and positive mindset. To understand the importance of mindset in creating transformational experiences that create breakthroughs in old patterns and habits of limitation and lack. To use your experience to help others learn how to build a daily practice that helps entrain Heart and action in a state of creative coherence. To use your experience to lead others to breakthroughs and transformation. To learn to harness the power of mindset to align with the grace necessary to break free from limiting patterns and habits.

Resiliency Keys:

Vitality, Decisiveness, Courage, Empowerment, Authenticity, Self-Trust, Emotional Wisdom

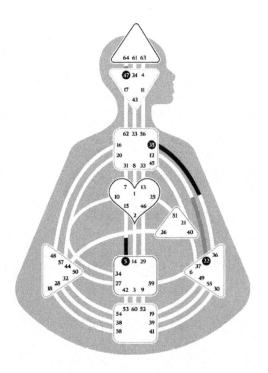

Traditional HD IC Name: Right Angle Cross of Eden 3
Quantum HD IC Name: Right Angle Cross of Miracles 3

Quantum Description:

To explore, experiment with, and experience the pursuit of pure inspiration. To have impact by implementing new ideas that have the power to shatter the patterns of the past and that stretch the edges of the human story. To explore new ideas by trying them out and then sharing the experience with others as a way of inspiring. To use the power of your Divine connection to break free from past limiting patterns. To create miracles and consciously harness the fulfillment of the unexpected by trusting in Source and following Divine Inspiration.

Resiliency Keys:

Courage, Emotional Wisdom, Empowerment, Decisiveness, Authenticity, Vitality, Self-Trust

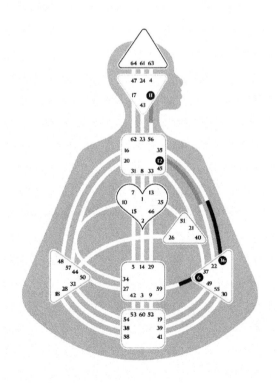

JUX Responsiveness
Conscious Sun Gate: 6
Conscious Earth Gate: 36
Unconscious Sun Gate: 15
Unconscious Earth Gate: 10

Traditional HD IC Name: Juxtaposition Cross of Conflict
Quantum HD IC Name: Juxtaposition Cross of Responsiveness

Quantum Description:

To embody and create a foundation of impact that allows you to help others break free from limiting patterns and habits that block self-love and compassion. To teach and share the knowledge necessary to liberate others from past patterns that keep them stuck or blocked. To heal and align the vibration of Love on the planet and to create and steer a new path that fully embodies the power and direction of Love.

Resiliency Keys:

Courage, Emotional Wisdom, Empowerment, Decisiveness, Lovability, Authenticity

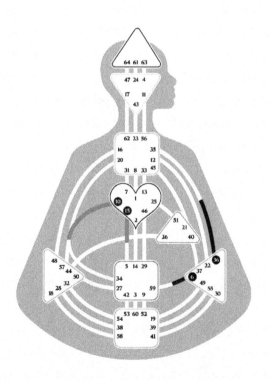

Traditional HD IC Name: Left Angle Cross of The Plane 2
Quantum HD IC Name: Left Angle Cross of Sustainability 2

Quantum Description:

To lead, teach, and inspire people by helping them break free from limiting patterns and habits that block self-love and compassion. To teach and share the knowledge necessary to liberate others from past patterns that keep them stuck or blocked. To heal and align the vibration of Love on the planet and to create and steer a new path that fully embodies the power and direction of Love. To shatter old patterns that bring the potential for collaboration and leadership that gives new direction to evolutionary ideas.

Resiliency Keys:

Courage, Emotional Wisdom, Empowerment, Decisiveness, Lovability, Authenticity

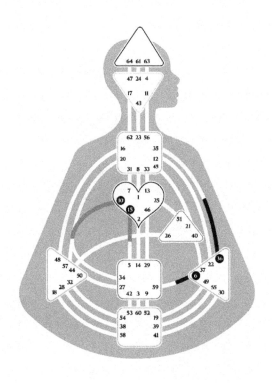

RAX Quantum Alignment 3
Conscious Sun Gate: 7
Conscious Earth Gate: 13
Unconscious Sun Gate: 2
Unconscious Earth Gate: 1

Traditional HD IC Name: Right Angle Cross of The Sphinx 3
Quantum HD IC Name: Right Angle Cross of Quantum Alignment 3

Quantum Description:

To model and help others live aligned with their authentic purpose in a relentlessly authentic way. To teach and model leadership that comes from the Heart. To help heal others by reconnecting them to their inherent value and remembering their worth, and to teach them how to reframe and take back control of their personal narrative so that they are open and receptive to all the good and support that the Universe has in store for them. To use your life experience to show others the way.

Resiliency Keys:

Lovability, Decisiveness, Courage, Authenticity

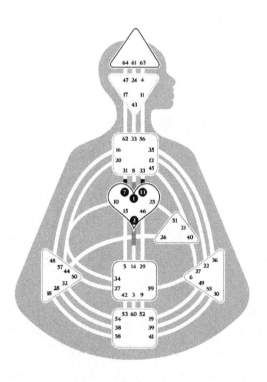

Traditional HD IC Name: Juxtaposition Cross of Interaction
Quantum HD IC Name: Juxtaposition Cross of Interpretation

Quantum Description:

To embody and create a foundation of leadership that is rooted in a transformative narrative that has the power to change the direction of humanity. To listen and bear witness to the stories of the past and to offer a new and transformational version of the story that embodies the theme of empowerment and sovereignty. To help others change their personal narrative by offering them new stories that better represent the truth of who they are. To change the world by helping the world change the narrative.

Resiliency Keys:

Lovability, Decisiveness, Courage Authenticity, Vitality, Self-Trust

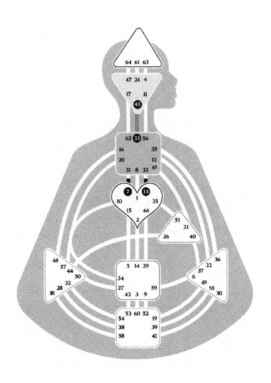

LAX The Narrative 2
Conscious Sun Gate: 7
Conscious Earth Gate: 13
Unconscious Sun Gate: 23
Unconscious Earth Gate: 43

Traditional HD IC Name: Left Angle Cross of Masks 2
Quantum HD IC Name: Left Angle Cross of The Narrative 2

Quantum Description:

To lead, teach, and inspire people by helping them redefine the themes of personal power and leadership. To help people tell a new story that is rooted in a transformative narrative that has the power to change the direction of humanity. To listen and bear witness to the stories of the past and to offer a new and transformational version of the story that embodies the theme of empowerment and sovereignty. To help others change their personal narrative by offering them new stories that better represent the truth of who they are. To change the world by helping the world change the narrative.

Resiliency Keys:

Lovability, Decisiveness, Courage, Authenticity, Vitality, Self-Trust

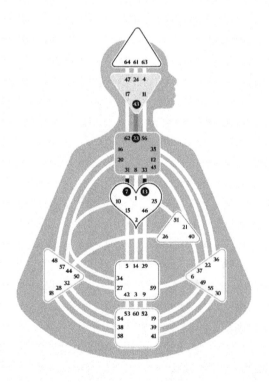

Traditional HD IC Name: Right Angle Cross of Contagion 2
Quantum HD IC Name: Right Angle Cross of Passion 2

Quantum Description:

To explore, learn about, and model the importance of living in alignment with purpose. To lead by understanding the importance and, ultimately, the fulfillment of creating in alignment with the Authentic Self. To have the courage to follow your Heart and to learn to trust and demonstrate that living true to who you are, creates abundance and flow. To show people how to live with passion and to use your passion to ignite the passion of others. To lead a relentlessly authentic life.

Resiliency Keys:

Authenticity, Vitality, Decisiveness, Courage, Empowerment, Emotional Wisdom

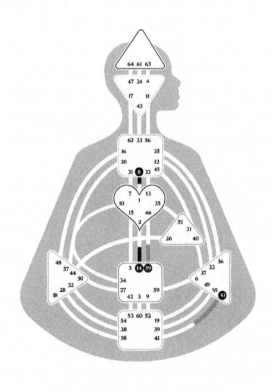

JUX Impact
Conscious Sun Gate: 8
Conscious Earth Gate: 14
Unconscious Sun Gate: 55
Unconscious Earth Gate: 59

Traditional HD IC Name: Juxtaposition Cross of Contribution

Quantum HD IC Name: Juxtaposition Cross of Impact

Quantum Description:

To embody and create a foundation for living a relentlessly authentic life. To cultivate the faith and trust that your unique contribution to the world is vital and worthy of support. To have faith in your own value and to relentlessly pursue the expression of your Authentic Self to the degree to which you trust—without a doubt—that you are fully supported. To show people how to be authentic without compromise.

Resiliency Keys:

Authenticity, Vitality, Decisiveness, Courage, Empowerment, Emotional Wisdom

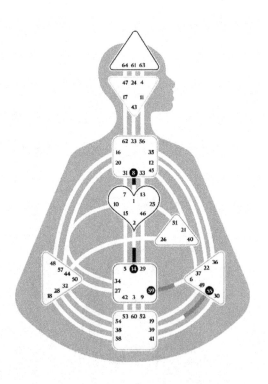

Traditional HD IC Name: Left Angle Cross of Uncertainty
Quantum HD IC Name: Left Angle Cross of Abundance

Quantum Description:

To lead, teach, and inspire people by creating a foundation for living a relentlessly authentic life. To cultivate the faith and trust that your unique contribution to the world is vital and worthy of support. To have faith in your own value and to relentlessly pursue the expression of your Authentic Self to the degree to which you trust—without a doubt—that you are fully supported. To show people how to be authentic without compromise.

Resiliency Keys:

Authenticity, Vitality, Decisiveness, Courage, Empowerment, Emotional Wisdom

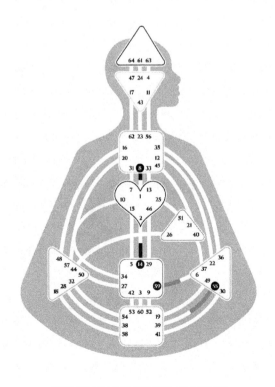

RAX Community 4
Conscious Sun Gate: 9
Conscious Earth Gate: 16
Unconscious Sun Gate: 40
Unconscious Earth Gate: 37

<hr>

Traditional HD IC Name: Right Angle Cross of Planning 4
Quantum HD IC Name: Right Angle Cross of Community 4

<hr>

Quantum Description:

To explore, learn about, and model the importance of focus, self-renewal, peace, and the willingness to try (even if the risk of failure is high) to create in a sustainable manner. To serve the world by helping people create healthy, agreements and contracts. To help people realize that the karma of self-worth must be healed and healthy for communities to build a sustainable future and a peaceful world.

Resiliency Keys:

Vitality, Decisiveness, Courage, Empowerment, Authenticity, Self-Worth, Emotional Wisdom

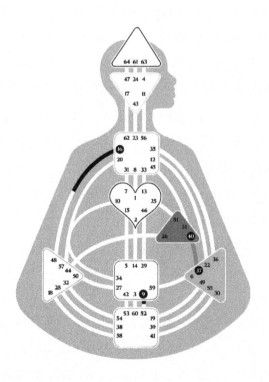

Traditional HD IC Name: Juxtaposition Cross of Focus
Quantum HD IC Name: Juxtaposition Cross of Confluence

Quantum Description:

To embody and create a foundation of intentional and focused enthusiasm for the sake of staying connected to the next new inspiration and idea that has the potential to transform the way we live. To consciously manage doubt and confusion by cultivating a mindset of curiosity and the willingness to explore whether an inspiration is worthy or not. To be willing, after research and deliberation, to explore new ideas for the sake of expansion. To inspire others to stretch and expand beyond their limitations.

Resiliency Keys:

Vitality, Decisiveness, Courage, Empowerment, Authenticity, Self-Trust

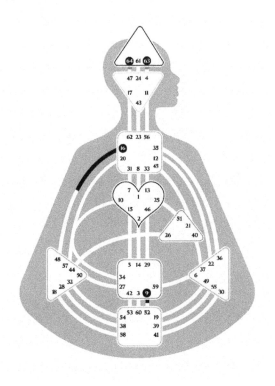

LAX Potential 2
Conscious Sun Gate: 9
Conscious Earth Gate: 16
Unconscious Sun Gate: 64
Unconscious Earth Gate: 63

Traditional HD IC Name: Left Angle Cross of Identification 2
Quantum HD IC Name: Left Angle Cross of Potential 2

Quantum Description:

To lead, teach, and inspire people to engage in exploration and experimentation and to resist doubt and confusion. To help people expand their thinking and their consciousness. To help people to be open-minded and inspired. To stay open-minded and inspired, and willing to explore new ideas with focused enthusiasm. To inspire others to experiment with and explore new ideas to find elegant solutions to the challenges facing humanity today. To lead people in the willingness to try.

Resiliency Keys:

Vitality, Decisiveness, Courage, Empowerment, Authenticity, Self-Trust

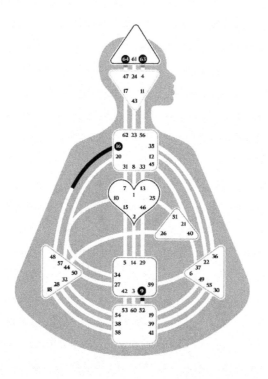

Traditional HD IC Name: Right Angle Cross of The Vessel of Love 4
Quantum HD IC Name: Right Angle Cross of Unity 4

Quantum Description:

To explore, learn about, and model the power of Love and the courage of the Heart. It is through the discipline of the Heart that one can lead others. To teach self-love, compassion, embodiment, and purpose by first learning, through personal experience, how to live and create from these energies. To become self-actualized and resilient by learning to love oneself and others. To know and teach that Love regulates how we lead, create and walk through our days. To embody and give direction to Love in every way.

Resiliency Keys:

Lovability, Decisiveness, Courage, Authenticity

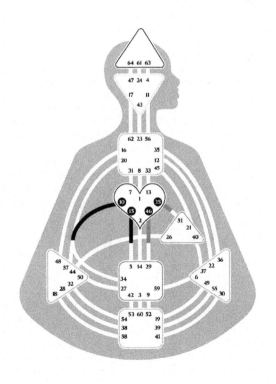

JUX Optimization
Conscious Sun Gate: 10
Conscious Earth Gate: 15
Unconscious Sun Gate: 18
Unconscious Earth Gate: 17

Traditional HD IC Name: Juxtaposition Cross of Behavior
Quantum HD IC Name: Juxtaposition Cross of Optimization

Quantum Description:

To embody and create a foundation of self-love and compassion. To help others by intuitively understanding the patterns that need to be shifted and aligned in order to help someone heal any limitations that may be keeping them from loving themselves and engaging in the world with compassion. To help others self-actualize by teaching them how to heal their hearts and cultivate resilience rooted in self-love and compassion.

Resiliency Keys:

Lovability, Decisiveness, Courage, Authenticity, Self-Trust

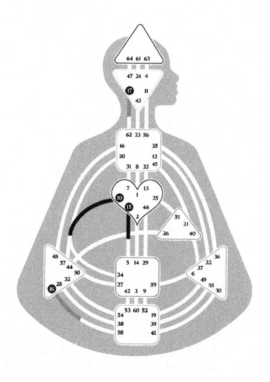

Traditional HD IC Name: Left Angle Cross of Prevention 2
Quantum HD IC Name: Left Angle Cross of Self-Actualization 2

Quantum Description:

To lead, teach, and inspire people to love themselves and to act with compassion. To see, embody and teach the potential of living with Heart. To show people the discipline of the Heart that can lead to greatness and resiliency. To help people connect to the courage of the Heart that is rooted in self-love and compassion. To show others the importance of being themselves by first loving yourself enough to be who you were born to be and then teaching others to do the same. To help people break free from the trauma of forgetting their lovability, courage, and conviction.

Resiliency Keys:

Lovability, Decisiveness, Courage, Authenticity, Self-Trust

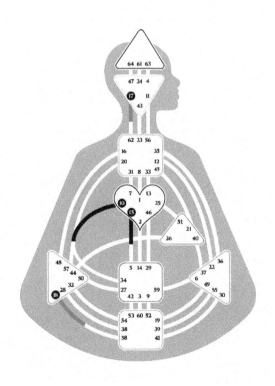

RAX Miracles 4
Conscious Sun Gate: 11
Conscious Earth Gate: 12
Unconscious Sun Gate: 6
Unconscious Earth Gate: 36

Traditional HD IC Name: Right Angle Cross of Eden 4
Quantum HD IC Name: Right Angle Cross of Miracles 4

Quantum Description:

To explore, experiment with, and experience the pursuit of pure inspiration. To have an impact by implementing new ideas that have the power to shatter the patterns of the past and that stretch the edges of the human story. To explore new ideas by trying them out and then sharing the experience with others as a means to inspire. To use the power of your Divine connection to break free from past limiting patterns. To create miracles and consciously harness the fulfillment of the unexpected by trusting in Source and following Divine Inspiration.

Resiliency Keys:

Decisiveness, Self-Trust, Authenticity, Vitality, Courage, Emotional Wisdom, Empowerment

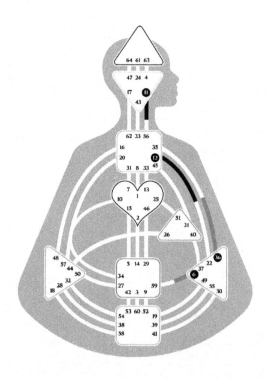

Traditional HD IC Name: Juxtaposition Cross of Ideas
Quantum HD IC Name: Juxtaposition Cross of The Multiverse

Quantum Description:

To be a spiritual teacher and leader and inspire people to fully embody their Divine connection to Source. To be the Divine Spark that initiates others into higher states of alignment with Source and greater states of alignment with wellbeing. To help others remember their natural state of divinity. To give people the ideas and inspirations necessary to remember their own Divine connection and to help them remove limitations, blocks, and habits that create cycles of pain in order to see new potentials and possibilities.

Resiliency Keys:

Self-Trust, Decisiveness, Authenticity, Vitality, Lovability, Courage

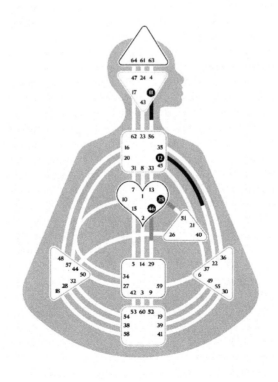

LAX Originality 2
Conscious Sun Gate: 11
Conscious Earth Gate: 12
Unconscious Sun Gate: 46
Unconscious Earth Gate: 25

Traditional HD IC Name: Left Angle Cross of Education 2
Quantum HD IC Name: Left Angle Cross of Originality 2

Quantum Description:

To be a spiritual teacher and leader and inspire people to fully embody their Divine connection to Source. To be the Divine Spark that initiates others into higher states of alignment with Source and greater states of alignment with wellbeing. To help others remember their natural state of divinity. To give people the ideas and inspirations necessary to remember their own Divine connection and to help them remove limitations, blocks, and habits that create cycles of pain in order to see new potentials and possibilities.

Resiliency Keys:

Self-Trust, Decisiveness, Authenticity, Vitality, Lovability, Courage

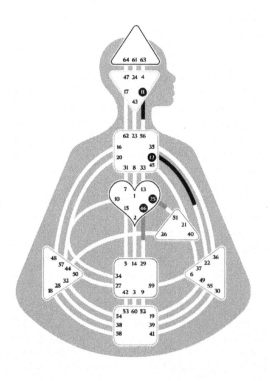

Traditional HD IC Name: Right Angle Cross of Eden 2
Quantum HD IC Name: Right Angle Cross of Miracles 2

Quantum Description:

To explore, experiment with, and experience the pursuit of pure inspiration. To have an impact by implementing new ideas that have the power to shatter the patterns of the past and that stretch the edges of the human story. To explore new ideas by trying them out and then sharing the experience with others as a way of inspiring. To use the power of your Divine connection to break free from past limiting patterns. To create miracles and consciously harness the fulfillment of the unexpected by trusting in Source and following Divine Inspiration.

Resiliency Keys:

Courage, Emotional Wisdom, Empowerment, Decisiveness, Authenticity, Vitality, Self-Trust

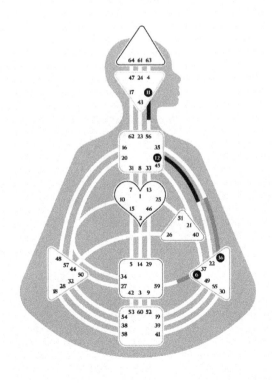

JUX Received Wisdom
Conscious Sun Gate: 12
Conscious Earth Gate: 11
Unconscious Sun Gate: 25
Unconscious Earth Gate: 46

<hr>

Traditional HD IC Name: Juxtaposition Cross of Articulation
Quantum HD IC Name: Juxtaposition Cross of Received Wisdom

<hr>

Quantum Description:

To embody and create a foundation for the embodiment of Spirit. To have the power to share words and ideas that are directly inspired by your spiritual connection. These words offer the power to heal and align others. To live in the flow of Spirit and Divine Timing. To be a channel for Divine Wisdom. To know exactly which words and ideas to share with others in the name of healing and aligning people with a deeper spiritual connection and truth.

Resiliency Keys:

Self-Trust, Decisiveness, Authenticity, Vitality, Lovability, Courage

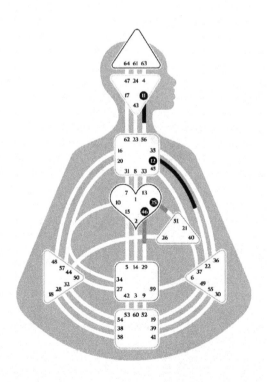

Traditional HD IC Name: Left Angle Cross of Education
Quantum HD IC Name: Left Angle Cross of Originality

Quantum Description:

To be a spiritual teacher and leader and inspire people to fully embody their Divine connection to Source. To be the Divine Spark that initiates others into higher states of alignment with Source and greater states of alignment with wellbeing. To help others remember their natural state of divinity. To give people the ideas and inspirations necessary to remember their own Divine connection and to help them remove limitations, blocks, and habits that create cycles of pain in order to see new potentials and possibilities.

Resiliency Keys:

Self-Trust, Decisiveness, Authenticity, Vitality, Lovability, Courage

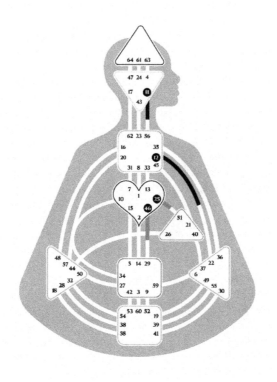

RAX Quantum Alignment
Conscious Sun Gate: 13
Conscious Earth Gate: 7
Unconscious Sun Gate: 1
Unconscious Earth Gate: 2

Traditional HD IC Name: Right Angle Cross of The Sphinx

Quantum HD IC Name: Right Angle Cross of Quantum Alignment

Quantum Description:

To model and help others live aligned with their authentic purpose in a relentlessly authentic way. To teach and model leadership that comes from the Heart. To help heal others by reconnecting them to their inherent value and remembering their worth, and to teach them how to reframe and take back control of their personal narrative so that they are open and receptive to all the good and support that the Universe has in store for them. To use your life experience to show others the way.

Resiliency Keys:

Lovability, Decisiveness, Courage, Authenticity

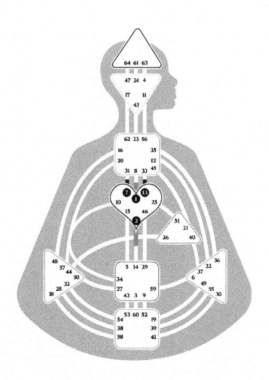

Traditional HD IC Name: Juxtaposition Cross of Listening
Quantum HD IC Name: Juxtaposition Cross of The Chronicle

Quantum Description:

To embody and create a foundation for bearing witness to the stories of others. Listening deeply to personal narratives and offering a mindset-shift so they can take back sovereignty and control by reframing their story and identity. Collaborating and sharing information creates mindset shifts that change the story of what we think is possible. To know the collective's stories and how to reframe the narrative to redefine what we think is possible.

Resiliency Keys:

Lovability, Decisiveness, Courage, Authenticity, Vitality, Self-Trust

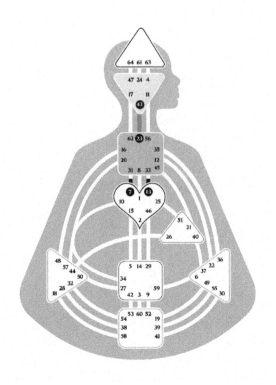

LAX The Narrative
Conscious Sun Gate: 13
Conscious Earth Gate: 7
Unconscious Sun Gate: 43
Unconscious Earth Gate: 23

Traditional HD IC Name: Left Angle Cross of Masks
Quantum HD IC Name: Left Angle Cross of The Narrative

Quantum Description:

To lead, teach, and inspire people by helping them redefine the themes of personal power and leadership. To help people tell a new story that is rooted in a transformative narrative that has the power to change the direction of humanity. To listen and bear witness to the stories of the past and to offer a new and transformational version of the story that embodies the theme of empowerment and sovereignty. To help others change their personal narrative by offering them new stories that better represent the truth of who they are. To change the world by helping the world change the narrative.

Resiliency Keys:

Lovability, Decisiveness, Courage, Authenticity, Vitality, Self-Trust

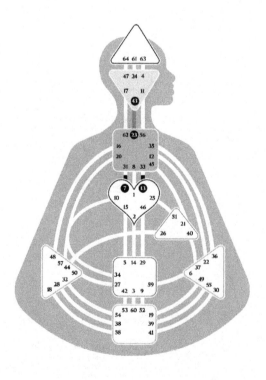

RAX Passion 4
Conscious Sun Gate: 14
Conscious Earth Gate: 8
Unconscious Sun Gate: 29
Unconscious Earth Gate: 30

Traditional HD IC Name: Right Angle Cross of Contagion 4
Quantum HD IC Name: Right Angle Cross of Passion 4

Quantum Description:

To explore, learn about, and model the importance of living in alignment with purpose. To lead by understanding the importance and, ultimately, the fulfillment of creating in alignment with the Authentic Self. To have the courage to follow your Heart and to learn to trust and demonstrate that living true to who you are creates abundance and flow. To show people how to live with passion and to use your passion to ignite the passion of others. To lead a life that is relentlessly authentic.

Resiliency Keys:

Authenticity, Vitality, Decisiveness, Courage, Empowerment, Emotional Wisdom

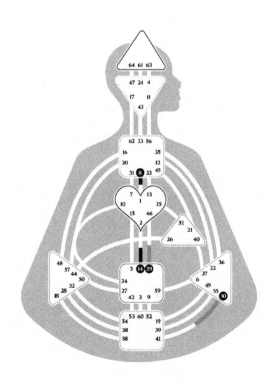

JUX Plentitude
Conscious Sun Gate: 14
Conscious Earth Gate: 8
Unconscious Sun Gate: 59
Unconscious Earth Gate: 55

Traditional HD IC Name: Juxtaposition Cross of Empowering
Quantum HD IC Name: Juxtaposition Cross of Plentitude

Quantum Description:

To embody and create a foundation of faith and purpose that aligns deeply with sustainable resources and support. To demonstrate to others the inextricable relationship between purpose and abundance. To cultivate a deep faith in abundance that supports you in taking great leaps of faith in the name of fulfilling your Heart and your purpose. To embody what living in deep alignment with your purpose looks and feels like. To assure others that the path to "enough" is through being relentlessly authentic.

Resiliency Keys:

Authenticity, Vitality, Decisiveness, Courage, Empowerment, Emotional Wisdom

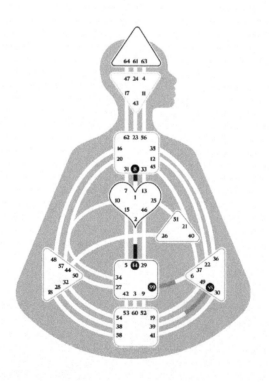

Traditional HD IC Name: Left Angle Cross of Uncertainty 2
Quantum HD IC Name: Left Angle Cross of Abundance 2

Quantum Description:

To lead, teach, and inspire people by creating a foundation for living a relentlessly authentic life. To cultivate the faith and trust that your unique contribution to the world is vital and worthy of support. To have faith in your own value and to relentlessly pursue the expression of your Authentic Self to the degree to which you trust—without a doubt—that you are fully supported. To show people how to be authentic without compromise.

Resiliency Keys:

Authenticity, Vitality, Decisiveness, Courage, Empowerment, Emotional Wisdom

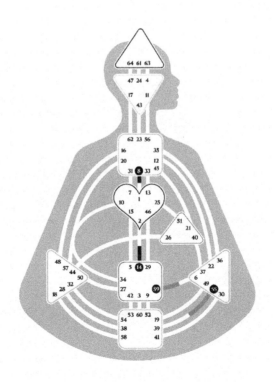

RAX Unity 2
Conscious Sun Gate: 15
Conscious Earth Gate: 10
Unconscious Sun Gate: 25
Unconscious Earth Gate: 46

Traditional HD IC Name: Right Angle Cross of The Vessel of Love 2
Quantum HD IC Name: Right Angle Cross of Unity 2

Quantum Description:

To explore, learn about, and model the power of Love and the courage of the Heart. It is through the discipline of the Heart that one can lead others. To teach self-love, compassion, embodiment, and purpose by first learning, through personal experience, how to live and create from these energies. To become self-actualized and resilient by learning to love oneself and others. To know and teach that Love regulates how we lead, create and walk through our days. To embody and give direction to Love in every way.

Resiliency Keys:

Lovability, Decisiveness, Courage, Authenticity

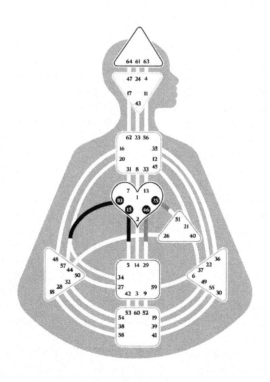

Traditional HD IC Name: Juxtaposition Cross of Extremes

Quantum HD IC Name: Juxtaposition Cross of Compassion

Quantum Description:

To embody and create a foundation of self-love and compassion. To fully overcome the shadow of self-judgment and self-criticism to discover that every incremental step is taking you to the fulfillment of your potential. To help others correct limiting patterns and beliefs that keep them from experiencing self-love and compassion. To intuitively understand patterns that create limitations and to help people break free from limiting patterns and habits. To open people up to the possibility of creating new patterns and habits that are expansive and loving.

Resiliency Keys:

Lovability, Decisiveness, Courage, Authenticity, Self-Trust, Courage

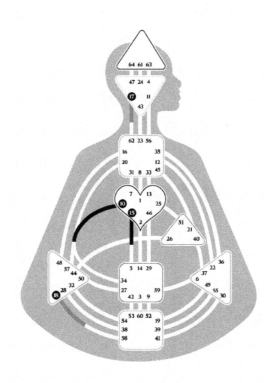

LAX Self-Actualization
Conscious Sun Gate: 15
Conscious Earth Gate: 10
Unconscious Sun Gate: 17
Unconscious Earth Gate: 18

Traditional HD IC Name: Left Angle Cross of Prevention
Quantum HD IC Name: Left Angle Cross of Self-Actualization

Quantum Description:

To lead, teach, and inspire people to love themselves and to act with compassion. To see, embody and teach the potential of living with Heart. To show people the discipline of the Heart that can lead to greatness and resiliency. To help people connect to the Heart's courage rooted in self-love and compassion. To show others the importance of being themselves by first loving yourself enough to be who you were born to be and then teaching others to do the same. To help people break free from the trauma of forgetting their lovability, courage, and conviction.

Resiliency Keys:

Lovability, Decisiveness, Courage, Authenticity, Self-Trust

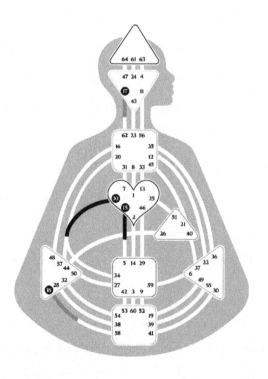

Traditional HD IC Name: Right Angle Cross of Planning 2
Quantum HD IC Name: Right Angle Cross of Community 2

Quantum Description:

To explore, learn about, and model the importance of focus, self-renewal, peace, and the willingness to try (even if the risk of failure is high) to create in a sustainable manner. To serve the world by helping people create healthy, agreements and contracts. To help people realize that the karma of self-worth must be healed and healthy for communities to build a sustainable future and a peaceful world.

Resiliency Keys:

Vitality, Decisiveness, Courage, Empowerment, Authenticity, Self-Worth, Emotional Wisdom

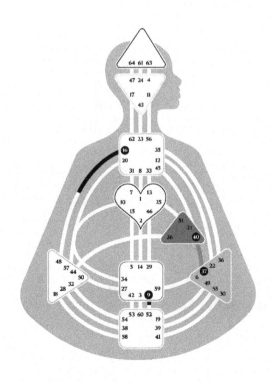

JUX Zest
Conscious Sun Gate: 16
Conscious Earth Gate: 9
Unconscious Sun Gate: 63
Unconscious Earth Gate: 64

Traditional HD IC Name: Juxtaposition Cross of Experimentation
Quantum HD IC Name: Juxtaposition Cross of Zest

Quantum Description:

The ability to take a big step back and see the big picture to understand that the corrections and alignments necessary in the moment, are essential to cultivating joy and exaltation. To discover what brings the greatest joy and to pursue its purest expression. To realize and demonstrate that this pursuit is a worthy contribution. To practice and perfect contributing to the world, in a way that brings the greatest joy. To teach the importance of joy.

Resiliency Keys:

Vitality, Decisiveness, Courage, Empowerment, Authenticity, Self-Trust

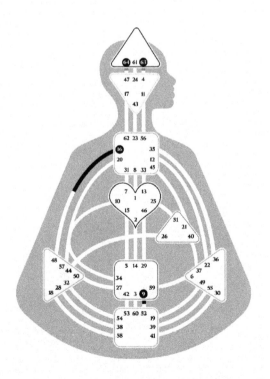

Traditional HD IC Name: Left Angle Cross of Identification
Quantum HD IC Name: Left Angle Cross of Potential

Quantum Description:

To lead, teach, and inspire people to engage in exploration and experimentation and to resist doubt and confusion. To help people expand their thinking and their consciousness. To help people to be open-minded and inspired. To stay open-minded and inspired, and willing to explore new ideas with focused enthusiasm. To inspire others to experiment with and explore new ideas to find elegant solutions to the challenges facing humanity today. To lead people in the willingness to try.

Resiliency Keys:

Vitality, Decisiveness, Courage, Empowerment, Authenticity, Self-Trust

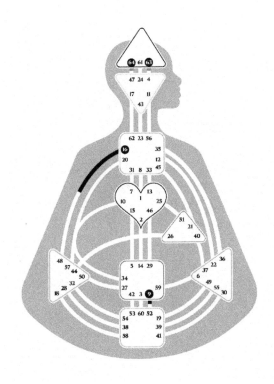

RAX Exaltation
Conscious Sun Gate: 17
Conscious Earth Gate: 18
Unconscious Sun Gate: 58
Unconscious Earth Gate: 52

Traditional HD IC Name: Right Angle Cross of Service
Quantum HD IC Name: Right Angle Cross of Exaltation

Quantum Description:

To explore, learn, and teach about the importance of perspective as a key element to cultivating self-actualization. The ability to take a big step back and see the big picture to understand that the corrections and alignments necessary in the moment are essential to cultivating joy and exaltation. To discover what brings the greatest joy and to pursue its purest expression. To realize and demonstrate that this pursuit is a worthy contribution. To practice and perfect contributing to the world, in a way that brings the greatest joy. To teach the importance of joy.

Resiliency Keys:

Self-Trust, Courage, Decisiveness, Vitality, Empowerment

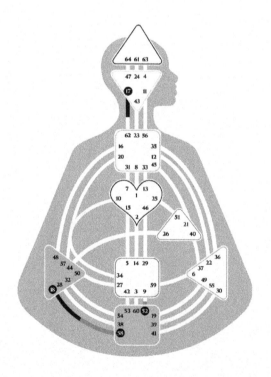

Traditional HD IC Name: Juxtaposition Cross of Opinions
Quantum HD IC Name: Juxtaposition Cross of Hope

Quantum Description:

To embody and create a foundation of hope built on understanding what patterns need to shift and change to make dreams a reality. To build the foundation of big dreams by knowing exactly what needs to shift to create expansion and which patterns and habits need to change to bring forth new and greater possibilities. To transform challenge and struggle into a wiser perspective that harnesses the wisdom of knowing what is worth fighting and struggling for, and understanding which patterns and habits need to shift and change to manifest the dream and its highest potential.

Resiliency Keys:

Self-Trust, Courage, Decisiveness, Vitality, Empowerment

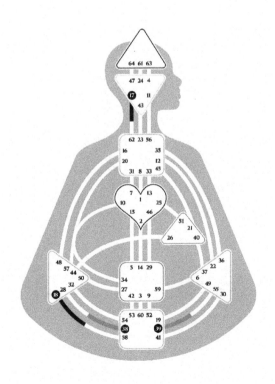

LAX Anticipation
Conscious Sun Gate: 17
Conscious Earth Gate: 18
Unconscious Sun Gate: 38
Unconscious Earth Gate: 39

Traditional HD IC Name: Left Angle Cross of Upheaval
Quantum HD IC Name: Left Angle Cross of Anticipation

Quantum Description:

To lead, teach, and inspire others to pursue their dreams and hopes. To share new possibilities and potentials that enable others to release limiting patterns and habits that keep people from dreaming large and allowing the full potential and expression of their abundance. To provoke and challenge limitations that keep people from fulfilling their dreams. To help others explore their limitations and, through practice and repetition, break free from old patterns and habits that keep people from fulfilling the full potential of their dreams.

Resiliency Keys:

Self-Trust, Courage, Decisiveness, Vitality, Empowerment

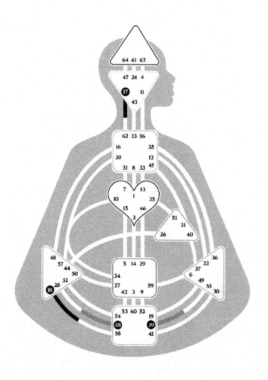

Traditional HD IC Name: Right Angle Cross of Service 3
Quantum HD IC Name: Right Angle Cross of Exaltation 3

Quantum Description:

To explore, learn, and teach about the importance of perspective as a key element to cultivating self-actualization. The ability to take a big step back and see the big picture to understand that the corrections and alignments necessary in the moment are essential to cultivating joy and exaltation. To discover what brings the greatest joy and to pursue its purest expression. To realize and demonstrate that this pursuit is a worthy contribution. To practice and perfect contributing to the world, in a way that brings the greatest joy. To teach the importance of joy.

Resiliency Keys:

Self-Trust, Courage, Decisiveness, Vitality, Empowerment

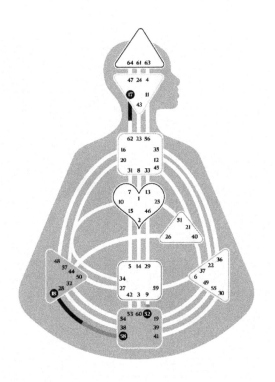

JUX Improvement
Conscious Sun Gate: 18
Conscious Earth Gate: 17
Unconscious Sun Gate: 39
Unconscious Earth Gate: 38

Traditional HD IC Name: Juxtaposition Cross of Correction
Quantum HD IC Name: Juxtaposition Cross of Improvement

Quantum Description:

To embody and create a foundation of hope built on understanding what patterns need to shift and change to make dreams a reality. To build the foundation of big dreams by knowing exactly what needs to shift to create expansion and which patterns and habits need to change to bring forth new and greater possibilities. To transform challenge and struggle into a wiser perspective that harnesses the wisdom of knowing what is worth fighting and struggling for and understanding which patterns and habits need to shift and change to manifest the dream and its highest potential.

Resiliency Keys:

Self-Trust, Courage, Decisiveness, Vitality, Empowerment

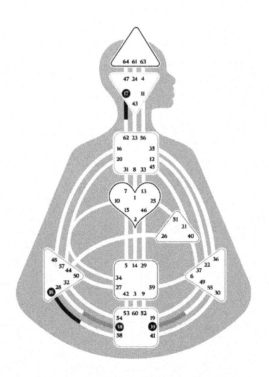

Traditional HD IC Name: Left Angle Cross of Upheaval 2
Quantum HD IC Name: Left Angle Cross of Anticipation 2

Quantum Description:

To lead, teach, and inspire others to pursue their dreams and hopes. To share new possibilities and potentials that enable others to release limiting patterns and habits that keep people from dreaming large and allowing the full potential and expression of their abundance. To provoke and challenge limitations that keep people from fulfilling their dreams. To help others explore their limitations and, through practice and repetition, break free from old patterns and habits that keep people from fulfilling the full potential of their dreams.

Resiliency Keys:

Self-Trust, Courage, Decisiveness, Vitality, Empowerment

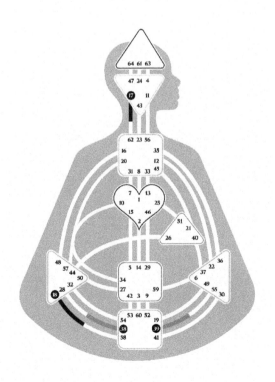

RAX Restoration 4
Conscious Sun Gate: 19
Conscious Earth Gate: 33
Unconscious Sun Gate: 44
Unconscious Earth Gate: 24

Traditional HD IC Name: Right Angle Cross of The Four Ways 4
Quantum HD IC Name: Right Angle Cross of Restoration 4

Quantum Description:

To explore, learn, and teach about the power and importance of narrative and story to set the tone and direction for life. To help others see patterns in old stories that may be causing them to rationalize and settle for less than what they deserve in their relationships. To use your natural sensitivity and intuition to be aware of where others may be settling and rationalize settling for less than what they want. To see the potential in others and to know how to change stories and narratives to support the fulfillment of potential. To help people stop playing small. To help others release the patterns and the pain of the past so they can better claim their true value and worth.

Resiliency Keys:

Vitality, Empowerment, Authenticity, Self-Trust, Courage, Decisiveness

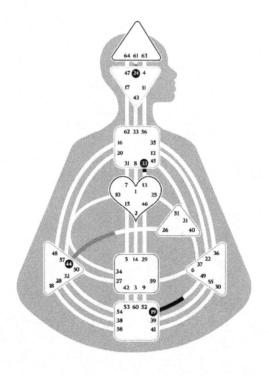

Traditional HD IC Name: Juxtaposition Cross of Need
Quantum HD IC Name: Juxtaposition Cross of Attunement

Quantum Description:

To embody and create a foundation of intimacy. Learning to use narrative power to reclaim and create authentic self-expression that facilitates true connection, community, and partnership. To teach and embody the importance of being relentlessly authentic as the only true path to intimacy. Use your intuitive attunement and awareness to see the potential in partnerships and community agreements and help others find ways to cultivate authentic and true intimacy in relationships.

Resiliency Keys:

Vitality, Empowerment, Authenticity, Lovability, Decisiveness, Courage

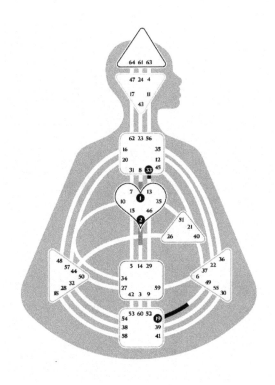

LAX Clarification 2
Conscious Sun Gate: 19
Conscious Earth Gate: 33
Unconscious Sun Gate: 1
Unconscious Earth Gate: 2

Traditional HD IC Name: Left Angle Cross of Refinement 2
Quantum HD IC Name: Left Angle Cross of Clarification 2

Quantum Description:

To lead, teach, and inspire others to be relentlessly authentic with their self-expression. To help others realize that the path to true intimacy and sustainable partnership and community can only be achieved when all parties are being authentic and on purpose. To help people realize their true potential for support and community by helping them rewrite their old relationship stories and expectations so that their new personal narrative and expectations about relationships reflect their value and their values. To redefine old perspectives on compromise, community, and relationships by demonstrating that there is always a win-win solution.

Resiliency Keys:

Vitality, Empowerment, Authenticity, Lovability, Decisiveness, Courage

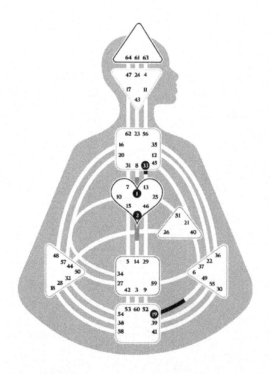

Traditional HD IC Name: Right Angle Cross of The Sleeping Phoenix 2
Quantum HD IC Name: Right Angle Cross of The Harbinger 2

Quantum Description:

To explore, learn, and teach about the true nature of power. To embody aligning yourself with Divine Timing in order to gather people around new ideas that have the potential to create sustainability. To create beyond what you know how to create by cultivating deep faith and trust in abundance. To use faith as a way of seeding the Quantum Field. To know how to read the signs and engage with the world in such a way that you know when it's time to respond to what's needed to create abundance for all. To organize people around new ideas and convictions that support the work and creation necessary to help people create sustainable, abundant resources and peace.

Resiliency Keys:

Authenticity, Decisiveness, Courage, Vitality, Empowerment, Emotional Wisdom

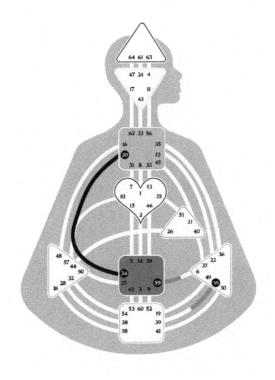

JUX The Epoch
Conscious Sun Gate: 20
Conscious Earth Gate: 34
Unconscious Sun Gate: 37
Unconscious Earth Gate: 40

Traditional HD IC Name: Juxtaposition Cross of The Now
Quantum HD IC Name: Juxtaposition Cross of The Epoch

Quantum Description:

To embody and create a foundation for creating empowered community agreements. To recognize that authentic community agreements and the benevolent use of power must be rooted in healthy self-worth, or else all expressions of community and power will be unsustainable and potentially lacking in peace. To build peaceful agreements rooted in a healthy understanding of the inherent value of life. To take leadership in building healthy, sustainable community agreements by teaching self-empowerment, authentic self-expression, and trusting in the capacity for win-win resolutions. To transform our collective definition of community by teaching the importance of empowerment for all community members.

Resiliency Keys:

Authenticity, Decisiveness, Courage, Vitality, Empowerment, Emotional Wisdom, Self-Worth

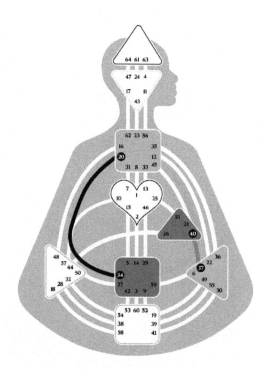

Traditional HD IC Name: Left Angle Cross of Duality

Quantum HD IC Name: Left Angle Cross of The Shift

Quantum Description:

To lead, teach and empower others by redefining the meaning of community. To build sustainable, equitable, and empowered communities and to support communities in building agreements that create and embody sustainability. To help others see that true community is rooted in authentic self-expression and that healthy communities must be composed of community members that feel empowered and have sovereignty over the community agreements. To recognize that communities cannot be sustainable without a deep understanding of the inherent value of each community member. To redefine community agreements to make them more equitable and sustainable.

Resiliency Keys:

Authenticity, Decisiveness, Courage, Vitality, Empowerment, Emotional Wisdom, Self-Worth

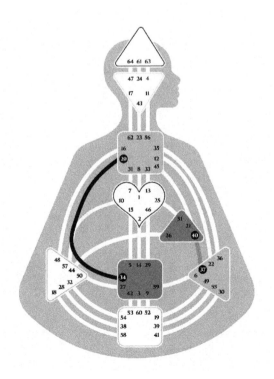

RAX Renewal
Conscious Sun Gate: 21
Conscious Earth Gate: 48
Unconscious Sun Gate: 38
Unconscious Earth Gate: 39

Traditional HD IC Name: Right Angle Cross of Tension
Quantum HD IC Name: Right Angle Cross of Renewal

Quantum Description:

To explore, learn, and teach from a depth of knowledge that comes from learning, studying, and investigating the importance and the power of self-regulation as a key element to accomplishing and fulfilling a dream. To instinctively know and understand what is out of alignment with abundance and to use your knowledge and wisdom to bring people back into harmony with the potential of support and sufficiency. To cultivate a vision of an abundant world, to practice self-regulation, and to study, learn and act upon exactly what needs to be done to fulfill that vision.

Resiliency Keys:

Self-Worth, Vitality, Empowerment, Self-Trust, Courage

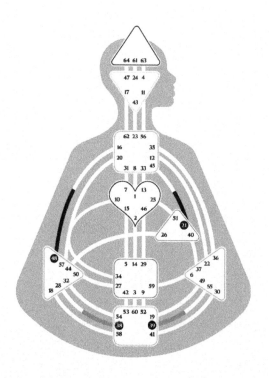

Traditional HD IC Name: Juxtaposition Cross of Control
Quantum HD IC Name: Juxtaposition Cross of Allocation

Quantum Description:

To embody and create a foundation of self-regulation rooted in a depth of knowledge and wisdom that comes from learning and studying. This depth of knowledge serves as a resource for sharing new ideas and potentials. To cultivate a deep spiritual practice of listening that sparks ideas that have the power to create new pathways to abundance. To be a source of new ideas that have the power to transform business, expand on the potential for abundance and make dreams come true.

Resiliency Keys:

Self-Worth, Vitality, Empowerment, Self-Trust, Courage

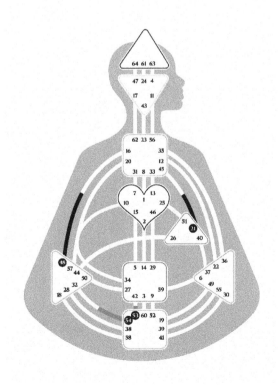

LAX Self-Regulation
Conscious Sun Gate: 21
Conscious Earth Gate: 48
Unconscious Sun Gate: 54
Unconscious Earth Gate: 53

Traditional HD IC Name: Left Angle Cross of Endeavor
Quantum HD IC Name: Left Angle Cross of Self-Regulation

Quantum Description:

To lead, teach, and inspire others to cultivate a practice of self-regulation that allows them to be inspired to follow new flows of abundance and inspiration. To create a depth of knowledge and wisdom from studying and learning that helps others manifest their dreams and do the work necessary to build new pathways of abundance. To model and teach the importance of patterns and habits that allow for conserving energy and creating sustainable wealth and wellbeing. To initiate others into healthy habits that help them create greater abundance and have access to more resources.

Resiliency Keys:

Self-Worth, Vitality, Empowerment, Self-Trust, Courage

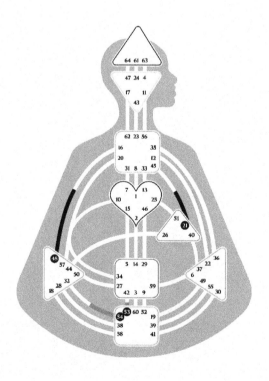

Traditional HD IC Name: Right Angle Cross of Rulership
Quantum HD IC Name: Right Angle Cross of Sovereignty

Quantum Description:

To explore, learn, and teach the importance of alignment and mindset in cultivating the energy necessary for creativity and manifestation. Understanding the relationship between self-worth, integrity, and mindset and teaching others how to regain sovereignty over their creations by healing any karma related to value and self-worth. To give people the resources they need to regain personal empowerment and control over their own lives and their own reality.

Resiliency Keys:

Courage, Emotional Wisdom, Empowerment, Decisiveness, Self-Trust, Authenticity, Vitality, Self-Worth

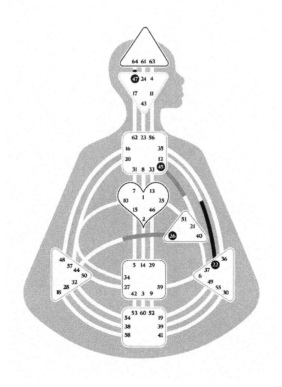

JUX Trust
Conscious Sun Gate: 22
Conscious Earth Gate: 47
Unconscious Sun Gate: 11
Unconscious Earth Gate: 12

Traditional HD IC Name: Juxtaposition Cross of Grace
Quantum HD IC Name: Juxtaposition Cross of Trust

Quantum Description:

To embody and create a foundation of understanding the relationship between mindset and creativity. To harness the power of mindset to nurture a deep connection to the flow of information, inspiration, and ideas. To be a source of ideas that enhance and inspire creativity in others. To be in the flow of receiving ideas and inspiration that contain the answers and instructions. To teach others the importance of mindset as an element of the creative process.

Resiliency Keys:

Self-Trust, Decisiveness, Courage, Emotional Wisdom, Empowerment, Authenticity, Vitality

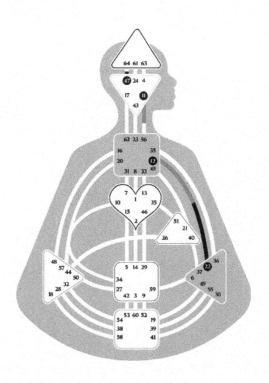

Traditional HD IC Name: Left Angle Cross of Informing

Quantum HD IC Name: Left Angle Cross of Metamorphosis

Quantum Description:

To lead, teach, and inspire others to understand the relationship between mindset and creativity. To give others ideas and Divine insights to help them heal their relationship with their creativity and to support people in learning to trust the power of their imagination. To teach people the importance of mindset in cultivating right timing. To have the right and Divine ideas and inspiration to help others heal their faith and activate their belief in support and sufficiency.

Resiliency Keys:

Self-Trust, Decisiveness, Courage, Emotional Wisdom, Empowerment, Authenticity, Vitality

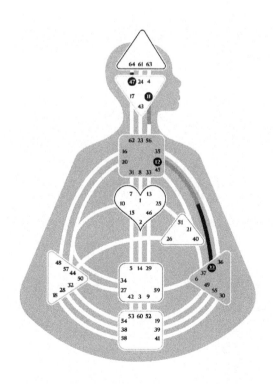

RAX The Divine Translator 2
Conscious Sun Gate: 23
Conscious Earth Gate: 43
Unconscious Sun Gate: 49
Unconscious Earth Gate: 4

Traditional HD IC Name: Right Angle Cross of Explanation 2
Quantum HD IC Name: Right Angle Cross of The Divine Translator 2

Quantum Description:

To share revolutionary ideas and possibilities that have the power to transform the way people think. To teach and transmit new ideas and possibilities that change how people understand and perceive the world. To transform old ideas into new possibilities when the timing and the energy are aligned. To serve the world by sharing new ideas that awaken planetary consciousness.

Resiliency Keys:

Self-Trust, Decisiveness, Courage, Emotional Wisdom, Empowerment, Authenticity, Vitality

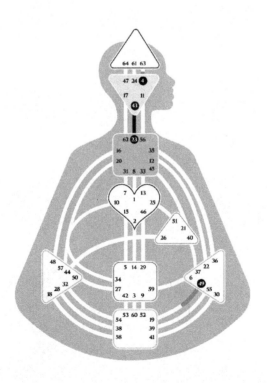

Traditional HD IC Name: Juxtaposition Cross of Assimilation

Quantum HD IC Name: Juxtaposition Cross of Fusion

Quantum Description:

To embody and create a foundation of information and understanding that has the capacity to support others in changing how they think and perceive the world. To ignite passion and possibility in others through your devotion and commitment. Commit to sharing your new and innovative ideas in the world to change how we think. To rethink and share powerful new insights that have the potential to change what we believe is possible.

Resiliency Keys:

Authenticity, Vitality, Decisiveness, Self-Trust, Courage, Vitality, Empowerment, Emotional Wisdom

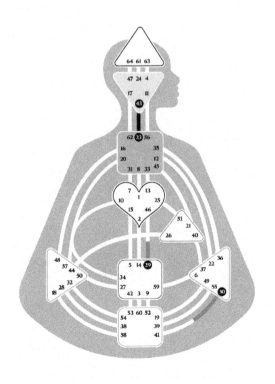

Conscious Sun Gate: 23
Conscious Earth Gate: 43
Unconscious Sun Gate: 30
Unconscious Earth Gate: 29

Traditional HD IC Name: Left Angle Cross of Dedication

Quantum HD IC Name: Left Angle Cross of Transmission

Quantum Description:

To lead, teach, and inspire others through your devotion and passion. To be a role model for dedication and commitment to a passionate cause. To share new ideas, insights, understandings, and ways of thinking to shift what people believe is possible and rethink old, outdated ideas that no longer fit. To teach and transmit new knowledge that promises to transform and evolve new potentials. To be dedicated to changing the world by changing personal and collective perceptions about what is possible.

Resiliency Keys:

Authenticity, Vitality, Decisiveness, Self-Trust, Courage, Vitality, Empowerment, Emotional Wisdom

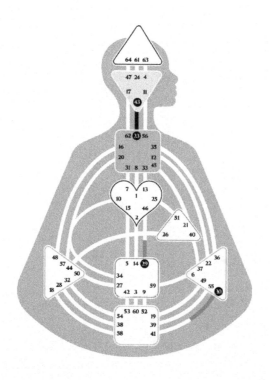

Traditional HD IC Name: Right Angle Cross of The Four Ways

Quantum HD IC Name: Right Angle Cross of Restoration

Quantum Description:

To explore, learn, and teach about the power and importance of narrative and story to set the tone and direction for life. To help others see patterns in old stories that may be causing them to rationalize and settle for less than what they deserve in their relationships. To use your natural sensitivity and intuition to be aware of where others may be settling and rationalize settling for less than what they want. To see the potential in others and to know how to change stories and narratives to support the fulfillment of potential. To help people stop playing small. To help others release the patterns and the pain of the past so they can better claim their true value and worth.

Resiliency Keys:

Vitality, Empowerment, Authenticity, Self-Trust, Courage, Decisiveness

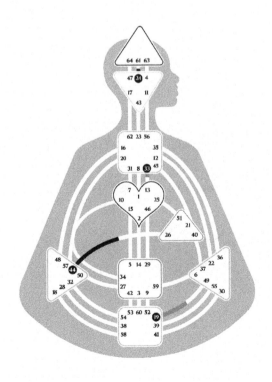

JUX Absolution
Conscious Sun Gate: 24
Conscious Earth Gate: 44
Unconscious Sun Gate: 13
Unconscious Earth Gate: 7

Traditional HD IC Name: Juxtaposition Cross of Rationalization
Quantum HD IC Name: Juxtaposition Cross of Absolution

Quantum Description:

To embody and build a foundation of knowledge that helps others create change and access abundant solutions by changing their personal narrative. To help people transform their stories by giving them support, helping them break free from the patterns of the past, and healing any experiences and traumas that keep them from seeing their value. To know how to help people find the gifts and the blessings from pain and to use this new understanding to rewrite their value story. To support people in breaking free from limiting rationalizations and settling for less than what they want and need.

Resiliency Keys:

Self-Trust, Decisiveness, Authenticity, Lovability, Courage

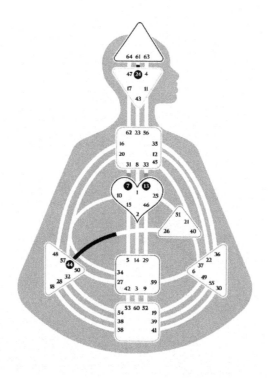

Traditional HD IC Name: Left Angle Cross of Incarnation
Quantum HD IC Name: Left Angle Cross of Remediation

Quantum Description:

To lead, teach, and inspire others to heal their self-worth and value story. To help others understand how to rewrite their personal narrative to reflect their true value, purpose, and worth. To help people break free from the patterns of the past that keep them stuck in old protective stories rooted in trauma. To help heal any trauma or trauma patterns that keep people settling and rationalizing receiving less than what they want and need. To support others in taking leadership in manifesting their dreams and cultivating a personal narrative that encompasses their true value and purpose. To help people change the direction of their lives by helping them heal their past and their old stories of limitation.

Resiliency Keys:

Self-Trust, Decisiveness, Authenticity, Lovability, Courage

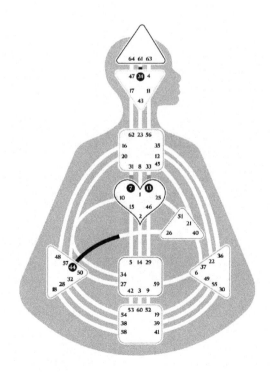

RAX Unity
Conscious Sun Gate: 25
Conscious Earth Gate: 46
Unconscious Sun Gate: 10
Unconscious Earth Gate: 15

Traditional HD IC Name: Right Angle Cross of The Vessel of Love
Quantum HD IC Name: Right Angle Cross of Unity

Quantum Description:

To explore, learn about, and model the power of Love and the courage of the Heart. It is through the discipline of the Heart that one can lead others. To teach self-love, compassion, embodiment, and purpose by first learning, through personal experience, how to live and create from these energies. To become self-actualized and resilient by learning to love oneself and others. To know and teach that Love regulates how we lead, create and walk through our days. To embody and give direction to Love in every way.

Resiliency Keys:

Lovability, Decisiveness, Courage, Authenticity

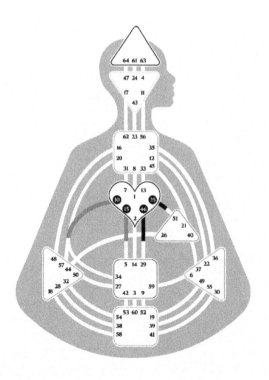

Traditional HD IC Name: Juxtaposition Cross of Innocence

Quantum HD IC Name: Juxtaposition Cross of Aliveness

Quantum Description:

To embody and build a foundation of joyful living through cultivating and studying how to build a strong relationship with Source and purpose. To help others heal their body and reclaim their joy by remembering their connection to Source and their natural state of wellbeing and abundance. To be able to give others a "big picture" perspective on the events of their life and to help them reframe their old perspectives to find the blessings and the lessons in the past experiences.

Resiliency Keys:

Lovability, Decisiveness, Courage, Authenticity, Vitality, Empowerment

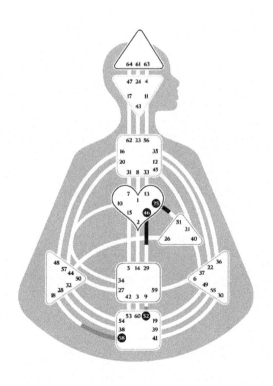

LAX The Heart
Conscious Sun Gate: 25
Conscious Earth Gate: 46
Unconscious Sun Gate: 58
Unconscious Earth Gate: 52

Traditional HD IC Name: Left Angle Cross of Healing

Quantum HD IC Name: Left Angle Cross of The Heart

Quantum Description:

To lead, teach, and inspire others to live and build a joyful life. To help others find a deep connection to the joy that comes from living and creating in alignment with their higher and spiritual purpose. To help people fully embody their purpose and take action to fulfill their purpose in the world. To heal by reconnecting to a higher purpose. To help others remember their higher purpose, support them in finding blessings, meaning, and new perspectives from past experiences.

Resiliency Keys:

Lovability, Decisiveness, Courage, Authenticity, Vitality, Empowerment

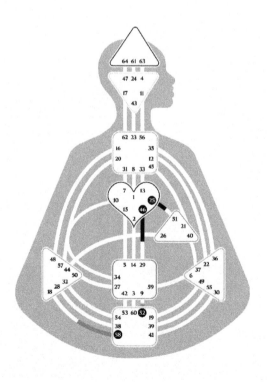

Traditional HD IC Name: Right Angle Cross of Rulership 4
Quantum HD IC Name: Right Angle Cross of Sovereignty 4

Quantum Description:

To explore, learn, and teach the importance of alignment and mindset in cultivating the energy necessary for creativity and manifestation. Understanding the relationship between self-worth, integrity, and mindset and teaching others how to regain sovereignty over their creations by healing any karma related to value and self-worth. To give people the resources they need to regain personal empowerment and control over their own lives and their own reality.

Resiliency Keys:

Courage, Emotional Wisdom, Empowerment, Decisiveness, Self-Trust, Authenticity, Vitality, Self-Worth

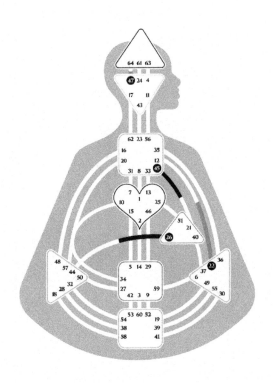

JUX Integrity
Conscious Sun Gate: 26
Conscious Earth Gate: 45
Unconscious Sun Gate: 6
Unconscious Earth Gate: 36

Traditional HD IC Name: Juxtaposition Cross of The Trickster
Quantum HD IC Name: Juxtaposition Cross of Integrity

Quantum Description:

To embody and build a foundation of creating with integrity and in alignment with high self-worth. To teach others the power and importance of healing self-worth. To penetrate deep into the personal stories of others and to help them rewrite those stories to help them break free from limiting patterns of the past. To demonstrate and teach how living in alignment with authenticity and high self-worth facilitates miracles and a life transcending limiting expectations.

Resiliency Keys:

Self-Worth, Vitality, Empowerment, Courage, Emotional Wisdom, Decisiveness, Authenticity

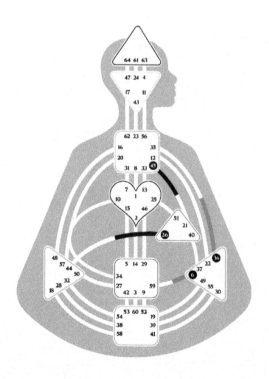

Traditional HD IC Name: Left Angle Cross of Confrontation 2
Quantum HD IC Name: Left Angle Cross of Breakthrough 2

Quantum Description:

To lead, teach, and inspire others to break free from limiting patterns and the pain of the past. To help people heal their self-worth and sense of value that supports them in living aligned with their true integrity. To help people harness the power of shattering old patterns and creating from outgrown expectations by showing them their value and helping them redefine their values. To help people create in alignment with physical, resource, identity, moral and energetic integrity. To do the work necessary to help the world redefine what is truly valuable.

Resiliency Keys:

Self-Worth, Vitality, Empowerment, Courage, Emotional Wisdom, Decisiveness, Authenticity

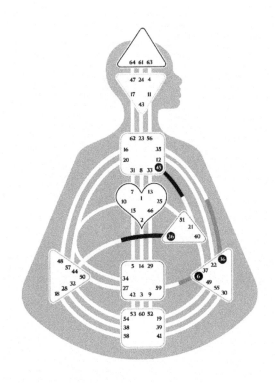

RAX Imagination
Conscious Sun Gate: 27
Conscious Earth Gate: 28
Unconscious Sun Gate: 41
Unconscious Earth Gate: 31

Traditional HD IC Name: Right Angle Cross of The Unexpected
Quantum HD IC Name: Right Angle Cross of Imagination

Quantum Description:

To explore, learn, and teach the values needed to transform experience into wisdom. To use your past experiences and challenges to redefine what you know is truly valuable. To use the power of your imagination to lay the foundation for something new that transcends the struggles and challenges of the past. To use past struggles as seeds to explore new possibilities and potentials. To take leadership in forging a new direction based on your wisdom from your past challenges and dreams about a better future.

Resiliency Keys:

Decisiveness, Courage, Vitality, Empowerment, Self-Trust, Authenticity

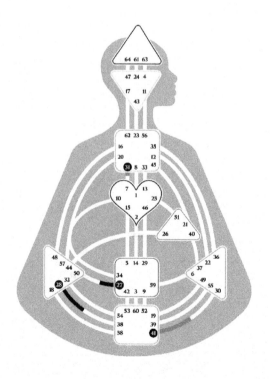

Traditional HD IC Name: Juxtaposition Cross of Caring

Quantum HD IC Name: Juxtaposition Cross of Intimacy

Quantum Description:

To embody and build a foundation of knowledge and wisdom that helps people reclaim their sovereignty over their personal narrative. To use your intuition and your natural awareness of people's emotional needs to help people reframe the perspective on their past experiences. To help people reinterpret their past experiences and to help them redefine their values to reflect what they've learned. To teach people the importance of personal narrative in creating intimacy, community, and high-quality relationships.

Resiliency Keys:

Decisiveness, Courage, Vitality, Empowerment, Self-Trust

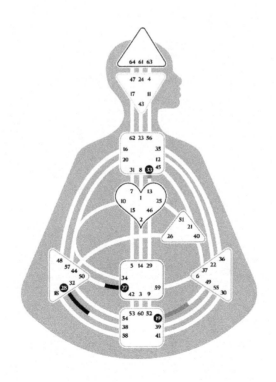

LAX Communion
Conscious Sun Gate: 27
Conscious Earth Gate: 28
Unconscious Sun Gate: 19
Unconscious Earth Gate: 33

Traditional HD IC Name: Left Angle Cross of Alignment
Quantum HD IC Name: Left Angle Cross of Communion

Quantum Description:

To lead, teach, and inspire others to rewrite old narratives and reframe past experiences. To teach others the power of personal narrative in creating community and relationships rooted in true intimacy. To use your intuition to sense and know what emotional needs must be met to create relationship agreements rooted in intimacy. To help people heal their sense of worth and value to be able to craft strong relationships. To help people redefine their values and build relationships, contracts, and agreements that reflect their value and their values.

Resiliency Keys:

Authenticity, Vitality, Self-Trust, Courage, Empowerment, Decisiveness

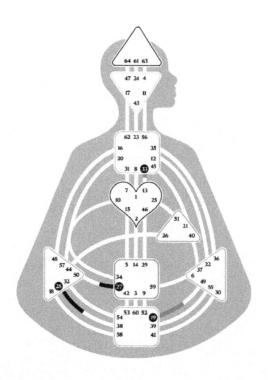

Traditional HD IC Name: Right Angle Cross of The Unexpected 3
Quantum HD IC Name: Right Angle Cross of Imagination 3

Quantum Description:

To explore, learn, and teach the values needed to transform experience into wisdom. To use your past experiences and challenges to redefine what you know is truly valuable. To use the power of your imagination to lay the foundation for something new that transcends the struggles and challenges of the past. To use past struggles as seeds to explore new possibilities and potentials. To take leadership in forging a new direction based on your wisdom from your past challenges and dreams about a better future.

Resiliency Keys:

Decisiveness, Courage, Vitality, Empowerment, Self-Trust, Authenticity

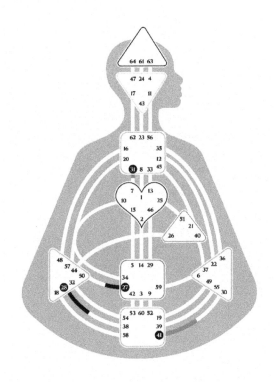

JUX Adventure
Conscious Sun Gate: 28
Conscious Earth Gate: 27
Unconscious Sun Gate: 33
Unconscious Earth Gate: 19

Traditional HD IC Name: Juxtaposition Cross of Risks
Quantum HD IC Name: Juxtaposition Cross of Adventure

Quantum Description:

To embody and build a foundation of learning how to integrate past experiences into a new set of values. To reframe old stories to reflect these new values. Use the power of your intuitive awareness and emotional wisdom to sense which narratives need to be rewritten to empower people to take back control of their stories. The ability to know which challenges are worthy of engaging in. The ability to know where the boundaries of an old story need to be challenged in order to create growth and evolution.

Resiliency Keys:

Decisiveness, Courage, Vitality, Empowerment, Self-Trust, Authenticity

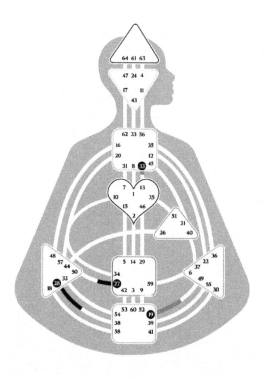

Traditional HD IC Name: Left Angle Cross of Alignment 2
Quantum HD IC Name: Left Angle Cross of Communion 2

Quantum Description:

To lead, teach, and inspire others to rewrite old narratives and reframe past experiences. To teach others the power of personal narrative in creating community and relationships rooted in true intimacy. Use your intuition to sense and know what emotional needs must be met to create relationship agreements rooted in intimacy. To help people heal their sense of worth and value to be able to craft strong relationships. To help people redefine their values and build relationships, contracts, and agreements that reflect their value and their values.

Resiliency Keys:

Decisiveness, Courage, Vitality, Empowerment, Self-Trust, Authenticity

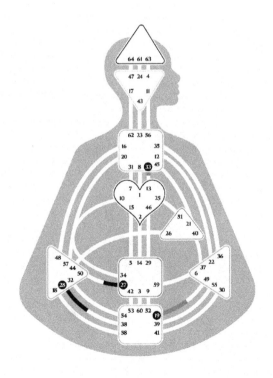

RAX Passion 3
Conscious Sun Gate: 29
Conscious Earth Gate: 30
Unconscious Sun Gate: 8
Unconscious Earth Gate: 14

Traditional HD IC Name: Right Angle Cross of Contagion 3
Quantum HD IC Name: Right Angle Cross of Passion 3

Quantum Description:

To explore, learn about, and model the importance of living in alignment with purpose. To lead by understanding the importance and, ultimately, the fulfillment of creating in alignment with the Authentic Self. To have the courage to follow your Heart and to learn to trust and demonstrate that living true to who you are creates abundance and flow. To show people how to live with passion and to use your passion to ignite the passion of others. To lead a relentlessly authentic life.

Resiliency Keys:

Authenticity, Vitality, Decisiveness, Courage, Empowerment, Emotional Wisdom

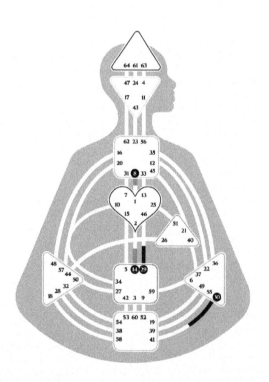

Traditional HD IC Name: Juxtaposition Cross of Commitment

Quantum HD IC Name: Juxtaposition Cross of Devotion

Quantum Description:

To embody and build a foundation rooted in commitment, consistency, and devotion. To explore the process of embodying power and charisma. To create and lead people through embodying the energy that sustains passion and devotion. To use your natural ability to lead and help people commit to their own evolution and their dreams. To organize people around common convictions that transform the collective definition of power.

Resiliency Keys:

Decisiveness, Courage, Vitality, Empowerment, Emotional Wisdom, Authenticity

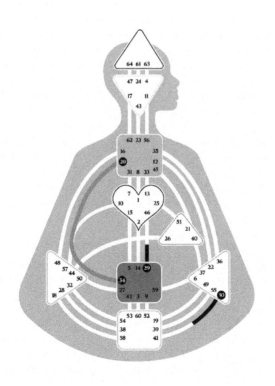

LAX Diligence 2
Conscious Sun Gate: 29
Conscious Earth Gate: 30
Unconscious Sun Gate: 20
Unconscious Earth Gate: 34

Traditional HD IC Name: Left Angle Cross of Industry 2
Quantum HD IC Name: Left Angle Cross of Diligence 2

Quantum Description:

To lead, teach, and inspire others to reclaim their true power. To lead with power and charisma. To devote yourself to inspiring others to follow their passion. To be passionate about helping others take leadership with their innate power. To redefine the collective definition of power. To organize others around passionate ideals and convictions. To live with passion and commit to leading with integrity and determination.

Resiliency Keys:

Decisiveness, Courage, Vitality, Empowerment, Emotional Wisdom, Authenticity

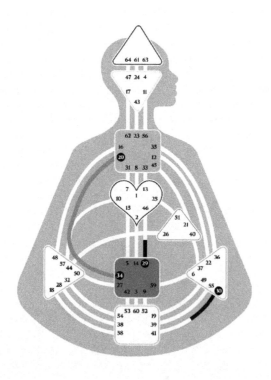

Traditional HD IC Name: Right Angle Cross of Contagion
Quantum HD IC Name: Right Angle Cross of Passion

Quantum Description:

To explore, learn about, and model the importance of living in alignment with purpose. To lead by understanding the importance and, ultimately, the fulfillment of creating in alignment with the Authentic Self. To have the courage to follow your Heart and learn to trust and demonstrate that living true to who you are creates abundance and flow. To show people how to live with passion and to use your passion to ignite the passion of others. To lead a relentlessly authentic life.

Resiliency Keys:

Authenticity, Vitality, Decisiveness, Courage, Empowerment, Emotional Wisdom

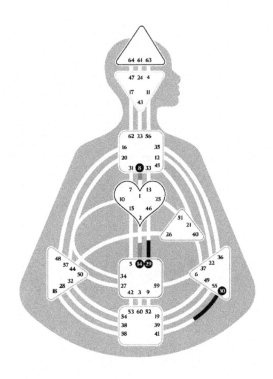

JUX Amplification
Conscious Sun Gate: 30
Conscious Earth Gate: 29
Unconscious Sun Gate: 34
Unconscious Earth Gate: 20

Traditional HD IC Name: Juxtaposition Cross of Fates
Quantum HD IC Name: Juxtaposition Cross of Amplification

Quantum Description:

To embody and build a foundation to lead others to discover their passion and purpose. To commit and devote yourself to unifying people around transformative ideas and redefining the collective definition of power and empowerment. To use your passion and intensity to connect people to their passion. To be determined and committed to awakening others to living in alignment with their passion and purpose. To follow your own conviction and to show others how to follow theirs.

Resiliency Keys:

Decisiveness, Courage, Vitality, Empowerment, Emotional Wisdom, Authenticity

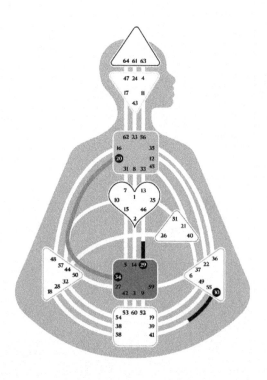

Traditional HD IC Name: Left Angle Cross of Industry

Quantum HD IC Name: Left Angle Cross of Diligence

Quantum Description:

To lead, teach, and inspire others to reclaim their true power. To lead with power and charisma. To devote yourself to inspiring others to follow their passion. To be passionate about helping others take leadership with their innate power. To redefine the collective definition of power. To organize others around passionate ideals and convictions. To live with passion and commit to leading with integrity and determination.

Resiliency Keys:

Decisiveness, Courage, Vitality, Empowerment, Emotional Wisdom, Authenticity

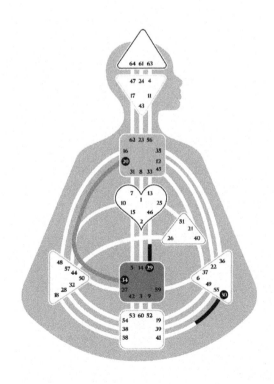

RAX Imagination 2
Conscious Sun Gate: 31
Conscious Earth Gate: 41
Unconscious Sun Gate: 27
Unconscious Earth Gate: 28

Traditional HD IC Name: Right Angle Cross of The Unexpected 2
Quantum HD IC Name: Right Angle Cross of Imagination 2

Quantum Description:

To explore, learn, and teach the values needed to transform experience into wisdom. To use your past experiences and challenges to redefine what you know is truly valuable. To use the power of your imagination to lay the foundation for something new that transcends the struggles and challenges of the past. To use past struggles as seeds to explore new possibilities and potentials. To take leadership in forging a new direction based on your wisdom from your past challenges and dreams about a better future.

Resiliency Keys:

Decisiveness, Courage, Vitality, Empowerment, Self-Trust, Authenticity

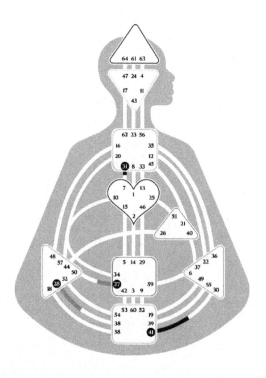

Traditional HD IC Name: Juxtaposition Cross of Influence
Quantum HD IC Name: Juxtaposition Cross of Stewardship

Quantum Description:

To embody and build a foundation of leadership rooted in the initiation of new ideas. To support others in releasing limiting stories and the patterns from the past so they can take their rightful place as leaders. To teach others the importance and the power of using your imagination to generate new possibilities that change our collective direction. To initiate authentic leadership and teach empowerment rooted in healthy values and high self-worth.

Resiliency Keys:

Authenticity, Vitality, Empowerment, Self-Trust, Courage, Decisiveness

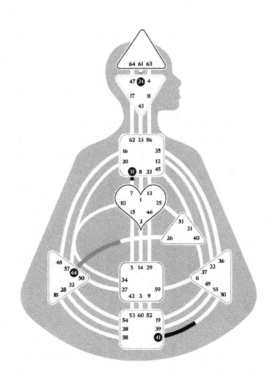

LAX Democracy
Conscious Sun Gate: 31
Conscious Earth Gate: 41
Unconscious Sun Gate: 24
Unconscious Earth Gate: 44

Traditional HD IC Name: Left Angle Cross of The Alpha
Quantum HD IC Name: Left Angle Cross of Democracy

Quantum Description:

To lead, teach, and inspire others to disentangle themselves from and heal the patterns of the past that keep them settling for less than what they deserve. To lead others to heal their sense of value and to create healthy values that support self-empowerment and the authentic embodiment of personal and collective sovereignty. To learn and teach the importance of imagination as the gateway to birthing new possibilities. To remind people of their innate creative power and help them heal limiting beliefs and patterns that keep them from taking leadership in their own lives and in setting the tone and the direction for their life.

Resiliency Keys:

Authenticity, Vitality, Empowerment, Self-Trust, Courage, Decisiveness

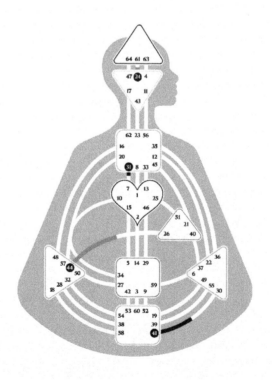

Traditional HD IC Name: Right Angle Cross of The Maya 3
Quantum HD IC Name: Right Angle Cross of Endurance 3

Quantum Description:

To explore, learn, and teach the importance of aligning with right timing in order to manifest and implement the next key steps to creation. To plan, prepare, and clear the path for the next step and to teach the importance of conscious readiness. To help others learn to set the stage and be prepared for what is next. To align yourself with the long haul. To be sure that all the necessary action steps are ready to align with the manifestation of a dream. To know that part of bringing the idea into form is to "act as if" and doing all the things necessary to be prepared for when the timing is right.

Resiliency Keys:

Authenticity, Self-Trust, Decisiveness, Courage, Vitality, Empowerment

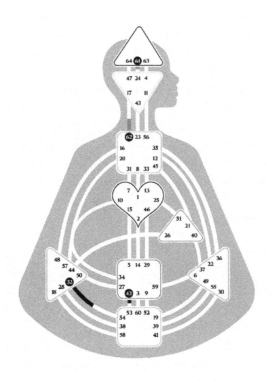

JUX Tenacity
Conscious Sun Gate: 32
Conscious Earth Gate: 42
Unconscious Sun Gate: 56
Unconscious Earth Gate: 60

Traditional HD IC Name: Juxtaposition Cross of Conservation
Quantum HD IC Name: Juxtaposition Cross of Tenacity

Quantum Description:

To embody and build a foundation rooted in the wisdom to acknowledge and focus on what IS working, the capacity to inspire others to stay aligned with possibility and potential, and to clear the path necessary for the manifestation of a new idea or an evolution of possibility. To use the power of storytelling and narrative to shift perspectives to help people focus with gratitude on what they seek to create and manifest. To use the power of narrative and focused gratitude to influence time and timing. To help people bring old ideas and situations to a conclusion to make room for the construction of a foundation for something new and better.

Resiliency Keys:

Authenticity, Self-Trust, Decisiveness, Courage, Vitality, Empowerment

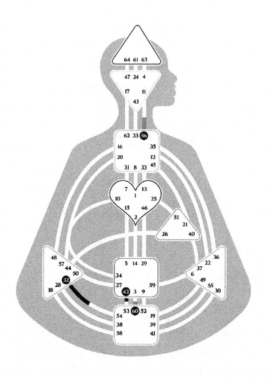

Traditional HD IC Name: Left Angle Cross of Limitation 2
Quantum HD IC Name: Left Angle Cross of Stamina 2

Quantum Description:

To lead, teach, and inspire others to learn to influence time and timing by demonstrating the importance of finishing tasks in order to create space for greater possibilities, by learning to share narratives filled with potential and possibility, and consciously focusing on growing what IS working. To leverage the power of gratitude as a skill that increases focus, enhances productivity, and helps to sustain the bigger vision that leads to the creation and manifestation of the fulfillment of a dream. To know how to build the infrastructure of a dream, lay the foundation in physical form for the manifestation of the dream, and cultivate the wisdom of waiting patiently for the right timing to take action.

Resiliency Keys:

Authenticity, Self-Trust, Decisiveness, Courage, Vitality, Empowerment

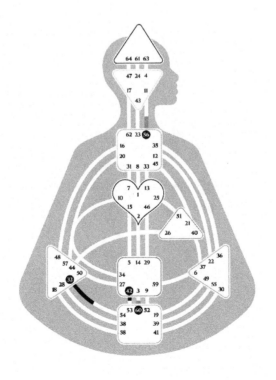

RAX Restoration 2
Conscious Sun Gate: 33
Conscious Earth Gate: 19
Unconscious Sun Gate: 24
Unconscious Earth Gate: 44

Traditional HD IC Name: Right Angle Cross of The Four Ways 2
Quantum HD IC Name: Right Angle Cross of Restoration 2

Quantum Description:

To explore, learn, and teach about the power and importance of narrative and story to set the tone and direction for life. To help others see patterns in old stories that may be causing them to rationalize and settle for less than what they deserve in their relationships. To use your natural sensitivity and intuition to be aware of where others may be settling and rationalizing settling for less than what they want. To see the potential in others and know how to change stories and narratives to support the fulfillment of potential. To help people stop playing small. To help others release the patterns and the pain of the past so they can better claim their true value and worth.

Resiliency Keys:

Vitality, Empowerment, Authenticity, Self-Trust, Courage, Decisiveness

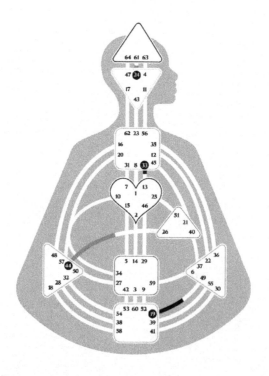

Traditional HD IC Name: Juxtaposition Cross of Retreat

Quantum HD IC Name: Juxtaposition Cross of Testimony

Quantum Description:

To embody and build a foundation of living aligned with purpose and relentlessly authentic self-expression. To use your intuitive understanding of the emotional needs of others to help them rewrite their personal narrative so that it fully encompasses their true value and their values and help them build relationships and communities that fully support their authentic self-expression. To support people in healing their self-worth to help them transform their personal narrative into a story that embodies their receptivity to support and resources that help them fulfill their true purpose and their authentic self-expression.

Resiliency Keys:

Vitality, Empowerment, Authenticity, Lovability, Decisiveness, Courage

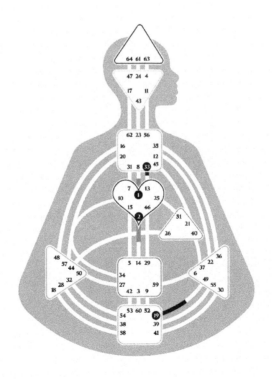

LAX Clarification
Conscious Sun Gate: 33
Conscious Earth Gate: 19
Unconscious Sun Gate: 2
Unconscious Earth Gate: 1

Traditional HD IC Name: Left Angle Cross of Refinement
Quantum HD IC Name: Left Angle Cross of Clarification

Quantum Description:

To lead, teach, and inspire others to be relentlessly authentic with their self-expression. To help others realize that the path to true intimacy and sustainable partnership and community can only be achieved when all parties are being authentic and on purpose. To help people realize their true potential for support and community by helping them rewrite their old relationship stories and expectations so that their new personal narrative and expectations about relationships reflect their value and their values. To redefine old perspectives on compromise, community, and relationships by demonstrating that there is always a win-win solution.

Resiliency Keys:

Vitality, Empowerment, Authenticity, Lovability, Decisiveness, Courage

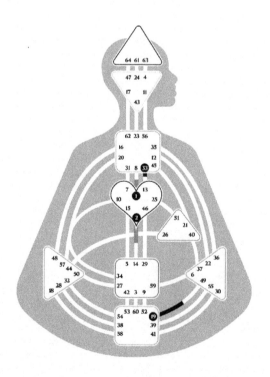

Traditional HD IC Name: Right Angle Cross of The Sleeping Phoenix 4
Quantum HD IC Name: Right Angle Cross of The Harbinger 4

Quantum Description:

To explore, learn, and teach about the true nature of power. To embody aligning yourself with Divine Timing in order to gather people around new ideas that have the potential to create sustainability. To create beyond what you know how to create by cultivating deep faith and trust in abundance. To use faith as a way of seeding the Quantum Field. To know how to read the signs and engage with the world in such a way that you know when it's time to respond to what's needed to create abundance for all. To organize people around new ideas and convictions that support the work and creation necessary to help people create sustainable, abundant resources and peace.

Resiliency Keys:

Authenticity, Decisiveness, Courage, Vitality, Empowerment, Emotional Wisdom

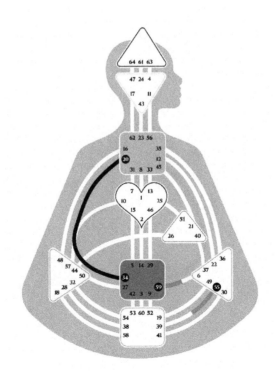

JUX Potentiality
Conscious Sun Gate: 34
Conscious Earth Gate: 20
Unconscious Sun Gate: 40
Unconscious Earth Gate: 37

Traditional HD IC Name: Juxtaposition Cross of Power

Quantum HD IC Name: Juxtaposition Cross of Potentiality

Quantum Description:

To embody and build a foundation of an empowered community and to empower community members to organize themselves around new ideas and convictions that support the creation and the manifestation of new ways of living together in peace. To stand on the edge between the past and the future and to know what needs to happen, re-engineer agreements, contracts, and relationships to make them more progressive and resilient. To help empower people so that they can serve their community and their relationships without hidden agendas and in an equitable, just, and sustainable way.

Resiliency Keys:

Authenticity, Decisiveness, Courage, Vitality, Empowerment, Emotional Wisdom, Self-Worth

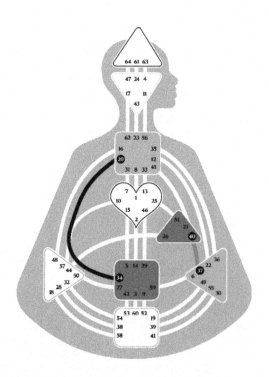

Traditional HD IC Name: Left Angle Cross of Duality 2
Quantum HD IC Name: Left Angle Cross of The Shift 2

Quantum Description:

To lead, teach and empower others by redefining the meaning of community. To build sustainable, equitable, and empowered communities and to support communities in building agreements that create and embody sustainability. To help others see that true community is rooted in authentic self-expression and that healthy communities must be comprised of community members that feel empowered and have sovereignty over the community agreements. To recognize that communities cannot be sustainable without a deep understanding of the inherent value of each community member. To redefine community agreements to make them more equitable and sustainable.

Resiliency Keys:

Authenticity, Decisiveness, Courage, Vitality, Empowerment, Emotional Wisdom, Self-Worth

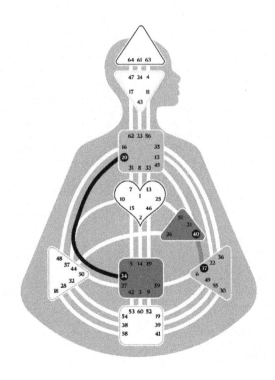

RAX The Quantum Pulse 2
Conscious Sun Gate: 35
Conscious Earth Gate: 5
Unconscious Sun Gate: 63
Unconscious Earth Gate: 64

Traditional HD IC Name: Right Angle Cross of Consciousness 2
Quantum HD IC Name: Right Angle Cross of The Quantum Pulse 2

Quantum Description:

To explore, experiment with, and experience the habits and rhythms necessary to implement new ideas and possibilities. To share and demonstrate the habits and consistency born of experience that set the stage for exploring new ideas. To embody and teach others how to be consistent and habitual. To teach from experience and to use your experience to know which new ideas to explore and experiment with. To lay the foundation of rhythm and consistency as the medium for exponential growth and compassionate expansion.

Resiliency Keys:

Decisiveness, Self-Trust, Authenticity, Vitality, Courage, Empowerment

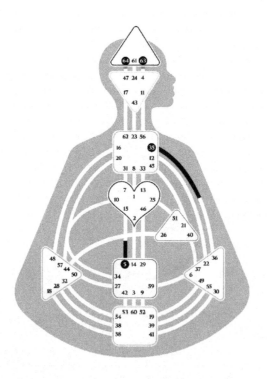

Traditional HD IC Name: Juxtaposition Cross of Experience
Quantum HD IC Name: Juxtaposition Cross of Maturity

Quantum Description:

To embody and build a foundation of practiced experience that supports others in knowing how to use routine and rhythm as a tool to help sustain a healthy and empowered mindset. To understand the power and importance of mindset as the spark that initiates miraculous and aligned experiences that have the capacity to transform what we believe is possible. To teach and share your experiences. To cultivate a practice and a rhythm that is so consistent that it stabilizes and supports intentional and deliberate growth.

Resiliency Keys:

Vitality, Decisiveness, Courage, Empowerment, Emotional Wisdom, Self-Trust, Authenticity

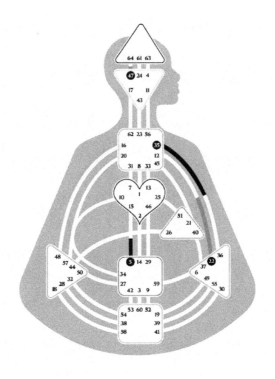

LAX Coherence
Conscious Sun Gate: 35
Conscious Earth Gate: 5
Unconscious Sun Gate: 22
Unconscious Earth Gate: 47

Traditional HD IC Name: Left Angle Cross of Separation
Quantum HD IC Name: Left Angle Cross of Coherence

Quantum Description:

To lead, teach, and inspire others to build a deliberate and intentional practice that supports the maintenance and the ability to sustain a constructive and positive mindset. To understand the importance of mindset in creating transformational experiences that create breakthroughs in old patterns and habits of limitation and lack. To use your experience to help others learn how to build a daily practice that helps entrain Heart and action in a state of creative coherence. To use your experience to lead others to breakthroughs and transformation. To learn to harness the power of mindset to align with the grace necessary to break free from limiting patterns and habits.

Resiliency Keys:

Vitality, Decisiveness, Courage, Empowerment, Emotional Wisdom, Self-Trust, Authenticity

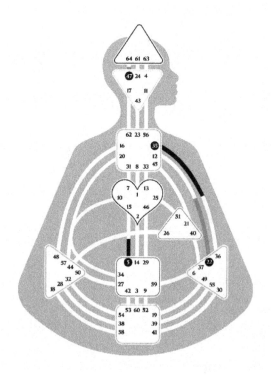

Traditional HD IC Name: Right Angle Cross of Eden
Quantum HD IC Name: Right Angle Cross of Miracles

Quantum Description:

To explore, experiment with, and experience the pursuit of pure inspiration. To have an impact by implementing new ideas that have the power to shatter the patterns of the past and that stretch the edges of the human story. To explore new ideas by trying them out and then sharing the experience with others as a way of inspiring. To use the power of your Divine connection to break free from past limiting patterns. To create miracles and consciously harness the fulfillment of the unexpected by trusting in Source and following Divine Inspiration.

Resiliency Keys:

Decisiveness, Self-Trust, Authenticity, Vitality, Courage, Emotional Wisdom, Empowerment

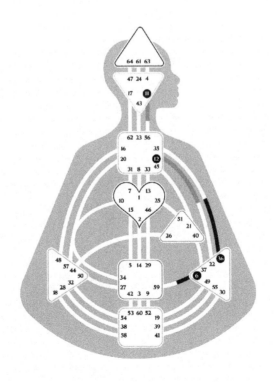

JUX Expectation
Conscious Sun Gate: 36
Conscious Earth Gate: 6
Unconscious Sun Gate: 10
Unconscious Earth Gate: 15

Traditional HD IC Name: Juxtaposition Cross of Crisis
Quantum HD IC Name: Juxtaposition Cross of Expectation

Quantum Description:

To embody and build a foundation of self-love and compassion that leads to the capacity to break free from limiting and hurtful patterns of the past. To have the ability to impact people by showing them new possibilities and potentials that lead them to expect a breakthrough. To harness the power of imagination and faith to build an energy template that supports the manifestation of new pathways of creative living. To help people solidify their self-love and strengthen it to the degree that they can redirect their creative power and use their authentic self-expression as a gift to the world for the betterment of others.

Resiliency Keys:

Courage, Emotional Wisdom, Empowerment, Decisiveness, Lovability, Authenticity

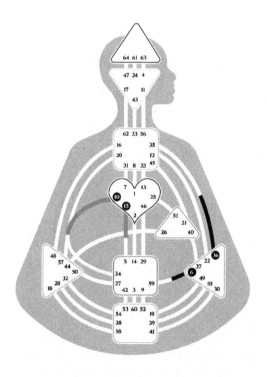

Traditional HD IC Name: Left Angle Cross of The Plane
Quantum HD IC Name: Left Angle Cross of Sustainability

Quantum Description:

To lead, teach, and inspire people by helping them break free from limiting patterns and habits that block self-love and compassion. To teach and share the knowledge necessary to liberate others from past patterns that keep them stuck or blocked. To heal and align the vibration of Love on the planet and to create and steer a new path that fully embodies the power and direction of Love. To shatter old patterns that bring the potential for collaboration and leadership that gives new direction to evolutionary ideas.

Resiliency Keys:

Courage, Emotional Wisdom, Empowerment, Decisiveness, Lovability, Authenticity

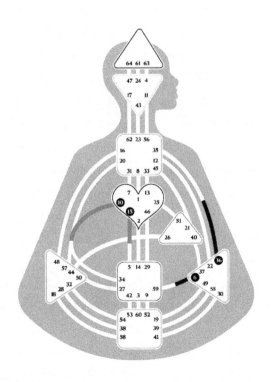

RAX Community
Conscious Sun Gate: 37
Conscious Earth Gate: 40
Unconscious Sun Gate: 9
Unconscious Earth Gate: 16

Traditional HD IC Name: Right Angle Cross of Planning
Quantum HD IC Name: Right Angle Cross of Community

Quantum Description:

To explore, learn about, and model the importance of focus, self-renewal, peace, and the willingness to try (even if the risk of failure is high) to create in a sustainable manner. To serve the world by helping people create healthy, agreements and contracts. To help people realize that the karma of self-worth must be healed and healthy for communities to build a sustainable future and a peaceful world.

Resiliency Keys:

Vitality, Decisiveness, Courage, Empowerment, Authenticity, Self-Worth, Emotional Wisdom

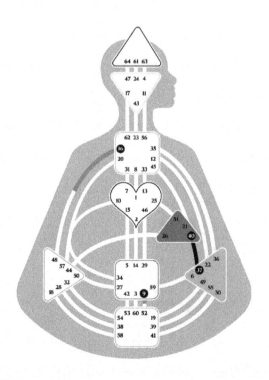

Traditional HD IC Name: Juxtaposition Cross of Bargains
Quantum HD IC Name: Juxtaposition Cross of Harmony

Quantum Description:

To embody and build a foundation of peace rooted in the cultivation of practices and habits that allow others to regulate their response to living with great intention and deliberation. To cultivate the wisdom and experience necessary to support people in creating equitable and just agreements that support the creation of sustainable and healthy communities. To be a bringer of peace. To know how to balance being IN a community with rest and renewal to bring to the community what is necessary to sustain it without hidden agendas and low expressions of ego. To serve the betterment of the world by knowing how to strengthen and heal self-worth and value to create aligned community and relationship agreements.

Resiliency Keys:

Courage, Emotional Wisdom, Empowerment, Decisiveness, Self-Worth, Authenticity, Vitality

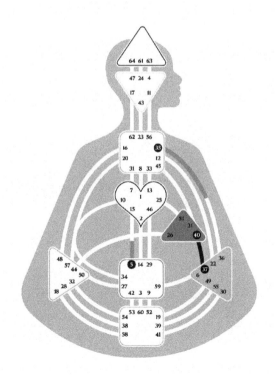

LAX Transaction
Conscious Sun Gate: 37
Conscious Earth Gate: 40
Unconscious Sun Gate: 5
Unconscious Earth Gate: 35

Traditional HD IC Name: Left Angle Cross of Migration

Quantum HD IC Name: Left Angle Cross of Transaction

Quantum Description:

To lead, teach, and inspire others to build sustainable and healthy community and relationship agreements through healing self-worth and alignment around common values. To understand and teach the importance of healthy self-worth as a key ingredient to sustainable relationship agreements and community. To understand and teach the balance between self, self-care, and contribution. To be able to bring sustainable resources to the community by first becoming self-sustaining. To create healthy, sustainable transactions that include mutual respect, dignity, and honor to build strong and resilient communities and relationships.

Resiliency Keys:

Courage, Emotional Wisdom, Empowerment, Decisiveness, Self-Worth, Authenticity, Vitality

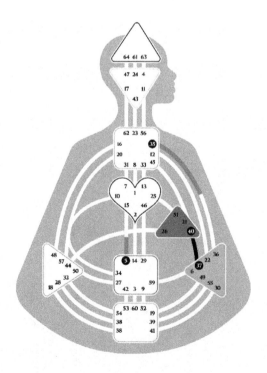

Traditional HD IC Name: Right Angle Cross of Tension 4
Quantum HD IC Name: Right Angle Cross of Renewal 4

Quantum Description:

To explore, learn, and teach from a depth of knowledge that comes from learning, studying, and investigating the importance and the power of self-regulation as a key element to accomplishing and fulfilling a dream. To instinctively know and understand what is out of alignment with abundance and to use your knowledge and wisdom to bring people back into harmony with the potential of support and sufficiency. To cultivate a vision of an abundant world, to practice self-regulation, and to study, learn, and act upon exactly what needs to be done to fulfill that vision.

Resiliency Keys:

Self-Worth, Vitality, Empowerment, Self-Trust, Courage

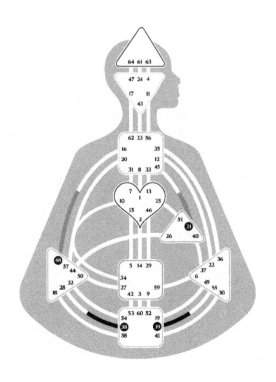

JUX The Idealist
Conscious Sun Gate: 38
Conscious Earth Gate: 39
Unconscious Sun Gate: 57
Unconscious Earth Gate: 51

Traditional HD IC Name: Juxtaposition Cross of Opposition
Quantum HD IC Name: Juxtaposition Cross of The Idealist

Quantum Description:

To embody and build a foundation rooted in a natural understanding of the need for a deep connection to Source. The trust that there is a bigger plan at hand and that dreams are essential and vital components to conscious and deliberate creation. The trust, faith, and intuitive knowingness that dreams can and will become a reality. The trust, faith, and intuitive knowingness support realigning any pattern, thought, or experience not rooted in abundance and trust in Source.

Resiliency Keys:

Vitality, Empowerment, Self-Worth, Self-Trust, Courage

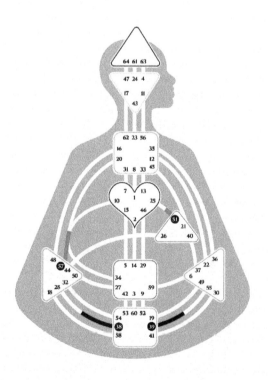

Traditional HD IC Name: Left Angle Cross of Individualism 2

Quantum HD IC Name: Left Angle Cross of The Visionary 2

Quantum Description:

To lead, teach, and inspire others to follow their dreams. To use your intuitive awareness to help people connect more deeply with their higher purpose. To initiate others into their higher purpose and to build a strong and trusting relationship with Source. To realign any perceptions that are rooted in lack. To use your experiences to craft a vision or a dream that is big enough to call you forward. To lead others towards fulfilling a vision of abundance, meaning, and possibility. To know when the timing and the circumstances are right to take aligned action to fulfill a vision. To be a visionary leader in every way.

Resiliency Keys:

Vitality, Empowerment, Self-Worth, Self-Trust, Courage

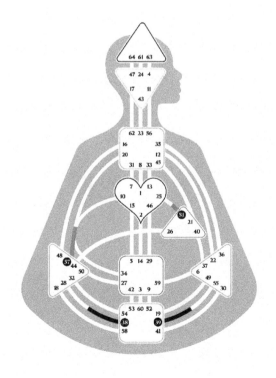

RAX Renewal 2
Conscious Sun Gate: 39
Conscious Earth Gate: 38
Unconscious Sun Gate: 21
Unconscious Earth Gate: 48

Traditional HD IC Name: Right Angle Cross of Tension 2
Quantum HD IC Name: Right Angle Cross of Renewal 2

Quantum Description:

To explore, learn, and teach from a depth of knowledge that comes from learning, studying, and investigating the importance and the power of self-regulation as a key element to accomplishing and fulfilling a dream. To instinctively know and understand what is out of alignment with abundance and to use your knowledge and wisdom to bring people back into harmony with the potential of support and sufficiency. To cultivate a vision of an abundant world, to practice self-regulation, and to study, learn and act upon exactly what needs to be done to fulfill that vision.

Resiliency Keys:

Self-Worth, Vitality, Empowerment, Self-Trust, Courage

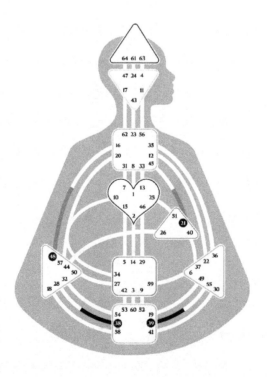

Traditional HD IC Name: Juxtaposition Cross of Provocation

Quantum HD IC Name: Juxtaposition Cross of Uncovering

Quantum Description:

To intuitively sense when something is out of alignment with abundance. To know what needs to be healed, released, aligned, or brought to someone's awareness to help them restore themselves to the energy of alignment with abundance. To understand and hold a vision of the highest potential of a dream and to intuitively know what needs to be restored or revealed to hold the aligned energy for the dream to be made manifest.

Resiliency Keys:

Vitality, Empowerment, Self-Worth, Self-Trust, Courage

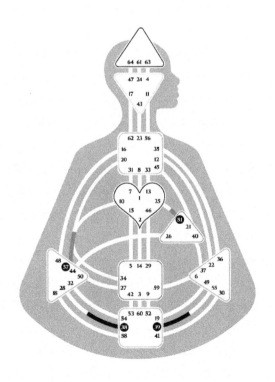

LAX The Visionary
Conscious Sun Gate: 39
Conscious Earth Gate: 38
Unconscious Sun Gate: 51
Unconscious Earth Gate: 57

Traditional HD IC Name: Left Angle Cross of Individualism
Quantum HD IC Name: Left Angle Cross of The Visionary

Quantum Description:

To lead, teach, and inspire others to follow their dreams. To use your intuitive awareness to help people connect more deeply with their higher purpose. To initiate others into their higher purpose and to build a strong and trusting relationship with Source. To realign any perceptions that are rooted in lack. To use your experiences to craft a vision or a dream that is big enough to call you forward. To lead others towards fulfilling a vision of abundance, meaning, and possibility. To know when the timing and the circumstances are right to take aligned action to fulfill a vision. To be a visionary leader in every way.

Resiliency Keys:

Vitality, Empowerment, Self-Worth, Self-Trust, Courage

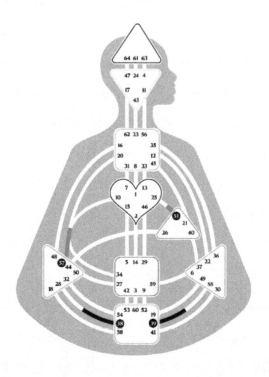

Traditional HD IC Name: Right Angle Cross of Planning 3
Quantum HD IC Name: Right Angle Cross of Community 3

Quantum Description:

To explore, learn about, and model the importance of focus, self-renewal, peace, and the willingness to try (even if the risk of failure is high) to create sustainably and sustainability in the world. To serve the world by helping people create healthy, agreements and contracts. To help people realize that the karma of self-worth must be healed and healthy for communities to build a sustainable future and a peaceful world.

Resiliency Keys:

Vitality, Decisiveness, Courage, Empowerment, Authenticity, Self-Worth, Emotional Wisdom

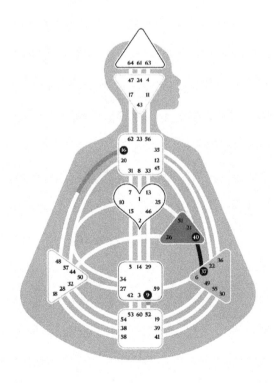

JUX Replenishing
Conscious Sun Gate: 40
Conscious Earth Gate: 37
Unconscious Sun Gate: 35
Unconscious Earth Gate: 5

Traditional HD IC Name: Juxtaposition Cross of Denial
Quantum HD IC Name: Juxtaposition Cross of Replenishing

Quantum Description:

To embody and build a foundation of experience rooted in consistency and practice that leads to the replenished and sustainable energy to engage in community and relationships without projection and hidden agendas. To understand innately that consistent patterns of self-care and self-renewal are essential to making healthy agreements with others as well as contracts and building strong communities. To heal self-worth and instill in people their value to consistently stay nurtured, replenished, and sustainable. Understanding and teaching that the root of deliberate relations, emotional alignment, and peace is a consistent practice of self-renewal that ensures sustainability.

Resiliency Keys:

Courage, Emotional Wisdom, Empowerment, Decisiveness, Self-Worth, Authenticity, Vitality

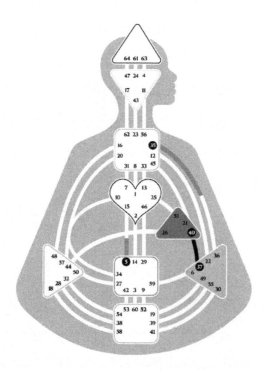

Traditional HD IC Name: Left Angle Cross of Migration 2
Quantum HD IC Name: Left Angle Cross of Transaction 2

Quantum Description:

To lead, teach, and inspire others to build sustainable and healthy communities and relationship agreements through healing self-worth and alignment around common values. To understand and teach the importance of healthy self-worth as a key ingredient to sustainable relationship agreements and community. To understand and teach the balance between self, self-care, and contribution. To be able to bring sustainable resources to the community by first becoming self-sustaining. Creating healthy, sustainable transactions that include mutual respect, dignity, and honor builds strong and resilient communities and relationships.

Resiliency Keys:

Courage, Emotional Wisdom, Empowerment, Decisiveness, Self-Worth, Authenticity, Vitality

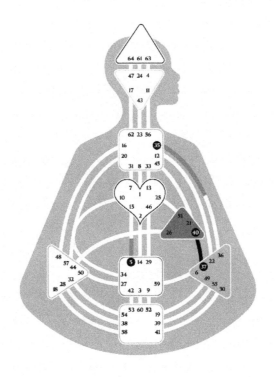

RAX Imagination 4
Conscious Sun Gate: 41
Conscious Earth Gate: 31
Unconscious Sun Gate: 28
Unconscious Earth Gate: 27

Traditional HD IC Name: Right Angle Cross of The Unexpected 4
Quantum HD IC Name: Right Angle Cross of Imagination 4

Quantum Description:

To explore, learn, and teach the values needed to transform experience into wisdom. To use your past experiences and challenges to redefine what you know is truly valuable. To use the power of your imagination to lay the foundation for something new that transcends the struggles and challenges of the past. To use past struggles as seeds to explore new possibilities and potentials. To take leadership in forging a new direction based on your wisdom from your past challenges and dreams about a better future.

Resiliency Keys:

Decisiveness, Courage, Vitality, Empowerment, Self-Trust, Authenticity

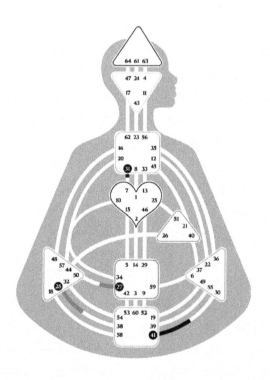

Traditional HD IC Name: Juxtaposition Cross of Fantasy
Quantum HD IC Name: Juxtaposition Cross of Creativity

Quantum Description:

To embody and lay the foundation for the power of imagination in creating new possibilities. To use your experiences to redefine values and take leadership in shifting and evolving values to align with the highest good and the betterment of humanity. To teach creativity and guide the creative process. To support others in the integration of values gleaned from enduring the challenges that come from pursuing the power of a dream. To use your capacity to respond to life with creativity as a value that you take the lead in transmitting.

Resiliency Keys:

Decisiveness, Courage, Vitality, Empowerment, Self-Trust, Authenticity

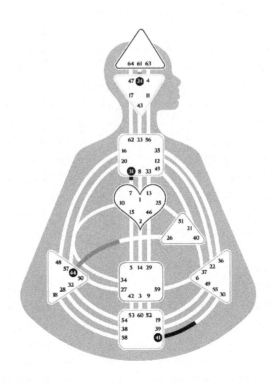

LAX Democracy 2
Conscious Sun Gate: 41
Conscious Earth Gate: 31
Unconscious Sun Gate: 44
Unconscious Earth Gate: 24

Traditional HD IC Name: Left Angle Cross of The Alpha 2
Quantum HD IC Name: Left Angle Cross of Democracy 2

Quantum Description:

To lead, teach, and inspire others to disentangle themselves from and heal the patterns from the past that keep them settling for less than what they deserve. To lead others to heal their sense of value and to create healthy values that support self-empowerment and the authentic embodiment of personal and collective sovereignty. To learn and teach the importance of imagination as the gateway to birthing new possibilities. To remind people of their innate creative power and help them heal limiting beliefs and patterns that keep them from taking leadership in their own lives and setting the tone and the direction for their life.

Resiliency Keys:

Decisiveness, Courage, Vitality, Empowerment, Self-Trust, Authenticity

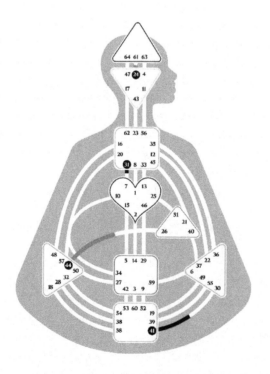

THE ENCYCLOPEDIA OF QUANTUM HUMAN DESIGN

Traditional HD IC Name: Right Angle Cross of The Maya
Quantum HD IC Name: Right Angle Cross of Endurance

Quantum Description:

To explore, learn, and teach the importance of aligning with right timing to manifest and implement the next key steps to creation. To plan, prepare, and clear the path for the next step and to teach the importance of conscious readiness. To help others learn to set the stage and be prepared for what is next. To align yourself with the long haul. To be sure that all the necessary action steps are ready to align with the manifestation of a dream. To know that part of bringing the idea into form is to "act as if" and doing all the things necessary to be prepared for when the timing is right.

Resiliency Keys:

Authenticity, Self-Trust, Decisiveness, Courage, Vitality, Empowerment

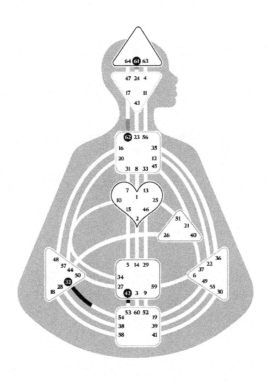

JUX Conclusion
Conscious Sun Gate: 42
Conscious Earth Gate: 32
Unconscious Sun Gate: 60
Unconscious Earth Gate: 56

Traditional HD IC Name: Juxtaposition Cross of Completion
Quantum HD IC Name: Juxtaposition Cross of Conclusion

Quantum Description:

To embody and build a foundation of knowing when to bring things to completion in order to make room for growth. Having the depth of knowledge necessary to understand that innovation is rooted in focusing on what IS working, building a new story around an already tested idea, and having the patience to take aligned action and wait for the right timing to share and transmit a new idea or an innovation. Knowing when to change course. Being able to come into a situation that is stalled or not working and bring it to a conclusion in a healthy and expansive way.

Resiliency Keys:

Self-Trust, Decisiveness, Courage, Vitality, Empowerment, Authenticity

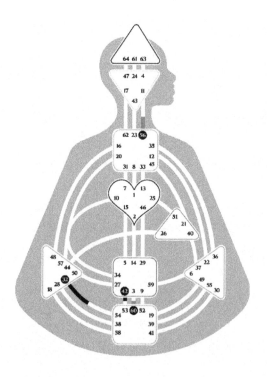

Traditional HD IC Name: Left Angle Cross of Limitation
Quantum HD IC Name: Left Angle Cross of Stamina

Quantum Description:

To lead, teach, and inspire others to learn to influence time and timing by demonstrating the importance of finishing tasks in order to create space for greater possibilities, learning to share narratives filled with potential and possibility, and by consciously focusing on growing what IS working. To leverage the power of gratitude as a skill that increases focus, enhances productivity, and helps to sustain the bigger vision that leads to the creation and manifestation of the fulfillment of a dream. To know how to build the infrastructure of a dream, lay the foundation in physical form for the manifestation of the dream, and cultivate the wisdom of knowing how to wait patiently for the right timing to take action.

Resiliency Keys:

Self-Trust, Decisiveness, Courage, Vitality, Empowerment, Authenticity

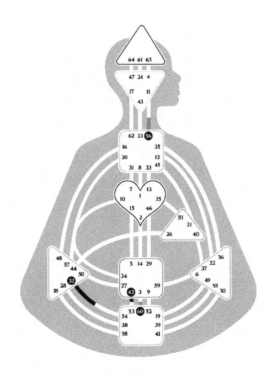

RAX The Divine Translator 4
Conscious Sun Gate: 43
Conscious Earth Gate: 23
Unconscious Sun Gate: 4
Unconscious Earth Gate: 49

Traditional HD IC Name: Right Angle Cross of Explanation 4
Quantum HD IC Name: Right Angle Cross of The Divine Translator 4

Quantum Description:

To share revolutionary ideas and possibilities that have the power to transform the way people think. To teach and transmit new ideas and possibilities that change how people understand and perceive the world. To transform old ideas into new possibilities when the timing and the energy are aligned. To serve the world by sharing new ideas that awaken planetary consciousness.

Resiliency Keys:

Self-Trust, Decisiveness, Courage, Emotional Wisdom, Empowerment, Authenticity, Vitality

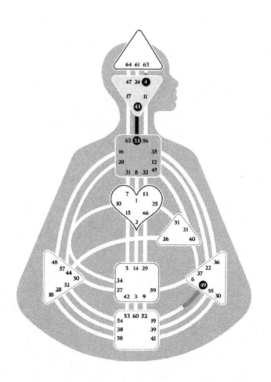

Traditional HD IC Name: Juxtaposition Cross of Insight
Quantum HD IC Name: Juxtaposition Cross of Insight

Quantum Description:

To embody and build a foundation of insight, awareness, and understandings that help transform people's thinking. To know how to trust your own knowingness and your intuitive connection to Cosmic Intelligence. To use your insights to support others in cultivating a practice of devotion that leads to living with passion. To use the spark of your passion and your knowingness to help others discover what is truly worth committing to. To say yes to new ideas and possibilities and to hold on to these new ideas long enough to see them transform collective beliefs about what is possible.

Resiliency Keys:

Authenticity, Decisiveness, Self-Trust, Courage, Vitality, Empowerment, Emotional Wisdom

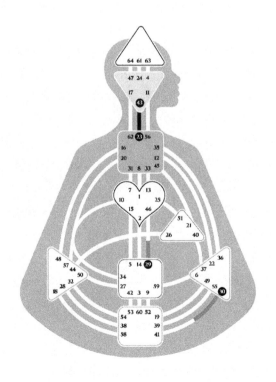

LAX Transmission 2
Conscious Sun Gate: 43
Conscious Earth Gate: 23
Unconscious Sun Gate: 29
Unconscious Earth Gate: 30

Traditional HD IC Name: Left Angle Cross of Dedication 2
Quantum HD IC Name: Left Angle Cross of Transmission 2

Quantum Description:

To lead, teach, and inspire others through your devotion and passion. To be a role model for dedication and commitment to a passionate cause. To share new ideas, insights, understandings, and ways of thinking to shift what people believe is possible and rethink old, outdated ideas that no longer fit. To teach and transmit new knowledge that promises to transform and evolve new potentials. To be dedicated to changing the world by changing personal and collective perceptions about what is possible.

Resiliency Keys:

Authenticity, Decisiveness, Self-Trust, Courage, Vitality, Empowerment, Emotional Wisdom

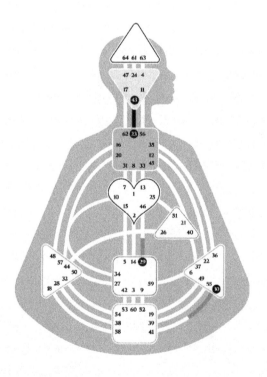

Traditional HD IC Name: Right Angle Cross of The Four Ways 3
Quantum HD IC Name: Right Angle Cross of Restoration 3

Quantum Description:

To explore, learn, and teach about the power and importance of narrative and story to set the tone and direction for life. To help others see patterns in old stories that may be causing them to rationalize and settle for less than what they deserve in their relationships. To use your natural sensitivity and intuition to be aware of where others may be rationalizing and settling for less than what they want. To see the potential in others and know how to change stories and narratives to support the fulfillment of potential. To help people stop playing small. To help others release the patterns and the pain of the past so they can better claim their true value and worth.

Resiliency Keys:

Vitality, Empowerment, Authenticity, Self-Trust, Courage, Decisiveness

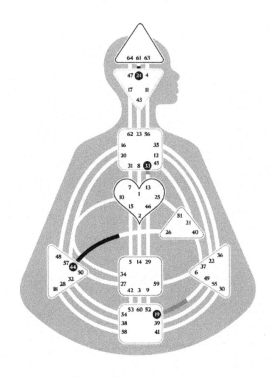

JUX Truth
Conscious Sun Gate: 44
Conscious Earth Gate: 24
Unconscious Sun Gate: 7
Unconscious Earth Gate: 13

Traditional HD IC Name: Juxtaposition Cross of Alertness
Quantum HD IC Name: Juxtaposition Cross of Truth

Quantum Description:

To embody and build a foundation rooted in your intuitive understanding of which patterns need to shift and be transformed to release limiting patterns from the past and to restore integrity. To heal by helping people recognize and claim their value and increase their self-worth. To help others see limiting patterns that keep them from owning their value. To collaborate and lead others to transform and realign their personal narrative so that their story includes their value and the full expression of their integrity. To show people the truth about their value and to help others heal their value story.

Resiliency Keys:

Self-Trust, Decisiveness, Courage, Lovability, Authenticity

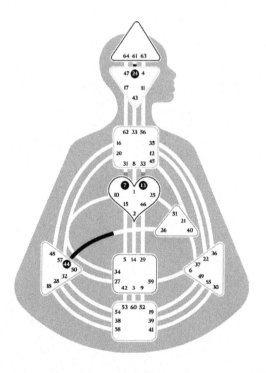

Traditional HD IC Name: Left Angle Cross of Incarnation 2
Quantum HD IC Name: Left Angle Cross of Remediation 2

Quantum Description:

To lead, teach, and inspire others to heal their self-worth and value story. To help others understand how to rewrite their personal narrative to reflect their true value, purpose, and worth. To help people break free from the patterns of the past that keep them stuck in old protective stories rooted in trauma. To help heal any trauma or trauma patterns that keep people settling and rationalizing receiving less than what they want and need. To support others in taking leadership in manifesting their dreams and cultivating a personal narrative that encompasses their true value and purpose. To help people change the direction of their lives by assisting them to heal their past and their old stories of limitation.

Resiliency Keys:

Self-Trust, Decisiveness, Courage, Lovability, Authenticity

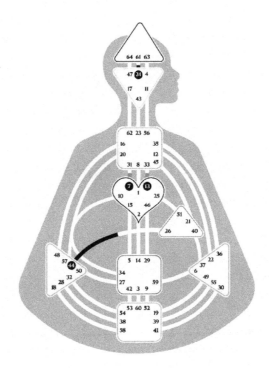

RAX Sovereignty 2
Conscious Sun Gate: 45
Conscious Earth Gate: 26
Unconscious Sun Gate: 22
Unconscious Earth Gate: 47

Traditional HD IC Name: Right Angle Cross of Rulership 2
Quantum HD IC Name: Right Angle Cross of Sovereignty 2

Quantum Description:

To explore, learn, and teach the importance of alignment and mindset in cultivating the energy necessary for creativity and manifestation. Understanding the relationship between self-worth, integrity, and mindset and teaching others how to regain sovereignty over their creations by healing any karma related to value and self-worth. To give people the resources they need to regain personal empowerment and control over their own lives and their own reality.

Resiliency Keys:

Courage, Emotional Wisdom, Empowerment, Decisiveness, Self-Trust, Authenticity, Vitality, Self-Worth

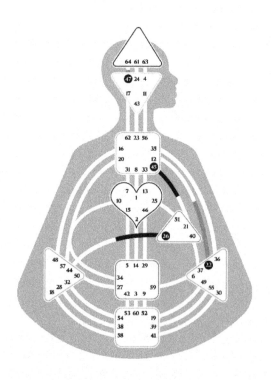

Traditional HD IC Name: Juxtaposition Cross of Possession

Quantum HD IC Name: Juxtaposition Cross of Distribution

Quantum Description:

To embody and build a foundation of teaching and sharing resources that help people reclaim and heal their value. To restore equitability and sustainability to distribute and share resources with integrity. To heal self-worth and redefine the metrics of value so that value is measured by quality, not quantity. To increase the quality of wellbeing for humanity by restoring integrity and value. To live sustainably and to teach sustainability to create greater value for others. To break old patterns that limit the distribution of value to create equitable, just, sustainable abundance for everyone.

Resiliency Keys:

Self-Worth, Vitality, Courage, Emotional Wisdom, Empowerment, Decisiveness, Authenticity

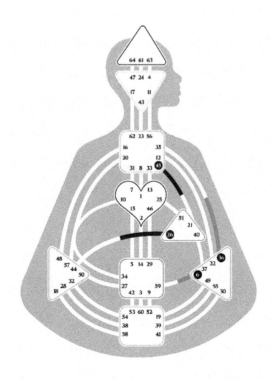

LAX Breakthrough

Conscious Sun Gate: 45
Conscious Earth Gate: 26
Unconscious Sun Gate: 36
Unconscious Earth Gate: 6

Traditional HD IC Name: Left Angle Cross of Confrontation

Quantum HD IC Name: Left Angle Cross of Breakthrough

Quantum Description:

To lead, teach, and inspire others to break free from limiting patterns and the pain of the past. To help people heal their self-worth and sense of value that supports them in living aligned with their true integrity. To help people harness the power of shattering old patterns and creating from outgrown expectations by showing them their value and helping them redefine their values. To help people create in alignment with physical, resource, identity, moral and energetic integrity. To do the work necessary to help the world redefine what is truly valuable.

Resiliency Keys:

Self-Worth, Vitality, Courage, Emotional Wisdom, Empowerment, Decisiveness, Authenticity

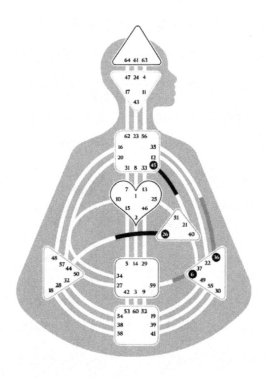

Traditional HD IC Name: Right Angle Cross of The Vessel of Love 3
Quantum HD IC Name: Right Angle Cross of Unity 3

Quantum Description:

To explore, learn about, and model the power of Love and the courage of the Heart. It is through the discipline of the Heart that one can lead others. To teach self-love, compassion, embodiment, and purpose by first learning, through personal experience, how to live and create from these energies. To become self-actualized and resilient by learning to love oneself and others. To know and teach that Love regulates how we lead, create, and walk through our days. To embody and give direction to Love in every way.

Resiliency Keys:

Lovability, Decisiveness, Courage, Authenticity

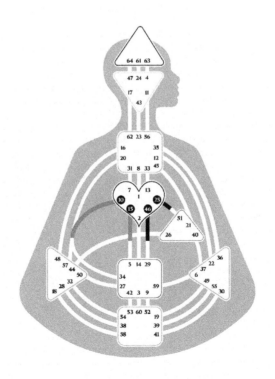

JUX Embodiment
Conscious Sun Gate: 46
Conscious Earth Gate: 25
Unconscious Sun Gate: 52
Unconscious Earth Gate: 58

Traditional HD IC Name: Juxtaposition Cross of Serendipity
Quantum HD IC Name: Juxtaposition Cross of Embodiment

Quantum Description:

To embody and build a foundation for connecting with the body's wisdom and sensual experience. To teach the importance of love for the body. To help people heal their bodies by helping them see the bigger message and purpose for their physical pain and reconnect them to their joy. To help others see the relationship between their experience of joy in their lives and the embodiment of their essence. To help people reconnect to the joy of physicality and support them in fully experiencing all the sensory and sensual aspects of being embodied. To help people reconnect to their purpose and to Source as a pathway to healing and using the body as a vehicle for their soul.

Resiliency Keys:

Lovability, Decisiveness, Courage, Authenticity, Vitality, Empowerment

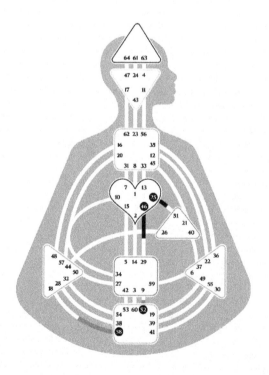

Traditional HD IC Name: Left Angle Cross of Healing 2
Quantum HD IC Name: Left Angle Cross of The Heart 2

Quantum Description:

To lead, teach, and inspire others to live and build a joyful life. To help others find a deep connection to the joy that comes from living and creating in alignment with their higher and spiritual purpose. To help people fully embody their purpose and take actions to fulfill their purpose in the world. To heal by reconnecting to a higher purpose. To help others remember their higher purpose, support them in finding blessings, meaning, and new perspectives from past experiences.

Resiliency Keys:

Lovability, Decisiveness, Courage, Authenticity, Vitality, Empowerment

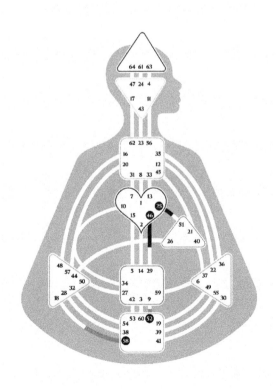

RAX Sovereignty 3
Conscious Sun Gate: 47
Conscious Earth Gate: 22
Unconscious Sun Gate: 45
Unconscious Earth Gate: 26

Traditional HD IC Name: Right Angle Cross of Rulership 3
Quantum HD IC Name: Right Angle Cross of Sovereignty 3

Quantum Description:

To explore, learn, and teach the importance of alignment and mindset in cultivating the energy necessary for creativity and manifestation. Understanding the relationship between self-worth, integrity, and mindset and teaching others how to regain sovereignty over their creations by healing any karma related to value and self-worth. To give people the resources they need to regain personal empowerment and control over their own lives and their reality.

Resiliency Keys:

Courage, Emotional Wisdom, Empowerment, Decisiveness, Self-Trust, Authenticity, Vitality, Self-Worth

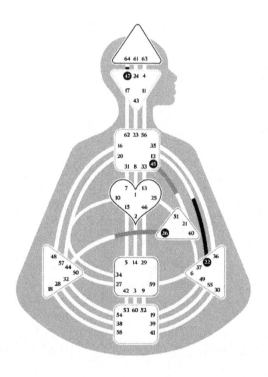

Traditional HD IC Name: Juxtaposition Cross of Oppression
Quantum HD IC Name: Juxtaposition Cross of Mindset

Quantum Description:

To embody and build a foundation of understanding and wisdom about the importance and creative power of mindset. To teach people how the attunement of mindset creates intuitive insights and inspirations that lead to the receptivity of ideas and inspirations that can potentially change worlds. To be a conduit for inspiration by trusting that the inspiration and the answer will appear. To see the relationship between ideas and thoughts in new ways as the intuitive spark and connection that brings ideas and inspirations together in new and inspiring ways. To be the source of intuitive knowing that shows people how to turn ideas and inspirations into reality.

Resiliency Keys:

Self-Trust, Decisiveness, Courage, Emotional Wisdom, Empowerment, Authenticity, Vitality

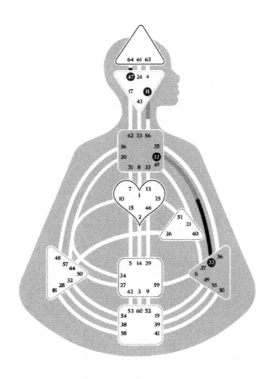

LAX Metamorphosis 2
Conscious Sun Gate: 47
Conscious Earth Gate: 22
Unconscious Sun Gate: 12
Unconscious Earth Gate: 11

Traditional HD IC Name: Left Angle Cross of Informing 2
Quantum HD IC Name: Left Angle Cross of Metamorphosis 2

Quantum Description:

To lead, teach, and inspire others to understand the relationship between mindset and creativity. To give others ideas and Divine insights to help them heal their relationship with their creativity and to support people in learning to trust the power of their imagination. To teach people the importance of mindset in cultivating right timing. To have the right and Divine ideas and inspiration to help others heal their faith and activate the belief in their support and sufficiency.

Resiliency Keys:

Self-Trust, Decisiveness, Courage, Emotional Wisdom, Empowerment, Authenticity, Vitality

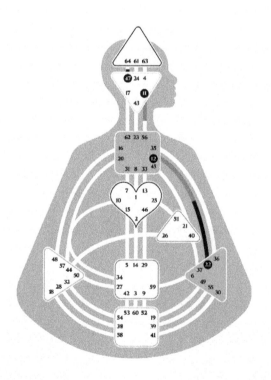

Traditional HD IC Name: Right Angle Cross of Tension 3
Quantum HD IC Name: Right Angle Cross of Renewal 3

Quantum Description:

To explore, learn, and teach from a depth of knowledge that comes from learning, studying, and investigating the importance and the power of self-regulation as a key element to accomplishing and fulfilling a dream. To instinctively know and understand what is out of alignment with abundance and to use your knowledge and wisdom to bring people back into harmony with the potential of support and sufficiency. To cultivate a vision of an abundant world, to practice self-regulation, and to study, learn and act upon exactly what needs to be done to fulfill that vision.

Resiliency Keys:

Self-Worth, Vitality, Empowerment, Self-Trust, Courage

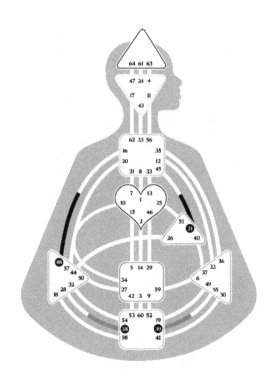

JUX Wisdom
Conscious Sun Gate: 48
Conscious Earth Gate: 21
Unconscious Sun Gate: 53
Unconscious Earth Gate: 54

Traditional HD IC Name: Juxtaposition Cross of Depth

Quantum HD IC Name: Juxtaposition Cross of Wisdom

Quantum Description:

To embody and build a foundation of understanding about the depth of knowledge and experience necessary to actualize talent and potential. To regulate the personal learning process to build a foundation of depth and wisdom. To cultivate a practice of deep connection with Cosmic Mind as a source of inspiration that is then, in turn, studied and practiced knowing which inspirations to initiate and make manifest on the physical plane. To use your embodiment of wisdom and learned knowledge to initiate others with new ideas and possibilities. To be the spark of initiation and the source of wisdom and ideas that help people begin the process of building a dream.

Resiliency Keys:

Self-Worth, Vitality, Empowerment, Self-Trust, Courage

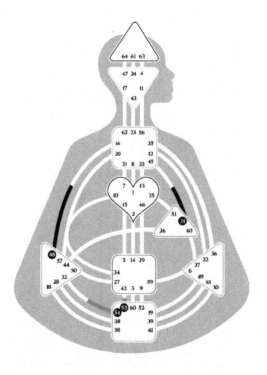

Traditional HD IC Name: Left Angle Cross of Endeavor 2
Quantum HD IC Name: Left Angle Cross of Self-Regulation 2

Quantum Description:

To lead, teach, and inspire others to cultivate a practice of self-regulation that allows them to be inspired to follow new flows of abundance and inspiration. To create a depth of knowledge and wisdom from studying and learning that helps others manifest their dreams and do the work necessary to build new pathways of abundance. To model and teach the importance of patterns and habits that allow for conserving energy and creating sustainable wealth and wellbeing. To initiate others into healthy habits that help them create greater abundance and have access to more resources.

Resiliency Keys:

Self-Worth, Vitality, Empowerment, Self-Trust, Courage

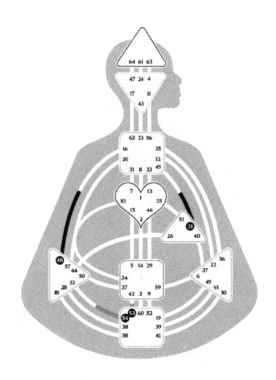

RAX The Divine Translator
Conscious Sun Gate: 49
Conscious Earth Gate: 4
Unconscious Sun Gate: 43
Unconscious Earth Gate: 23

Traditional HD IC Name: Right Angle Cross of Explanation
Quantum HD IC Name: Right Angle Cross of The Divine Translator

Quantum Description:

To share revolutionary ideas and possibilities that have the power to transform the way people think. To teach and transmit new ideas and possibilities that change how people understand and perceive the world. To transform old ideas into new possibilities when the timing and the energy are aligned. To serve the world by sharing new ideas that awaken planetary consciousness.

Resiliency Keys:

Self-Trust, Decisiveness, Courage, Emotional Wisdom, Empowerment, Authenticity, Vitality

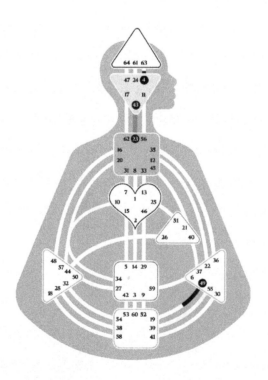

Traditional HD IC Name: Juxtaposition Cross of Principles

Quantum HD IC Name: Juxtaposition Cross of The Catalyst

Quantum Description:

To embody and build a foundation of exploration and experimentation with answers that have the potential to catalyze transformation and create revolutions in relationships and intimacy. To understand the importance of creating relationship agreements rooted in mutual respect, value, and common values. To catalyze relationships and contracts that lead to the manifestation of the common good. To redefine and create a revolution in how we create and generate money, wealth, and income. To catalyze and teach the importance of the relationship between working "on purpose" and creating true wealth. To teach the importance of not settling or rationalizing receiving less. To work to redefine personal and collective definitions of wealth and abundance to include alignment with purpose and meaning.

Resiliency Keys:

Courage, Emotional Wisdom, Empowerment, Decisiveness, Vitality, Authenticity, Self-Trust

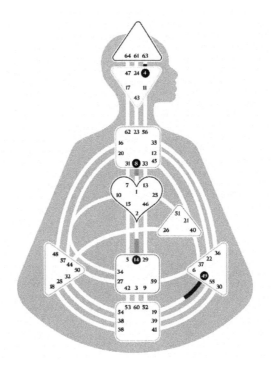

LAX Revelation
Conscious Sun Gate: 49
Conscious Earth Gate: 4
Unconscious Sun Gate: 14
Unconscious Earth Gate: 8

Traditional HD IC Name: Left Angle Cross of Revolution
Quantum HD IC Name: Left Angle Cross of Revelation

Quantum Description:

To lead, teach, and inspire people to catalyze transformation in their work. To help people align with the answers that help them create greater abundance when they express their true and authentic voice. To change the economic landscape, so that right work includes authentic self-expression. To help people break free from the idea that they have to compromise who they are to create abundance.

Resiliency Keys:

Courage, Emotional Wisdom, Empowerment, Decisiveness, Vitality, Authenticity, Self-Trust

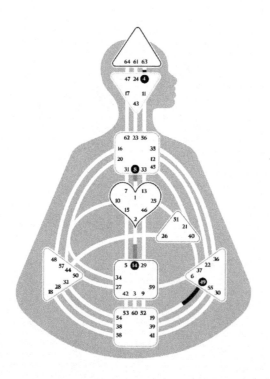

Traditional HD IC Name: Right Angle Cross of Laws 3
Quantum HD IC Name: Right Angle Cross of Evolution 3

Quantum Description:

To bring innovation and new possibilities to the world by using gratitude to expand on what already works. To learn to use the power of narrative, metaphor, and storytelling to transform the story of what is possible and to shift the collective definition of value. To bring innovative ideas to the world that increase our ability to support, nurture, feed, and care for each other.

Resiliency Keys:

Vitality, Decisiveness, Courage, Empowerment, Self-Trust, Authenticity

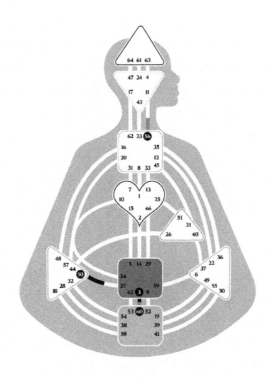

JUX Nurturing
Conscious Sun Gate: 50
Conscious Earth Gate: 3
Unconscious Sun Gate: 31
Unconscious Earth Gate: 41

Traditional HD IC Name: Juxtaposition Cross of Values
Quantum HD IC Name: Juxtaposition Cross of Nurturing

Quantum Description:

To embody and build a foundation of values that support the evolution of innovative ideas that help meet the needs of others. To lead with innovative and new ideas that have the potential to improve how we care for, provide for and educate others. Using the power of imagination and innovation that leads others to reframe and rethink the possibility of creating abundance and sufficiency for all. To embody and teach others the value of caring. To be nurturing and to value nurturing as a quality that creates a medium for growth and evolution.

Resiliency Keys:

Authenticity, Vitality, Decisiveness, Courage, Empowerment, Self-Trust

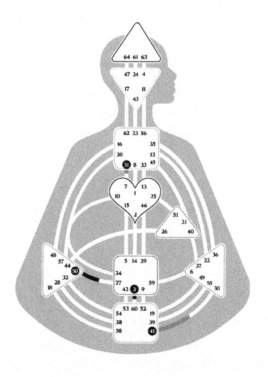

Traditional HD IC Name: Left Angle Cross of Wishes 2
Quantum HD IC Name: Left Angle Cross of Transformation 2

Quantum Description:

To lead, teach, and inspire others in adopting and adapting to new values that include the importance and the power of creativity and imagination as keystones to innovation. To lead others in integrating innovative ideas and creative possibilities. To begin establishing new laws and values that support growth and transformation. To usher in innovation and new ideas by establishing the value of creativity and imagination in the collective.

Resiliency Keys:

Vitality, Decisiveness, Courage, Empowerment, Self-Trust, Emotional Wisdom, Authenticity

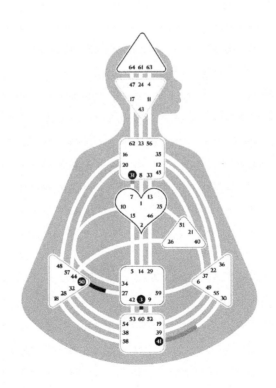

RAX Honesty
Conscious Sun Gate: 51
Conscious Earth Gate: 57
Unconscious Sun Gate: 54
Unconscious Earth Gate: 53

Traditional HD IC Name: Right Angle Cross of Penetration

Quantum HD IC Name: Right Angle Cross of Honesty

Quantum Description:

To explore, learn, and teach about new ideas that have the power to initiate others into new possibilities and potentials. To use your intuitive understanding and insights to initiate others into exploring new ideas. To use your intuitive, penetrating awareness to bring people back into alignment with what is true and what is truth. To use your intuitive awareness to help people begin the process of constructing the manifestation of their dreams. To initiate others by reconnecting them to their higher purpose and their innate connection with Source. To be a spiritual teacher whose insights help people quickly dismantle illusions that keep them from fulfilling their true potential.

Resiliency Keys:

Self-Worth, Vitality, Empowerment, Self-Trust, Courage

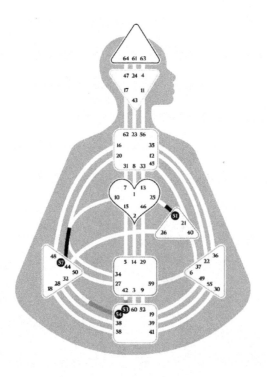

Traditional HD IC Name: Juxtaposition Cross of Shock
Quantum HD IC Name: Juxtaposition Cross of Higher Purpose

Quantum Description:

To embody and build a foundation of practical understandings that help people reconnect with their higher purpose. To use your intuitive awareness and penetrating understanding to help people know what needs to shift and change for them to align with their true value and purpose. To help people remove blocks and limitations that keep them from fulfilling that purpose. To help people see their place in the Cosmic Plan and to give them practical steps to begin fulfilling that purpose. To be a teacher of the importance of living with purpose.

Resiliency Keys:

Self-Worth, Vitality, Empowerment, Self-Trust, Courage, Decisiveness

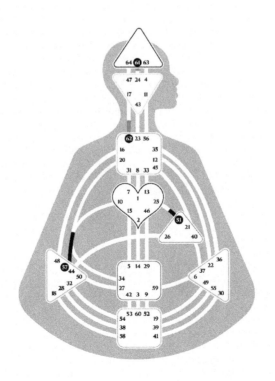

LAX Initiation
Conscious Sun Gate: 51
Conscious Earth Gate: 57
Unconscious Sun Gate: 61
Unconscious Earth Gate: 62

Traditional HD IC Name: Left Angle Cross of The Clarion
Quantum HD IC Name: Left Angle Cross of Initiation

Quantum Description:

To lead, teach, and inspire others by initiating them into powerful spiritual truths. To help people discover practical ways to live in alignment with their higher purpose. To see the bigger Cosmic and Spiritual Perspective and to share your understanding of this perspective in practical and powerful ways. To be a practical mystic. To use your penetrating intuitive awareness to initiate others into their higher purpose and the bigger perspective of the meaning of their life. To be a spiritual teacher and initiator. To help people discover the meaning of their challenges and to help them reconnect with their spiritual purpose.

Resiliency Keys:

Self-Worth, Vitality, Empowerment, Self-Trust, Courage, Decisiveness

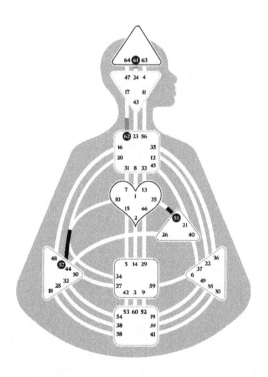

Traditional HD IC Name: Right Angle Cross of Service 2
Quantum HD IC Name: Right Angle Cross of Exaltation 2

Quantum Description:

To explore, learn, and teach about the importance of perspective as a key element to cultivating self-actualization. The ability to take a big step back and see the big picture to understand that the corrections and alignments necessary in the moment are essential to cultivating joy and exaltation. To discover what brings the greatest joy and to pursue its purest expression. To realize and demonstrate that this pursuit is a worthy contribution. To practice and perfect contributing to the world, in a way that brings the greatest joy. To teach the importance of joy.

Resiliency Keys:

Self-Trust, Courage, Decisiveness, Vitality, Empowerment

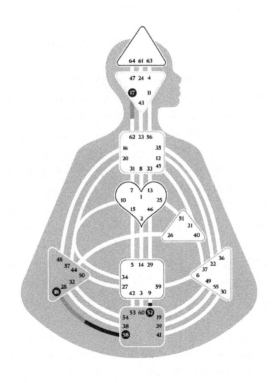

JUX Perspective
Conscious Sun Gate: 52
Conscious Earth Gate: 58
Unconscious Sun Gate: 21
Unconscious Earth Gate: 48

Traditional HD IC Name: Juxtaposition Cross of Stillness
Quantum HD IC Name: Juxtaposition Cross of Perspective

Quantum Description:

To embody and build a foundation of understanding of the power of stillness. To use your depth of knowledge and wisdom to help others cultivate a practice that supports them in cultivating joy and aligning with that which brings them joy. To connect with Source through cultivating a practice of stillness. To see the entire perspective and to know where to focus right action. In right timing, to know how to actualize joy and wisdom best.

Resiliency Keys:

Vitality, Empowerment, Self-Trust, Courage, Self-Worth

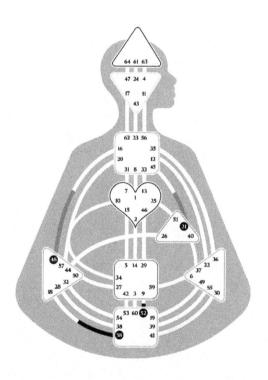

Traditional HD IC Name: Left Angle Cross of Demands
Quantum HD IC Name: Left Angle Cross of Process

Quantum Description:

To lead, teach, and inspire people to create a practice of self-renewal and self-regulation that supports them in the process of continuing to practice, align and repeat until they actualize their talents and skills. To become an expert at teaching others how to become an expert. To coach others to build a practice of cultivating joy and expertise. To innately understand the process of pursuing that which brings joy. To understand and cultivate a practice that cultivates joy into expertise and actualization. To support others in cultivating their talent into fully expressing their potential. To understand and lead people through turning talent into expertise and fulfillment.

Resiliency Keys:

Vitality, Empowerment, Self-Trust, Courage, Self-Worth

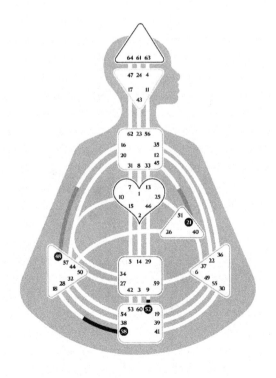

RAX Honesty 2
Conscious Sun Gate: 53
Conscious Earth Gate: 54
Unconscious Sun Gate: 51
Unconscious Earth Gate: 57

Traditional HD IC Name: Right Angle Cross of Penetration 2
Quantum HD IC Name: Right Angle Cross of Honesty 2

Quantum Description:

To explore, learn, and teach about new ideas that have the power to initiate others into new possibilities and potentials. To use your intuitive understanding and insights to initiate others into exploring new ideas. To use your intuitive, penetrating awareness to bring people back into alignment with what is true and what is truth. To use your intuitive awareness to help people begin the process of constructing the manifestation of their dreams. To initiate others by reconnecting them to their higher purpose and their innate connection with Source. To be a spiritual teacher whose insights help people quickly dismantle illusions that keep them from fulfilling their true potential.

Resiliency Keys:

Self-Worth, Vitality, Empowerment, Self-Trust, Courage

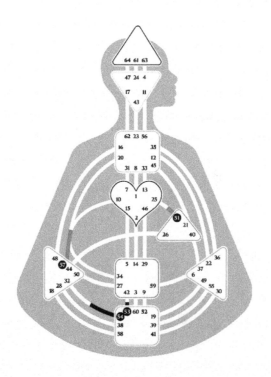

Conscious Sun Gate: 53
Conscious Earth Gate: 54
Unconscious Sun Gate: 42
Unconscious Earth Gate: 32

Traditional HD IC Name: Juxtaposition Cross of Beginnings
Quantum HD IC Name: Juxtaposition Cross of Patience

Quantum Description:

To embody and build a foundation for initiating new ideas. To understand the importance of creating with a clean slate. To have the energy, intuition, and drive to complete what has come before to have space to create something new. To begin the building process and to have the endurance and patience to wait for the right timing to initiate the idea into the world. To teach the importance of completion as a vital aspect of starting new things. To understand how to begin something new and how to endure the process of creating for the length of time it takes to bring a project to fruition and completion.

Resiliency Keys:

Vitality, Empowerment, Decisiveness, Courage, Self-Trust

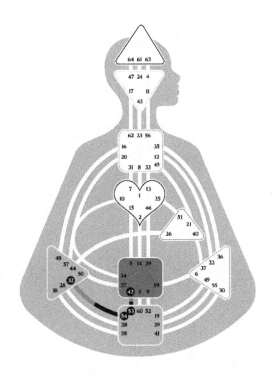

LAX Stewardship
Conscious Sun Gate: 53
Conscious Earth Gate: 54
Unconscious Sun Gate: 42
Unconscious Earth Gate: 32

Traditional HD IC Name: Left Angle Cross of Cycles
Quantum HD IC Name: Left Angle Cross of Stewardship

Quantum Description:

To lead, teach, and inspire others to nurture and protect their dreams and inspirations. To help others initiate the manifestation of their ideas but encourage them first to complete anything that may be holding them back. To understand the importance of creating space to initiate a new idea. To value and be a steward of new ideas and to know that the manifestation of an idea is worth the time and effort it takes to bring it forth. To intuitively understand the importance of Divine and right timing to bring an idea into form. To do the work necessary to lay the foundation for the manifestation of a dream or an idea. Diligence.

Resiliency Keys:

Vitality, Empowerment, Decisiveness, Courage, Self-Trust

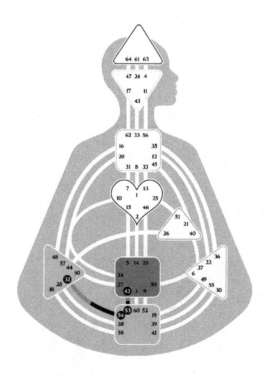

Traditional HD IC Name: Right Angle Cross of Penetration 4
Quantum HD IC Name: Right Angle Cross of Honesty 4

Quantum Description:

To explore, learn, and teach about new ideas that have the power to initiate others into new possibilities and potentials. To use your intuitive understanding and insights to initiate others into exploring new ideas. To use your intuitive, penetrating awareness to bring people back into alignment with what is true and what is truth. To use your intuitive awareness to help people begin the process of constructing the manifestation of their dreams. To initiate others by reconnecting them to their higher purpose and their innate connection with Source. To be a spiritual teacher whose insights help people quickly dismantle illusions that keep them from fulfilling their true potential.

Resiliency Keys:

Self-Worth, Vitality, Empowerment, Self-Trust, Courage

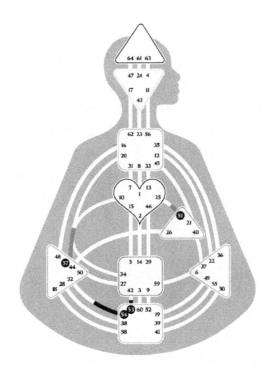

JUX Divine Inspiration
Conscious Sun Gate: 54
Conscious Earth Gate: 53
Unconscious Sun Gate: 32
Unconscious Earth Gate: 42

Traditional HD IC Name: Juxtaposition Cross of Ambition

Quantum HD IC Name: Juxtaposition Cross of Divine Inspiration

---

Quantum Description:

To embody and build a foundation of knowing how to cultivate a deep attunement to Source to understand the timing and work necessary to bring inspiration into form. To see the relationships between ideas and understand which ideas are worth pursuing. To understand the process of bringing an idea into form and to completion. To support the creation and manifestation of new ideas by first completing whatever needs to be brought to completion to create space for something new. To have the drive, ambition, and patience to build the foundation for a dream and bring it into form when the time and timing are aligned.

Resiliency Keys:

Vitality, Empowerment, Decisiveness, Courage, Self-Trust

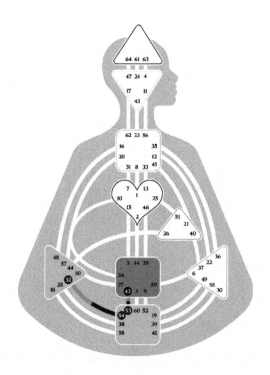

Traditional HD IC Name: Left Angle Cross of Cycles 2
Quantum HD IC Name: Left Angle Cross of Stewardship 2

Quantum Description:

To lead, teach, and inspire others to nurture and protect their dreams and inspirations. To help others initiate the manifestation of their ideas but encourage them first to complete anything that may be holding them back. To understand the importance of creating space to initiate a new idea. To value and be a steward of new ideas and to know that the manifestation of an idea is worth the time and effort it takes to bring it forth. To intuitively understand the importance of Divine and right timing to bring an idea into form. To do the work necessary to lay the foundation for the manifestation of a dream or an idea. Diligence.

Resiliency Keys:

Vitality, Empowerment, Decisiveness, Courage, Self-Trust

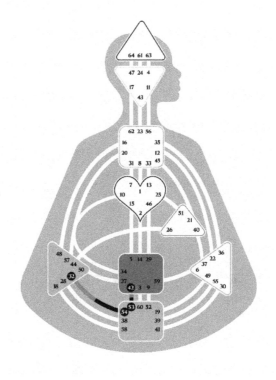

RAX The Harbinger
Conscious Sun Gate: 55
Conscious Earth Gate: 59
Unconscious Sun Gate: 34
Unconscious Earth Gate: 20

Traditional HD IC Name: Right Angle Cross of The Sleeping Phoenix
Quantum HD IC Name: Right Angle Cross of The Harbinger

Quantum Description:

To explore, learn, and teach about the true nature of power. To embody aligning yourself with Divine Timing to gather people around new ideas that have the potential to create sustainability. To create beyond what you know how to create by cultivating deep faith and trust in abundance. To use faith as a way of seeding the Quantum Field. To know how to read the signs and engage with the world in such a way that you know when it's time to respond to what's needed to create abundance for all. To organize people around new ideas and convictions that support the work and creation necessary to help people create sustainable, abundant resources and peace.

Resiliency Keys:

Authenticity, Decisiveness, Courage, Vitality, Empowerment, Emotional Wisdom

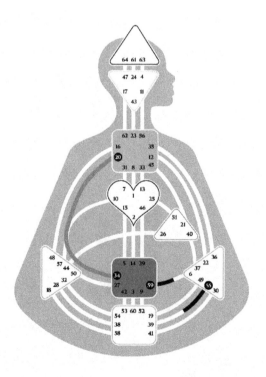

Traditional HD IC Name: Juxtaposition Cross of Moods
Quantum HD IC Name: Juxtaposition Cross of Sufficiency

Quantum Description:

To embody and build a foundation of trust in Source as a key element of cultivating abundance and sufficiency. To operate in the world with zest and focus, knowing that exploration and experimentation are vital to growth and expansion. Trusting the growth process with a deep understanding rooted in the awareness that there is no risk in trying when you trust that you are supported. Being willing to take leaps of faith because you trust in the foundation of your abundance.

Resiliency Keys:

Courage, Emotional Wisdom, Empowerment, Decisiveness, Vitality, Authenticity

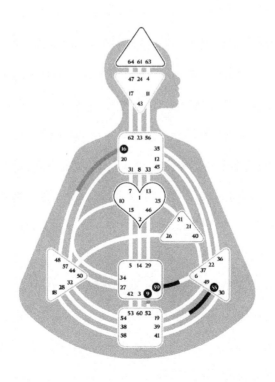

LAX Faith
Conscious Sun Gate: 55
Conscious Earth Gate: 59
Unconscious Sun Gate: 9
Unconscious Earth Gate: 16

Traditional HD IC Name: Left Angle Cross of Spirit
Quantum HD IC Name: Left Angle Cross of Faith

Quantum Description:

To lead, teach, and inspire people to cultivate faith and trust in their own sufficiency. To use the power of zestful focus to create vibrational alignment with abundance. To uplift others and penetrate their energy field with a high degree and frequency of faith in abundance. To not be afraid to try and take risks in the name of growth and evolution because you implicitly trust your abundance and your connection with Source. To be a teacher and role model of creating with faith. To be willing to create beyond the limitations of the human experience. To know how to inspire others to take leaps of faith.

Resiliency Keys:

Courage, Emotional Wisdom, Empowerment, Decisiveness, Vitality, Authenticity

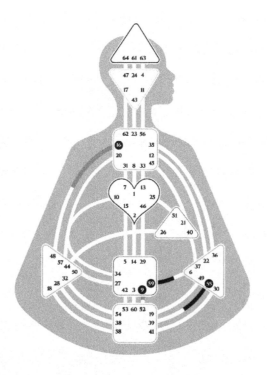

Traditional HD IC Name: Right Angle Cross of Laws 2
Quantum HD IC Name: Right Angle Cross of Evolution 2

Quantum Description:

To bring innovation and new possibilities to the world by using gratitude to expand on what already works. To learn to use the power of narrative, metaphor, and storytelling to transform the story of what is possible and to shift the collective definition of value. To bring innovative ideas to the world that increase our ability to support, nurture, feed, and care for each other.

Resiliency Keys:

Vitality, Decisiveness, Courage, Empowerment, Self-Trust, Authenticity

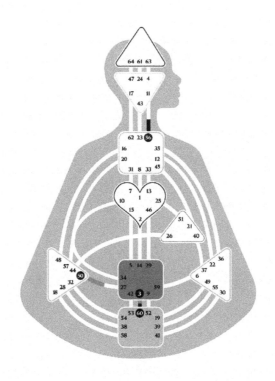

JUX The Narrator
Conscious Sun Gate: 56
Conscious Earth Gate: 60
Unconscious Sun Gate: 27
Unconscious Earth Gate: 28

Traditional HD IC Name: Juxtaposition Cross of Stimulation
Quantum HD IC Name: Juxtaposition Cross of The Narrator

Quantum Description:

To embody and build a foundation of a deep wisdom of what is truly worthy of pursuing and what is truly valuable in life based on your own explorations, challenges, adventures, and experiences. To use your challenges as metaphors to help others redefine their past experiences. To know what's worth the challenge. To use gratitude as a pathway to gain sovereignty over past experiences and old narratives of victimhood. To understand the power of narrative and storytelling as a tool to help people shift their perspective and align their values with what's truly important.

Resiliency Keys:

Vitality, Decisiveness, Courage, Empowerment, Self-Trust, Authenticity

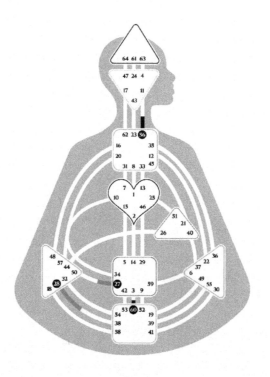

Traditional HD IC Name: Left Angle Cross of Distraction
Quantum HD IC Name: Left Angle Cross of Expansion

Quantum Description:

To lead, teach, and inspire others to translate their past experiences of challenge and struggle into new understandings that help them regain control and sovereignty over their lives. To use the power of narrative and storytelling to help others craft an empowered personal narrative that helps them reimagine and reinterpret their lives. To educate others about how the power of language and the words we use become the frame for what we create tomorrow. To help others stay focused on growth and expansion and not let themselves be distracted by outdated stories of victimhood and struggle.

Resiliency Keys:

Vitality, Decisiveness, Courage, Empowerment, Self-Trust, Authenticity

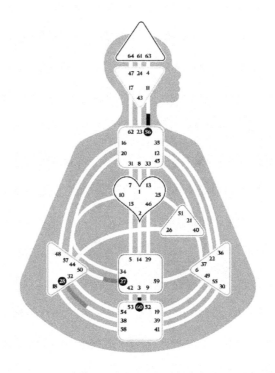

RAX Honesty 3
Conscious Sun Gate: 57
Conscious Earth Gate: 51
Unconscious Sun Gate: 53
Unconscious Earth Gate: 54

Traditional HD IC Name: Right Angle Cross of Penetration 3
Quantum HD IC Name: Right Angle Cross of Honesty 3

Quantum Description:

To explore, learn, and teach about new ideas that have the power to initiate others into new possibilities and potentials. To use your intuitive understanding and insights to initiate others into exploring new ideas. To use your intuitive, penetrating awareness to bring people back into alignment with what is true and what is truth. To use your intuitive awareness to help people begin the process of constructing the manifestation of their dreams. To initiate others by reconnecting them to their higher purpose and their innate connection with Source. To be a spiritual teacher whose insights help people quickly dismantle illusions that keep them from fulfilling their true potential.

Resiliency Keys:

Self-Worth, Vitality, Empowerment, Self-Trust, Courage

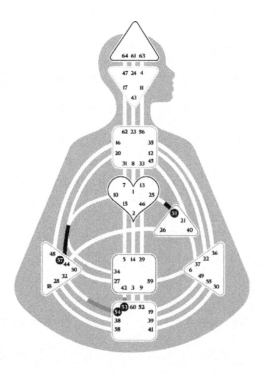

Traditional HD IC Name: Juxtaposition Cross of Intuition

Quantum HD IC Name: Juxtaposition Cross of Knowingness

Quantum Description:

To embody and build a foundation of deep trust in your own inner knowingness. To use your intuitive knowingness and penetrating intuitive awareness to help others find a practical path to awakening their connection to the Cosmos and Cosmic Mind: a practical mystical teacher. To initiate others onto their own path of inner knowingness by teaching others how to trust their intuition. To serve as a conduit for Divine knowledge.

Resiliency Keys:

Self-Trust, Decisiveness, Courage, Authenticity, Vitality, Self-Worth, Empowerment

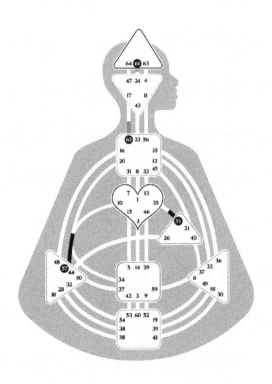

LAX Initiation 2
Conscious Sun Gate: 57
Conscious Earth Gate: 51
Unconscious Sun Gate: 62
Unconscious Earth Gate: 61

Traditional HD IC Name: Left Angle Cross of The Clarion 2
Quantum HD IC Name: Left Angle Cross of Initiation 2

Quantum Description:

To lead, teach, and inspire others by initiating them into powerful spiritual truths. To help people discover practical ways to live in alignment with their higher purpose. To see the bigger Cosmic and Spiritual Perspective and to share your understanding of this perspective in practical and powerful ways. To be a practical mystic. To use your penetrating intuitive awareness to initiate others into their higher purpose and the bigger perspective of the meaning of their life. To be a spiritual teacher and initiator. To help people discover the meaning of their challenges and to help them reconnect with their spiritual purpose.

Resiliency Keys:

Self-Trust, Decisiveness, Courage, Authenticity, Vitality, Self-Worth, Empowerment

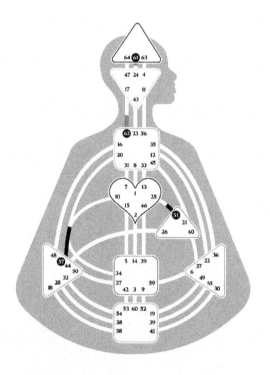

Traditional HD IC Name: Right Angle Cross of Service 4
Quantum HD IC Name: Right Angle Cross of Exaltation 4

Quantum Description:

To explore, learn, and teach about the importance of perspective as a key element to cultivating self-actualization. The ability to take a big step back and see the big picture to understand that the corrections and alignments necessary in the moment are essential to cultivating joy and exaltation. To discover what brings the greatest joy and to pursue its purest expression. To realize and demonstrate that this pursuit is a worthy contribution. To practice and perfect contributing to the world, in a way that brings the greatest joy. To teach the importance of joy.

Resiliency Keys:

Self-Trust, Courage, Decisiveness, Vitality, Empowerment

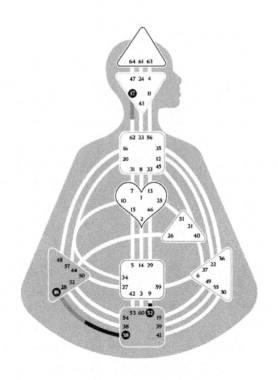

JUX Joy
Conscious Sun Gate: 58
Conscious Earth Gate: 52
Unconscious Sun Gate: 48
Unconscious Earth Gate: 21

Traditional HD IC Name: Juxtaposition Cross of Vitality
Quantum HD IC Name: Juxtaposition Cross of Joy

Quantum Description:

To embody and build a foundation of living in joy. To let your joy drive your creative process. To use your understanding of the process of self-actualization to help you cultivate the drive and resilience necessary to follow and develop what brings you joy in cultivating and perfecting the expression of joy. To understand the practice and repetition required to cultivate talent and bring it to a mature expression. To help others deepen the wise and mature expression of their talent by helping them connect with their joy and to help them permit themselves to pursue that which is joyful to them.

Resiliency Keys:

Vitality, Empowerment, Self-Trust, Courage, Self-Worth

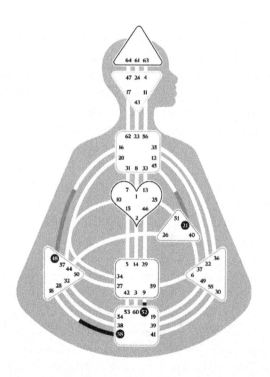

Traditional HD IC Name: Left Angle Cross of Demands 2
Quantum HD IC Name: Left Angle Cross of Process 2

Quantum Description:

To lead, teach, and inspire people to create a practice of self-renewal and self-regulation that supports them in the process of continuing to practice, align and repeat until they actualize their talents and skills. To become an expert at teaching others how to become an expert. To coach others to build a practice of cultivating joy and expertise. To innately understand the process of pursuing that which brings joy. To understand and cultivate a practice that cultivates joy into expertise and actualization. To support others in cultivating their talent into fully expressing their potential. To understand and lead people through turning talent into expertise and fulfillment.

Resiliency Keys:

Vitality, Empowerment, Self-Trust, Courage, Self-Worth

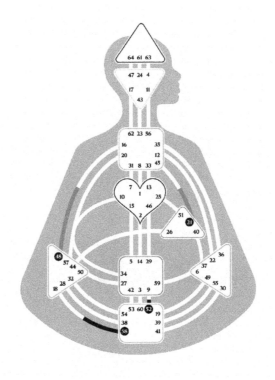

RAX The Harbinger 3
Conscious Sun Gate: 59
Conscious Earth Gate: 55
Unconscious Sun Gate: 20
Unconscious Earth Gate: 34

Traditional HD IC Name: Right Angle Cross of The Sleeping Phoenix 3

Quantum HD IC Name: Right Angle Cross of The Harbinger 3

Quantum Description:

To explore, learn, and teach about the true nature of power. To embody aligning yourself with Divine Timing in order to gather people around new ideas that have the potential to create sustainability. To create beyond what you know how to create by cultivating deep faith and trust in abundance. To use faith as a way of seeding the Quantum Field. To know how to read the signs and engage with the world in such a way that you know when it's time to respond to what's needed to create abundance for all. To organize people around new ideas and convictions that support the work and creation necessary to help people create sustainable, abundant resources and peace.

Resiliency Keys:

Authenticity, Decisiveness, Courage, Vitality, Empowerment, Emotional Wisdom

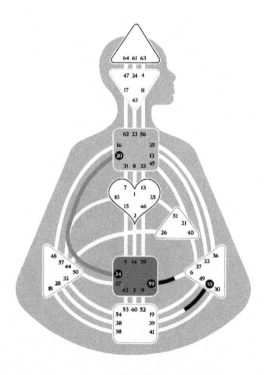

Traditional HD IC Name: Juxtaposition Cross of Strategy
Quantum HD IC Name: Juxtaposition Cross of Generation

Quantum Description:

To embody and build a foundation of unshakable faith rooted in focus, impact, and amplified with zest and enthusiasm. To understand that faith is the foundation that grounds and roots you in the freedom to explore and experiment. To learn risk assessment and management while recognizing faith as a metaphorical safety net. Understanding that focus and the willingness to take action with aligned circumstances and right timing create the matrix within which exponential growth can happen. To know the importance and cultivate the courage to take leaps of faith consistently.

Resiliency Keys:

Courage, Emotional Wisdom, Empowerment, Decisiveness, Vitality, Authenticity

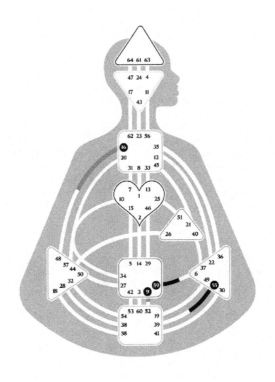

LAX Faith 2
Conscious Sun Gate: 59
Conscious Earth Gate: 55
Unconscious Sun Gate: 16
Unconscious Earth Gate: 9

Traditional HD IC Name: Left Angle Cross of Spirit 2
Quantum HD IC Name: Left Angle Cross of Faith 2

Quantum Description:

To lead, teach, and inspire people to cultivate faith and trust in their own sufficiency. To use the power of zestful focus to create vibrational alignment with abundance. To uplift others and penetrate their energy field with a high degree and frequency of faith in abundance. To not be afraid to try and take risks in the name of growth and evolution because you implicitly trust your abundance and your connection with Source. To be a teacher and role model of creating with faith. To be willing to create beyond the limitations of the human experience. To know how to inspire others to take leaps of faith.

Resiliency Keys:

Courage, Emotional Wisdom, Empowerment, Decisiveness, Vitality, Authenticity

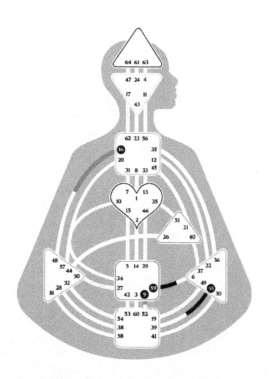

Traditional HD IC Name: Right Angle Cross of Laws 4
Quantum HD IC Name: Right Angle Cross of Evolution 4

Quantum Description:

To bring innovation and new possibilities to the world by using gratitude to expand on what already works. To learn to use the power of narrative, metaphor, and storytelling to transform the story of what is possible and to shift the collective definition of value. To bring innovative ideas to the world that increase our ability to support, nurture, feed, and care for each other.

Resiliency Keys:

Vitality, Decisiveness, Courage, Empowerment, Self-Trust, Authenticity

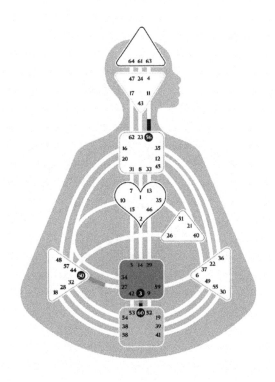

JUX Gratitude
Conscious Sun Gate: 60
Conscious Earth Gate: 56
Unconscious Sun Gate: 28
Unconscious Earth Gate: 27

Traditional HD IC Name: Juxtaposition Cross of Limitation
Quantum HD IC Name: Juxtaposition Cross of Gratitude

Quantum Description:

To embody and build a foundation of gratitude that helps transform struggle and pain into lessons and blessings that redefine what is truly valuable and worthy of creating in life. To reframe personal narratives by discovering that life happens for you, not against you. To realize that there are blessings and things to be grateful for in all circumstances. To use gratitude as a skill to help redefine the pain of the past. To teach and share lessons about the importance of enduring and sustaining during challenges while pursuing dreams and essential innovations.

Resiliency Keys:

Self-Trust, Courage, Authenticity, Vitality, Decisiveness, Empowerment

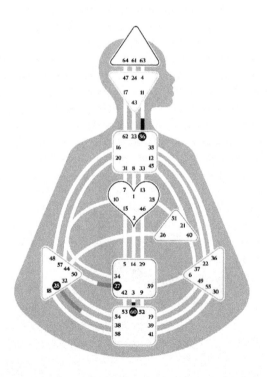

Traditional HD IC Name: Left Angle Cross of Distraction 2
Quantum HD IC Name: Left Angle Cross of Expansion 2

Quantum Description:

To lead, teach, and inspire others to translate their past experiences of challenge and struggle into new understandings that help them regain control and sovereignty over their lives. To use the power of narrative and storytelling to help others craft an empowered personal narrative that helps them reimagine and reinterpret their lives. To educate others about how the power of language and the words we use become the frame for what we create tomorrow. To help others stay focused on growth and expansion and not let themselves be distracted by outdated stories of victimhood and struggle.

Resiliency Keys:

Self-Trust, Courage, Authenticity, Vitality, Decisiveness, Empowerment

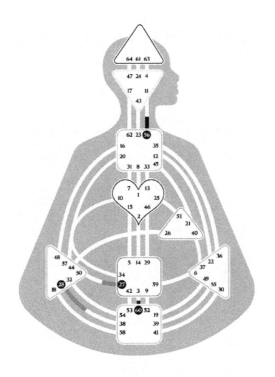

RAX Endurance 4
Conscious Sun Gate: 61
Conscious Earth Gate: 62
Unconscious Sun Gate: 32
Unconscious Earth Gate: 42

Traditional HD IC Name: Right Angle Cross of The Maya 4
Quantum HD IC Name: Right Angle Cross of Endurance 4

Quantum Description:

To explore, learn, and teach the importance of aligning with right timing to manifest and implement the next key steps to creation. To plan, prepare, and clear the path for the next step and to teach the importance of conscious readiness. To help others learn to set the stage and be prepared for what is next. To align yourself with the long haul. To ensure all the necessary action steps are ready to align with the manifestation of a dream. To know that part of bringing the idea into form is to "act as if" and doing all the things necessary to be prepared for when the timing is right.

Resiliency Keys:

Authenticity, Self-Trust, Decisiveness, Courage, Vitality, Empowerment

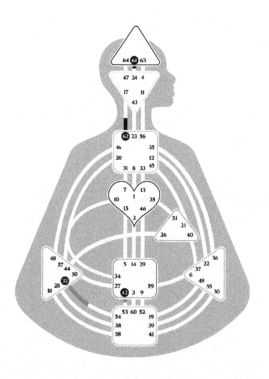

Traditional HD IC Name: Juxtaposition Cross of Thinking
Quantum HD IC Name: Juxtaposition Cross of Contemplation

Quantum Description:

To embody and build a foundation of innovation by serving as a conduit for Divine Inspiration. To teach and share that all information, including innovative ideas and breakthrough concepts, are contained within Cosmic Mind and to show people how to harness the power of Cosmic Intelligence. To learn to spark Cosmic Intelligence by cultivating thoughtful and deep connection practice. To spark innovative solutions to humanity's challenges by sustaining a mystical and spiritual connection to Cosmic Intelligence.

Resiliency Keys:

Decisiveness, Self-Trust, Authenticity, Vitality, Courage, Empowerment

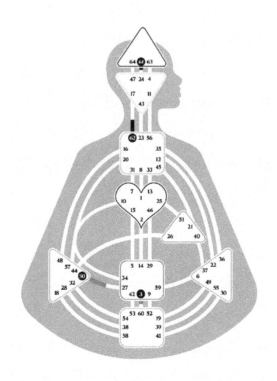

LAX Wonder 2
Conscious Sun Gate: 61
Conscious Earth Gate: 62
Unconscious Sun Gate: 50
Unconscious Earth Gate: 3

Traditional HD IC Name: Left Angle Cross of Obscuration 2
Quantum HD IC Name: Left Angle Cross of Wonder 2

Quantum Description:

To lead, teach, and inspire others to tap into the flow of Cosmic Intelligence to source innovative answers to humanity's challenges. To teach people about the power of staying in wonder and active curiosity for the solutions and the inspirational spark for innovation to be revealed. To remain in a state of innocence and wonder as an essential state of conscious expansion and exploration of potential and possibility. To take time away from daily existence to plug into Cosmic Intelligence and intuition as a source of innovation and inspiration.

Resiliency Keys:

Decisiveness, Self-Trust, Authenticity, Vitality, Courage, Empowerment

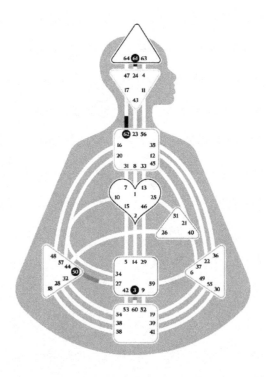

Traditional HD IC Name: Right Angle Cross of The Maya 2
Quantum HD IC Name: Right Angle Cross of Endurance 2

Quantum Description:

To explore, learn, and teach the importance of aligning with right timing to manifest and implement the next key steps to creation. To plan, prepare, and clear the path for the next step and to teach the importance of conscious readiness. To help others learn to set the stage and be prepared for what is next. To align yourself with the long haul. To ensure all the necessary action steps are ready to align with the manifestation of a dream. To know that part of bringing the idea into form is to "act as if" and doing all the things necessary to be prepared for when the timing is right.

Resiliency Keys:

Authenticity, Self-Trust, Decisiveness, Courage, Vitality, Empowerment

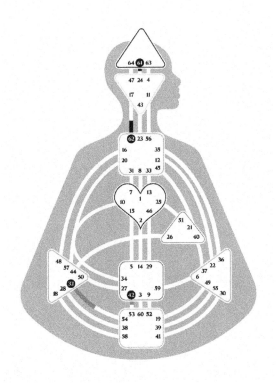

JUX Readiness
Conscious Sun Gate: 62
Conscious Earth Gate: 61
Unconscious Sun Gate: 3
Unconscious Earth Gate: 50

Traditional HD IC Name: Juxtaposition Cross of Detail
Quantum HD IC Name: Juxtaposition Cross of Readiness

Quantum Description:

To embody and build a foundation of knowledge that helps people find practical solutions that support innovation and activation of solutions to the challenges facing humanity today. To see the bigger Cosmic Perspective and the confluence of past lessons and current needs that spark innovation and a shift in perspective that changes the direction of our work to change the future. To cultivate a deep understanding of all possibilities and potential blended with innovation and new possibilities to teach and lead people into innovating how we work and provide resources and nurturing for others.

Resiliency Keys:

Decisiveness, Self-Trust, Authenticity, Vitality, Courage, Empowerment

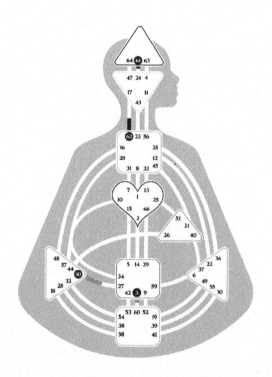

Traditional HD IC Name: Left Angle Cross of Obscuration
Quantum HD IC Name: Left Angle Cross of Wonder

Quantum Description:

To lead, teach, and inspire others to tap into the flow of Cosmic Intelligence to source innovative answers to humanity's challenges. To teach people about the power of staying in wonder and active curiosity for the solutions and the inspirational spark for innovation to be revealed. To remain in a state of innocence and wonder as an essential state of conscious expansion and exploration of potential and possibility. To take time away from daily existence to plug into Cosmic Intelligence and intuition as a source of innovation and inspiration.

Resiliency Keys:

Decisiveness, Self-Trust, Authenticity, Vitality, Courage, Empowerment

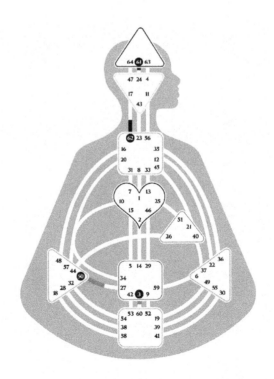

RAX The Quantum Pulse
Conscious Sun Gate: 63
Conscious Earth Gate: 64
Unconscious Sun Gate: 5
Unconscious Earth Gate: 35

Traditional HD IC Name: Right Angle Cross of Consciousness
Quantum HD IC Name: Right Angle Cross of The Quantum Pulse

Quantum Description:

To explore, experiment with, and experience the habits and rhythms necessary to implement new ideas and possibilities. To share and demonstrate the habits and consistency born of experience that set the stage for exploring new ideas. To embody and teach others how to be consistent and habitual. To teach from experience and to use your experience to know which new ideas to explore and experiment with. To lay the foundation of rhythm and consistency as the medium for exponential growth and compassionate expansion.

Resiliency Keys:

Vitality, Decisiveness, Courage, Empowerment, Authenticity, Self-Trust

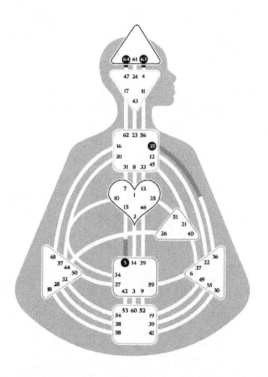

Traditional HD IC Name: Juxtaposition Cross of Doubts
Quantum HD IC Name: Juxtaposition Cross of Curiosity

Quantum Description:

To embody and build a foundation of open-mindedness that supports the possibility of new thoughts and ideas that have the potential to change the quality and quantity of our resources and our capacity for sustainable wellbeing. To be willing to suspend doubt and expand upon curiosity and wonder as part of cultivating an essential mindset that supports learning new ways of creating resources. To know that healing self-worth and value issues supports the expansion of possibility thinking and tapping into the limitless abundance of the Cosmic Mind.

Resiliency Keys:

Decisiveness, Self-Trust, Authenticity, Self-Worth, Vitality, Empowerment

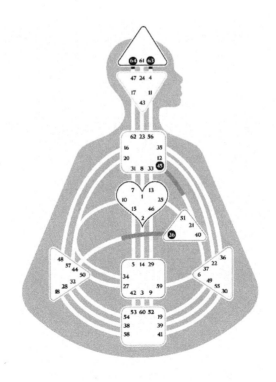

LAX Co-Creation
Conscious Sun Gate: 63
Conscious Earth Gate: 64
Unconscious Sun Gate: 26
Unconscious Earth Gate: 45

Traditional HD IC Name: Left Angle Cross of Dominion
Quantum HD IC Name: Left Angle Cross of Co-Creation

Quantum Description:

To lead, teach, and inspire others to maintain and sustain a countenance and aura of curiosity and wonder. To know that curiosity and wonder are key components of creating receptivity to cosmically inclusive thinking. To teach the importance of healing self-worth and aligning with the value of sustainable wellbeing as the key to being receptive to new ideas and information that have the potential to change the world. Understanding that the power of co-creation comes from knowing your unique, vital, and irreplaceable role in the Cosmic Plan. To be able to create in harmony with Higher Intelligence when you serve your higher purpose.

Resiliency Keys:

Decisiveness, Self-Trust, Authenticity, Self-Worth, Vitality, Empowerment

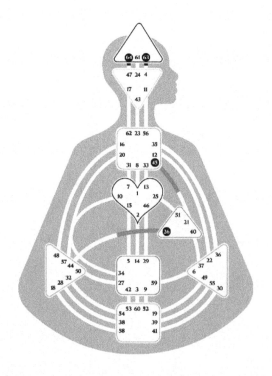

Traditional HD IC Name: Right Angle Cross of Consciousness 3
Quantum HD IC Name: Right Angle Cross of The Quantum Pulse 3

Quantum Description:

To explore, experiment with, and experience the habits and rhythms necessary to implement new ideas and possibilities. To share and demonstrate the habits and consistency born of experience that set the stage for exploring new ideas. To embody and teach others how to be consistent and habitual. To teach from experience and to use your experience to know which new ideas to explore and experiment with. To lay the foundation of rhythm and consistency as the medium for exponential growth and compassionate expansion.

Resiliency Keys:

Vitality, Decisiveness, Courage, Empowerment, Authenticity, Self-Trust

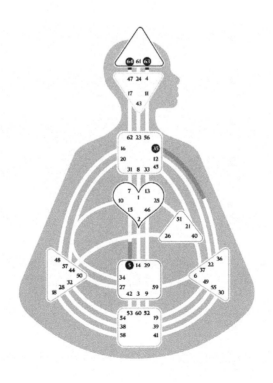

JUX Divine Transference
Conscious Sun Gate: 64
Conscious Earth Gate: 63
Unconscious Sun Gate: 45
Unconscious Earth Gate: 26

Traditional HD IC Name: Juxtaposition Cross of Confusion
Quantum HD IC Name: Juxtaposition Cross of Divine Transference

---

Quantum Description:

To embody and build a foundation of self-trust and trust in Source rooted in the deep understanding of your unique, vital and irreplaceable role in the Cosmic Plan. To be open and receptive to Cosmic Intelligence as a result of valuing your contribution to the world. To serve as a conduit for Cosmic Intelligence and inspirations. To help others heal their self-worth in order to create with integrity. To consciously co-create with Source as a way of shifting and changing personal and global value stories. To co-create sustainable resources, to collaborate, and share what you have and know for the betterment of the world.

Resiliency Keys:

Decisiveness, Self-Trust, Authenticity, Self-Worth, Vitality, Empowerment

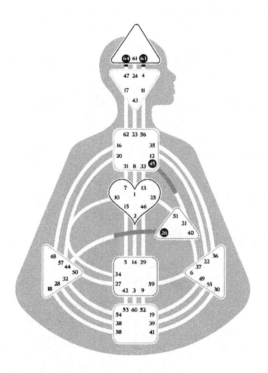

Traditional HD IC Name: Left Angle Cross of Dominion 2

Quantum HD IC Name: Left Angle Cross of Co-Creation 2

Quantum Description:

To lead, teach, and inspire others to maintain and sustain a countenance and aura of curiosity and wonder. To know that curiosity and wonder are key components of creating receptivity to cosmically inclusive thinking. To teach the importance of healing self-worth and aligning with the value of sustainable wellbeing as the key to being receptive to new ideas and information that have the potential to change the world. Understanding that the power of co-creation comes from knowing your unique, vital, and irreplaceable role in the Cosmic Plan. To be able to create in harmony with Higher Intelligence when you serve your higher purpose.

Resiliency Keys:

Decisiveness, Self-Trust, Authenticity, Self-Worth, Vitality, Empowerment

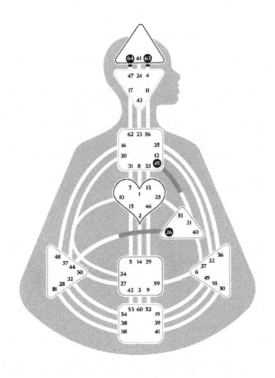

CONCLUSIONS   398

Conclusion

It is time that we remember the power of narrative over the power of muscle. As we emerge and push into the final thrust of the Solar Plexus Mutation and the actualization of our creative ability rooted in faith versus fear, we need high-quality, high-frequency stories to help entrain our brains to the solution-finding brilliance of the Cosmic Mind. The vocabulary of Quantum Human Design begins the process of helping ourselves and others construct a scaffolding of energy that supports the manifestation of a life rooted in wellbeing and conscious evolution.

The more we lift ourselves up, proclaim our value, and amplify the frequency of our stories by using empowered language, the more we align with the purity of creativity that comes from the cosmically inclusive mind. Good stories are not the only step, but they are a vital first step in constructing the temple of tomorrow and a world rooted in equitable, just, sustainable, abundance, and peace.

Quantum Human Design was created for helping you and your clients rethink the archetypes and stories you've been told about who and how you are. Suppose the character and the role that you play in your own story include the story of your unique, vital, and irreplaceable role in the Cosmic Plan. In that case, you will be maximizing the potential of the deconditioning process and increasing the power of your story.

Stories are comprised of archetypes packed with meanings and perspectives. Think of a rose. The idea of a rose may include thoughts such as romance, colors, thorns, funerals, leaves, gardens, fragrance, and more. The word *rose* is packed with meaning based on perception and history.

We give our idea of *rose* the meaning most aligned with our personal experience. The deconditioning process allows us to shift our perspective from the rose's potential thorns and enable us to see and sense the potential colors and fragrance.

The role of the human brain is to basically build a database of memory rooted in our personal and collective experiences. Memory, much like the idea of *rose*, is mutable. Do we remember the pain or the lessons we gleaned? Do we see the past as a springboard to our future and redefine it in a way that empowers us, or do we let the story of our victimhood recreate the metaphor of our condition again and again and again?

When we are conditioned, our brain and our thinking are ego-inclusive. The brain fights to hold onto old perceptions of stories as a way of protecting us from experiencing the same pain over and over again. This holding on is instinctual and limiting. The true power of the mind happens when we heal our thinking patterns. This is the importance of the deconditioning process and the power of rewriting our personal narrative. When we remember our natural state of wellbeing, the Cosmic Importance of our life, and our inherent value rooted in our very existence, then we learn to serve the Cosmic Mind. We release the ego-inclusive thinking of a defensive brain and allow the Cosmic Mind to take over.

The Cosmic Mind can program the brain. Allowing your brain to be rewired to serve the betterment of your world and consequently the betterment of the planet is the most important work you can do on the planet at this time. Good stories create a rich, powerful medium for the evolution of true human nature—beings created to fulfill the potential of the Divine in form.

I hope this book has given you new thoughts and perspectives on your story. I hope that you have found the beauty and the power that is the true story of Who You Are. I hope you've found the words that help you codify your magnificence and the beauty that is YOU.

From My Heart to Yours,
Karen

Index of Incarnation Crosses

Resources

Find out more
QuantumAlignmentSystem.com

Enroll in courses
KarenCurryParker.Teachable.com

Join the community
KarenCurryParker.Circle.so

Want to become a Certified Quantum Human Design Specialist?
Enroll in Professional Training here:
QuantumAlignmentSystem.com/ProTraining

Acknowledgments

As always, thank you to the amazing GracePoint Publishing Team especially, Tascha Yoder, Debby Levering, and Clementine Kornder who so carefully and lovingly guided the creation of this book. Your vision and your dedication to turning ideas into manuscripts, manuscripts into books, and books into evolutionary missives that change the world is humbling.

I am so deeply grateful to all of my team, Kristin Steele, Jamie McComas, Betsy Batista, Michelle Wolff, Jessica Murrell, David Nadler, Michelle René Robinson, Kendra Woods, Teresa Miller, and Hannah Sawicky for their tireless devotion and faith in the future of the world and for working so hard to get my message out to the world.

None of this work would exist without the initiation from my teacher, Ra Uru Hu, and the insistence of The Voice which guided him to share Human Design with the world (even though he was reluctant at times).

Every day I log into a virtual world that is filled with the rich heart and soul of my students, Human Design Specialists and Quantum Alignment System Practitioners. Their questions, explorations and contemplations keep me inspired and in service. I hope I've answered some of your questions in this book!

In 2019, I held my first grandchild in my arms. In that single second, I entered into an entirely new dance with infinity. When it all feels so very complex and difficult, my grandchildren help me remember the future we're building and that my excuses are irrelevant.

As always, thank you to my husband and my last kiddo living at home, Ayelet. Your patience with my hiding out in my writing "cave" and your willingness to order pizza over and over again gave me the space and the time to complete this book.

Lastly, somewhere anchored in infinity, but probably more like around ten years ago, the Universe positioned me to meet my best friend, collaborator, and visionary, Michelle Vandepas. A long walk around Cedar Lake and many downloads later, she continues to be my collaborator, my biggest cheerleader and the one who really gets me. Thank you for finding me and restoring my faith. Also, thank you for all the downloads...

About the Author

Karen Curry Parker is a Transformational Teacher, Speaker & Coach. She is a multiple Best-Selling Author, EFT (Emotional Freedom Techniques) Practitioner since 2000, Life Coach since 1998, Original student of Ra Uru Hu, and one of the world's leading Human Design teachers since 1999. She is also a Quantum University PhD Student/Guest Lecturer and a TEDx Presenter.

Karen is the Founder & Creator of two professional trainings, the Quantum Human Design™ for Everyone Training System and The Quantum Alignment System™ and is also the Founder of the Understanding Human Design Membership Community. She is also the Host of the Quantum Evolution and Cosmic Revolution Podcasts and Co-Founder of GracePoint Publishing.

Karen has a deep love for helping people activate their highest potential, which in part is why she created Quantum Human Design™. Her core mission is to help people live the life they were designed to live by discovering who they are, what they are here to do and how to activate their authentic life path by waking them up to the power of their innate creativity and unlimited possibility.

Karen is a 4/6 Time Bender (Manifesting Generator), Mother of eight amazing Humans, Wife of a genius, and Grandmother of two emerging World Leaders. She has her BSN in Nursing, BA in Journalism, and is currently working on her PhD in Integrative Health at Quantum University.

For more great books from Human Design Press
Visit Books.GracePointPublishing.com

If you enjoyed reading *The Encyclopedia of Quantum Human Design™*, and
purchased it through an online retailer, please return to the site and write a
review to help others find the book.

CPSIA information can be obtained
at www.ICGtesting.com
Printed in the USA
LVHW051041031222
734517LV00008B/656